THE MARKET'S MEASURE

Industrials

AN ILLUSTRATED HISTORY OF AMERICA
TOLD THROUGH THE DOW JONES INDUSTRIAL AVERAGE

THE MARKET'S MEASURE

Edited by John A. Prestbo

Library of Congress Catalog Card Number: 99-66379

ISBN: 1-881944-25-5

Printed in the United States of America

CONTENTS

ACKNOWLEDGMENTS

This book has been a true collaborative effort of the reporters and editors of *The Wall Street Journal* and the staff of the Dow Jones Indexes group. Much of the material was previously published in *The Wall Street Journal* in a somewhat different format in connection with the centennial of the Dow Jones Industrial Average in 1996. Georgette Jasen, an assistant news editor of *The Wall Street Journal,* was charged with bringing it up to date and with adding new material to reflect the events of the past two years. Harold Seneker, publications editor at Dow Jones Indexes, was responsible for the section on the future of investing written by Peter Francese. Valerie Bowe, with the assistance of Bonnie Berrien, Maryanne Garcia-Hawthorne and Lisa Hargraves, turned everything into the beautiful book you have in your hands. Michael Jassmann and Ken Shannon arranged for production. Jim Hyatt and Gillian Shapiro in *The Wall Street Journal* statistics department provided invaluable assistance with numbers. Heather Bell helped with many tasks.

A number of *Wall Street Journal* reporters, past and present, contributed to the text, including Roger Lowenstein, Robert McGough, Vanessa O'Connell, Anita Raghavan, John Dorfman, Nancy Jeffrey, Bridget O'Brian, Susan Pulliam, Dave Kansas, Charles Gasparino, Ellen Schultz, Deborah Lohse, Karen Damato, Tom Herman, Jonathan Clements, Patrick McGeehan, Greg Ip, Jim Browning and Michael Sesit. We are especially indebted to our former colleague John Dorfman who, when he was with *The Wall Street Journal*, helped to create the special sections of the paper that led directly to this book and who has continued to be a trusted adviser. Ned Davis Research provided data for many of the charts and tables. We are saddened that Robert Sobel, a business historian and professor emeritus at Hofstra University, who was a patient and knowledgeable source of information, died just as we were completing production of this book.

Last, but not least, we thank Paul Steiger, managing editor of *The Wall Street Journal*, and Michael Petronella, managing director of Dow Jones Indexes, for their continued support of this project.

John A. Prestbo
Markets Editor, *The Wall Street Journal*
Editor, Dow Jones Indexes

INTRODUCTION

During the past one hundred-plus years, the Dow Jones Industrial Average has evolved from a newspaperman's practical tool into a globally recognized cultural icon. It is the daily symbol of the U.S. stock market, for people on Wall Street and on Main Street as well as for millions of people around the globe. Let someone say that the market is up or down, and he or she is usually referring to the movement of what is familiarly called the Dow. As the market has become important to the lives and business affairs of many millions of ordinary people in the United States, its oldest and most famous measure has become a part of their lives.

It was not always thus. You can trace the existence of stock exchanges from 1531, when something resembling one was started in Antwerp, but as late as the early 1860s, the New York Stock Exchange (NYSE) was trading all of 1,500 shares on an average day.

Finally the NYSE had its first million-share day, in 1886, and by 1896, traders in this burgeoning financial market felt the need for a way to take the measure of its rises and falls. Often it was clear that most of the activity on a given day was driving the majority of prices up or down. But there was no good way of measuring how much or of comparing one day's performance to another day's; one particular stock might run counter to the general trend.

And that's why a certain journalist named Charles H. Dow stepped in, introducing an initial stock average in 1884, and then the Dow Jones Industrial Average in 1896. In the process, he forever changed the world's way of perceiving and measuring its increasingly important invention, the stock market.

PART I

THE BIRTH
OF AN INDEX

CHARLES DOW'S VISION WAS WELL ABOVE THE AVERAGE

Charles H. Dow couldn't have known it, but 1896 was an auspicious time to begin producing his average of industrial shares. A bitter national depression, born of the panic of 1893, was close to having run its course. Deflation, the curse of farmers and wage earners, seemed ready to ease its icy grip.

Only the previous year, Mr. Dow could have been among those around New York harbor who watched freighters laden with gold steaming for London. He had surely known that the gold-depleted U.S. government was days from default. But as Mr. Dow's young newspaper had chronicled, financier J.P. Morgan, Sr., had saved the day by organizing a bond syndicate. President Grover Cleveland accepted the move reluctantly. But he had little choice. There was no Federal Reserve and no public safety net except for the intervention of Wall Street's reigning baron.

On May 26, 1896, when the Dow Jones Industrial Average first appeared, the genesis of a recovery was at hand. At the same time, a merger wave was reshaping American business. In industry after industry, giant cor-

Opposite page: South Street and harbor, New York, N.Y., 1895

porations were seeking national markets and, often, monopolies.

These companies, Mr. Dow predicted, would constitute "the great speculative market" of the future. A partial list of these newly formed "trusts" includes producers of copper, glue, hay, needles, flour, sugar, lead, whiskey, plate glass, wire nails, coal and steel. Yet the trend was hardly glimpsed by many. For most Americans, business was still local — the foundry, the store, the farm. The "national economy" seemed an abstraction.

Mr. Dow's index of 12 industrials (General Electric is the lone survivor among the current 30 Dow stocks) began at 40.94. A hostage to politics from the start, the average was buffeted by what historian Robert Sobel would call the most important election since the Civil War. William Jennings Bryan, giving poetic voice to farmers' and Westerners' fanatic hatred of tight money, campaigned for an end to "the cross of gold." In its place, he promised silver money and inflation.

Mr. Dow, though he had been born on a Connecticut farm, thought Mr. Bryan's platform "folly." Indeed, anyone with a mind to invest in shares of companies in his newly

concocted average — all of Wall Street, every banker, all the new industrialists — put in for gold and sound money.

The average, which Mr. Dow figured by pencil, fell a disastrous 30% as the campaign dragged on, touching 28.48 in August. William McKinley's victory saved the gold standard, and gold strikes in the Yukon and elsewhere soon restored liquidity. Mr. Dow's average would never sink so low again. Yet when prosperity returned, it was visited on a changed country. The previous half-century had been the age of rails. Their relentless steel ribbons had been the arsenal of growth, if not exactly of democracy (fixing rates and buying legislatures being vital to the business). Railroads had become the first great national corporations. Their shares were actively traded from Boston to San Francisco; indeed, theirs and virtually no others. On the New York Stock Exchange, 60% of the listed stocks were rails.

When Mr. Dow first cobbled together indexes of shares in 1884 and 1885, those lists, too, were dominated by rails. Industrial stocks with reasonable float and liquidity were scarce. Even National Cordage Co., a rope manufacturer and the most widely traded industrial of the Gilded Age, had, as the popular joke went, hung itself in the panic of '93, according to James Grant's evocative biography *Bernard Baruch.* General Electric itself had needed a Morgan bailout. Stocks in general were frowned on. Share prices, often controlled, cornered or otherwise stage-managed by Wall Street pools, were subject to spectacular rises and plunges. Trading on inside information was de rigueur, and little other information existed. In 1895, when the stock exchange gingerly proposed that companies distribute an annual statement of earnings to shareholders, it was a radical step.

Prudent investors bought bonds, which is what Mr. Dow would recommend to readers of the *Ladies' Home Journal.* Stocks were the playthings of raiders and speculators. In our own age, stocks are recommended for savers from toddlers on up, but one hundred years ago the notion of putting savings in industrial shares was hardly serious. It was simply too risky. The very concept of investing — and paying up — profits was foreign, according to Ron Chernow, author of a biography of John D. Rockefeller. Stocks selling for more than the issuing company's asset value were considered "watered." To gamble on them was un-

Victorian speculation. Investors bought into tangible assets and sought return from income. That is why bonds were the preferred vehicle. Among stocks, only the railroads paid dividends on a regular basis. Yet by 1890, the railroads had covered the country and the frontier had been tamed. In a landmark essay, "The Significance of the Frontier in American History," Frederick Jackson Turner warned that the entrepreneurial spirit of Americans could vanish with the open prairie.

Mr. Dow suspected otherwise.

A tall and bearded, taciturn journalist, Charles Dow had spent his first years reporting for various newspapers in Springfield, Mass., and Providence, R.I. His early work was diligent but unexceptional. In 1879, however, when Mr. Dow was 27 years old, he was sent to cover the silver rush in Leadville, Colo. He rode west with the president of the New York Stock Exchange and a group of financiers and journalists. In Leadville, Mr. Dow found a "gigantic lottery," where the ignorant fared as well as the educated. Astonished, he wrote that "Men sprang from poverty to affluence in an

Left: Bales of cotton fill flatbed railcars at the Texas Central Railway Yards in Houston, 1904
Opposite page: Pedestrians strolling on Brooklyn Bridge, Brooklyn, N.Y., 1898

hour." His letters from "the Magic City" described not only the silver ores but also the rampant gambling and the eighty-two saloons (vastly outnumbering churches). Breaking with his usual modesty, Mr. Dow observed that many mining claims bore the names of the attractive personnel of Leadville's lushly appointed brothel.

When Mr. Dow returned to the East, he moved to Brooklyn and struck out for Wall Street. He worked first as a mining-stock reporter, then in general financial news. After a few years he and a partner, Edward D. Jones, launched Dow Jones & Co. In 1889, they began *The Wall Street Journal,* with Mr. Dow as editor.

When Mr. Dow crossed the magnificent, spidery Brooklyn Bridge to Manhattan, he saw a speculative dynamism surpassing Leadville's. The streets were crowded with money men, deposited by trolley, elevated train and stage coach. There were markets for stocks, bonds, commodity futures and the raw stuff itself — fresh fish and coffee beans being off-loaded by the boatful. Stock-market volume and public interest in stocks surged, but for some time, shares would remain speculative, illiquid and subject to collusive manipulations. The notion of required disclosure was still years away. U.S. Steel, the giant trust organized at the century's turn and soon to be a part of the

industrial average, set a cautionary example. Its shares opened at $38 and promptly soared to $55. By 1903, they were quoted at a pitiful $9. Mr. Dow, no naif, limited his own stock purchases to ten-share lots.

What his average represented wasn't security, but popularization. Without an index — without a way for the ordinary investor to follow the broad market — today's age of financial democracy, in which employees are also future pensioners and corporate shareholders, would be unimaginable.

Mr. Dow's ambition for his average was more modest — that it take the temperature of markets and, by extension, of the new industrial economy. In an age when prosperity was regularly cut short by recessions and panics, he was acutely conscious of the rhythms of economic life. His prose, sometimes wooden, was at its best when he was describing the cycles of business, to him as inexorable and unalterable as forces of nature. He was fascinated by "the great swing of the market up or down," a tide so powerful that, as Mr. Dow put it, a man who had hardly dared put in his winter stock of coal would suddenly venture an entire mine. As he wrote in 1899, when seventy-five million people undergo such a shift "from feeling discouraged and doubtful to being confident and enterprising," the effect "is stupendous in its results upon all lines of business, including the stock market." It has been that way ever since.

AN UNASSUMING CHARLES DOW

Charles Henry Dow

Like the Dow Jones Industrial Average, which Charles H. Dow invented, it was Mr. Dow's nature to take the pulse of events rather than to directly stir them. Modest and reserved, he managed to start one of the country's great newspapers, yet leave only the barest trace of a personal record.

Although the journalism of the era is remembered by the modifier "yellow," Mr. Dow had not the bombast of a Hearst, but the grave bearing of a professor. When he died, at only fifty-one in 1902, *The Wall Street Journal* didn't run his picture. It hadn't occurred to Mr. Dow that the newspaper he edited might want his likeness.

He was born in 1851, in a farmhouse in Sterling, Conn. His father died when he was six, plunging the younger Dow into a succession of odd jobs. He was diligent, responsible to a fault — in short, Yankee to the core — but too cerebral for the farm.

In 1872, he landed work at the *Springfield Daily Republican,* run by a well-known editor of the day, Samuel Bowles. He got his break when the *Providence Journal* sent him to the West to cover a silver strike. Though put off by the loose morals of a mining town, Mr. Dow was energized by the glimpse of capitalism in the raw and fascinated by the alternating boom-and-bust business currents that his index would later chronicle.

In 1882, after a couple of jobs on Wall Street, Mr. Dow and his partner, Edward Jones, started Dow Jones & Co. From an unpainted basement office next to the New York Stock Exchange, they published the "Customer's Afternoon Letter," a precursor of *The Wall Street Journal.* Their first stock-market average, published in 1884, consisted mainly of rail shares. A decade later, in 1896, they began producing the Dow Jones Industrial Average.

An early recruit recalled the office as a place of high tension; Mr. Jones, upon finishing a bulletin, would summon messengers with the cry of "Boy! Boy!" Days passed before the employees saw that Mr. Jones had a partner — the tall, bearded, quiet Mr. Dow, secluded by a few pine boards put up for privacy.

THE INDEX'S HOT-BLOODED OTHER NAMESAKE

Edward Davis Jones ruled the newsroom of his fledgling Wall Street newspaper as a benevolent tyrant.

A hot-tempered, red-mustachioed six-footer, Mr. Jones was the fiery complement to Charles Dow's ice at newly formed Dow Jones & Co. The two men, with a third partner, Charles Bergstresser, were partners in the 1882 founding of Dow Jones & Co., publisher of the "Customer's Afternoon Letter," later known as *The Wall Street Journal.*

Edward Davis Jones

Although Mr. Dow was the preeminent partner, Mr. Jones was more visible. He dealt with messengers scurrying in and out of the office, wrote and edited bulletins, and spent nights scouring the city for tips, especially at the watering holes frequented by his racy friends, the pool operators and wheeler-dealers of Wall Street. Ironically, he had nothing to do with the devising of the Dow Jones Industrial Average that bears his name; that was entirely the creation of Mr. Dow.

According to Richard J. Stillman, professor emeritus at the University of New Orleans, who has written about the Dow Jones Industrial Average, Mr. Jones was "excitable, emotional and you never knew when [he] might explode" into profanity. But he also was quick with praise.

Mr. Jones met Mr. Dow while both were working in Providence. After Mr. Dow took a job at a market newsletter in New York, he brought in his friend, Eddie Jones.

The austere Mr. Dow, with his farming background, grew uncomfortable with the fast-track friends of Mr. Jones, who had grown up in more affluent social circles. Messrs. Dow and Bergstresser also disapproved of Mr. Jones's profane outbursts in the newsroom, though Mr. Jones took on an aura of calm and command during times of crisis.

Mr. Jones gradually felt estranged from his two partners. In January 1899, he left the newsletter for the glitter of Wall Street. (He worked in the brokerage business, but the present-day brokerage firm Edward D. Jones & Co. is named for an entirely different man.) Mr. Jones died in New York in 1920 at the age of sixty-five.

DOW JONES'S FORGOTTEN FOUNDER

He may have had "deep pockets and short arms," as one historian puts it, but Charles M. Bergstresser deserves credit for digging deep enough to bankroll a publishing venture with cash-poor Charles Dow and Edward Jones, beginning in 1882.

Unfortunately, he didn't get any of the credit. "Bergstresser" was too long to be included in the company's name, Dow Jones & Co., so he also missed out on being immortalized in the name of the Dow Jones Industrial Average, which Mr. Dow invented fourteen years later.

A Pennsylvania Dutchman, Mr. Bergstresser was born in 1859 into a large family in bucolic Lykens Valley. He worked while attending Lafayette College in Easton, Pa., and saved much of what he earned. After graduation in 1881, he moved to New York City and took a job covering the stock market as a reporter for the Kiernan News Agency.

Stocky and with thick-lensed glasses, Mr. Bergstresser easily won the confidence of the Wall Street executives who were his news sources, and he wowed his colleagues early in his career by landing an interview with the great financier John Pierpont Morgan, Sr. A pugnacious reporter, Mr. Bergstresser had a knack for getting bigwigs to spill details of their deals. "He could make a wooden Indian talk — and tell the truth," Mr. Jones used to say.

In 1882, Messrs. Dow and Jones were scheming to leave Kiernan to start their own news agency when "Buggy" got wind of their plan. He pestered them until they took him on as a partner. Within months, the three men began publishing the "Customer's Afternoon Letter" from an unpainted basement office next to the New York Stock Exchange.

They used Buggy's savings as seed money. Mr. Bergstresser was the "driving financial force behind the company during its formative years," says Richard J. Stillman.

When Dow Jones & Co. turned its business newsletter into a full-fledged newspaper in 1889, it was the firm's unnamed partner who named it. Mr. Bergstresser dubbed it *The Wall Street Journal*.

Opposite page: The Wall Street Journal *delivery wagon, 1890s*

Charles M. Bergstresser

PART II

HOW THE INDUSTRIAL AVERAGE WORKS

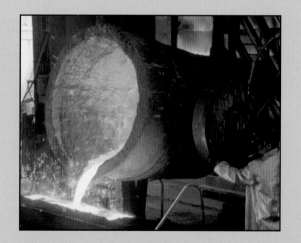

SO WHAT IS THE DOW JONES INDUSTRIAL AVERAGE, ANYWAY?

Quick. *How did the market do yesterday?*

If you're like most people, you'd probably answer by saying that the Dow Jones Industrial Average rose or fell. If you're a market junkie, you might even be able to quote the closing level.

Now more than one hundred years old, the Dow Jones Industrial Average has acquired a unique place in the collective consciousness of investors. It is the market barometer people talk about in the office, on the golf course, at the bar. It is the number quoted on the nightly news and remembered when the market takes a dive.

The industrial average has become a cultural icon. Personified, vilified and criticized, the measure has taken on a life of its own. "The Dow is a historical touchpoint," says John Rekenthaler, publisher of "Morningstar Mutual Funds," a Chicago newsletter. "It has a resonance none of the others has."

But enough superlatives. What is the Dow, exactly, and what does it do?

The first part is easy: The Dow is an average of 30 blue-chip U.S. stocks. As for what it does, there are about as many analogies for the Dow's role as there are stocks in the index (it's a thermometer, a barometer, a mile marker, a pulse, a magnifying glass). But perhaps the simplest explanation is this: It's a tool by which the general public can measure the overall performance of the U.S. stock market.

Even though the industrial average consists of only 30 stocks, the theory is that each one represents a particular sector of the economy and serves as a reliable bellwether for that industry. Thus, the Dow Jones roster is made up of giants such as International Business Machines (IBM) Corp., J.P. Morgan & Co. and AT&T Corp. Together, the 30 stocks reflect the market as a whole.

Left: Factory workers at a Boeing plant in Seattle, Wash., in 1938
Opposite page: AT&T workers hauling ashore a transatlantic telephone cable on the New Jersey coast, 1956. It was the first cable to connect the United States directly to continental Europe.

The Dow's movements "give the average investor some sense of what happens" in his or her portfolio each day, says Laszlo Birinyi, who heads a Greenwich, Conn., consulting firm that bears his name.

The Dow Jones Industrial Average made its debut on May 26, 1896, the brainchild of Charles Dow, the tall, bearded and unassuming journalist who cofounded Dow Jones & Co., publisher of *The Wall Street Journal*. (Although his partner, Edward Jones, has his name attached to the average, he had nothing to do with its creation.)

The industrial average wasn't Mr. Dow's first attempt to measure the market. In 1884, he devised a market measure made up of eleven stocks, mainly railroad companies. It was intermittently published in the "Customer's Afternoon Letter," a precursor to *The Wall Street Journal*.

But Mr. Dow believed that the rails presented only a partial picture of the economy and that industrial companies, whose stocks were then considered highly speculative, were crucial contributors to America's growth. And because the goods produced by the industrials were being delivered by the railroads, Mr. Dow figured that two separate measures could act as coconfirmers of any broad market trend.

So *The Wall Street Journal* began publishing the industrial average and the railroad average in every issue, and it has done so ever since. (With airplanes and trucks bringing competition to the railroads, the railroad average was changed to the Dow Jones Transportation Average in 1970. As of mid-1999, there were only four railroads in this 20-stock average. And in 1929, the *Journal* introduced a daily Dow Jones Utility Average.)

Initially, the industrial average included twelve companies. Only one, General Electric Co., remains in the average under its original name. Many of the others are extinct today, and some have mutated into different companies that are still active. But a century ago, the corporate titans of the time included American Cotton Oil, Distilling & Cattle Feeding Co., American Tobacco and Chicago Gas, to name a few.

As these companies gained greater success, editors of the *Journal* (who assumed management of the averages after Mr. Dow's death in 1902) added more industrials. On October 1, 1928, a year before the crash, the Dow was expanded to a 30-stock average.

But in the beginning, the Dow industrials didn't fare too well. The average began at a meager 40.94 and gradually declined to 28.48 by August. The culprit was the 1896 presidential elections, which featured a contentious debate about the gold standard. With the election of William McKinley, however, gold won out over silver, and the economy took off. So did the Dow average.

Ten years later, after some bumps along the way, the industrial average passed the 100-point mark for the first time. But there was little fanfare. Stocks were still considered speculative, and the average hadn't yet caught on as a popular stock-market barometer.

World War I and a devastating flu epidemic held back stocks during the next decade. But then came the 1920s, the age of Charles Lindbergh and flappers. The stock market roared, helped by the laissez-faire policies of "Silent Cal" Coolidge. The industrial average set a record in each of six consecutive years, the longest such string on record until the bull market of the 1990s. It hit a peak of 381.17 in September 1929.

When the market collapsed on October 28, the Dow industrials fell 13%; the next day, Black Tuesday, they dropped an additional 12%. In the depths of the Depression in 1932, the Dow hit a low of 41.22 — nearly where it had started thirty-six years earlier. It wouldn't recover the lost ground until 1954.

After decades of various market upheavals, the industrial average finally broke through the 1000 level in 1972, and in recent years it has been marching past milestones as if it were a marathon runner. It passed the 5000 mark on November 21, 1995; 6000 in October 1996, 7000 in February 1997 and 8000 just five months later. It closed above 9000 for the first time on April 6, 1998, and 10000 on March 29, 1999.

As times have changed, so have the makeup and mechanics of the Dow. Back in 1896, all Charles Dow needed was pencil and paper to compute the industrial average. He simply added up the prices of the twelve stocks and then divided by 12. In 1923, the task of working the numbers fell to Arthur "Pop" Harris, who had been hired in 1908 at the age of twenty-two.

For the next forty years, Pop calculated the Dow Jones average every hour on the hour for the Dow Jones News Service, sometimes, on busy trading days, bloodying his hands pulling out the ticker tape. Through all those years, the financial world would hold its breath for seven minutes after the New York Stock Exchange's closing bell, waiting for Pop, a small, skinny man, to finish his official calculations on a piece of newsprint.

Pop Harris retired in 1963, when the advent of computers made it possible to calculate the Dow Jones averages in a fraction of a second any time of the day.

Today, the first step in calculating the Dow is still totaling the prices of the component stocks. But the rest of the math isn't so easy anymore, because the divisor is continually being adjusted. The reason? To preserve historical continuity. In the past hundred years, there have been many stock splits, spinoffs and stock substitutions that, without adjustment, would distort the value of the Dow.

To understand how the formula works, consider a stock split. Say three stocks are trading at $15, $20 and $25; the average of the three is $20. But if the company with the $20 stock has a two-for-one split, its shares suddenly are priced at half of their previous level. That's not to say the value of the investment has changed; rather, the $20 stock simply sells for $10, with twice as many shares available. The average of the three stocks, meanwhile, falls to $16.66. So, the Dow divisor is adjusted to keep the average at $20 and reflect the continuing value of the investment represented by the gauge.

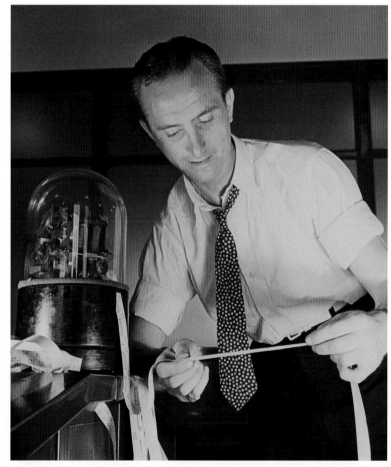

Opposite page: Workers assemble arc lamps at the West Lynn, Mass., General Electric plant in 1898
Above: Reading the tape from a ticker tape machine

Over time, the divisor has been adjusted several times, mostly downward (it stood at 0.24275214 at the end of 1998), which means that it has become, in effect, a multiplier. This explains why the average can be reported as, say, 9800, even though no single stock in the average is close to that price. A one-point move in any component stock pushes the average up or down a little more than four points.

"What the divisor does is keep things level with history," says Robert Dickey, a technical stock analyst at Minneapolis-based Dain Rauscher Inc. Current divisors for each of the Dow Jones averages appear on page C3 of *The Wall Street Journal* every day.

In another effort to preserve continuity, the guardians of the Dow, *The Wall Street Journal* editors, keep to a minimum any changes in the index's component stocks.

Most substitutions have arisen because of mergers, but from time to time, changes are made so the Dow is more representative of the broad market. As the economy has shifted from railroads to heavy industry to consumer goods to technology over the past century, the Dow's component stocks have reflected those changes.

The latest changes took place on March 17, 1997, when four stocks, Bethlehem Steel Corp., Texaco Inc., Westinghouse Electric Corp. and Woolworth Corp., were replaced by Hewlett-Packard Co., Johnson & Johnson, Travelers Group Inc. and Wal-Mart Stores Inc. The change enlarged representation of the technology, finance and health care sectors, which have become major propellants of the economy.

Since Charles Dow's time, several stock-market indexes have challenged the Dow Jones Industrial Average. In 1926, Standard & Poor's Corp. developed the S&P 90, which by the 1950s had evolved into the S&P 500, a benchmark widely used today by professional money managers. And now indexes abound. Wilshire Associates in Santa Monica, Calif., for example, uses computers to compile an index of nearly 7,000 stocks.

Nevertheless, the Dow remains unique. For one thing, it isn't market-weighted as other indicators are, which means it isn't adjusted to reflect the market capitalization of the component stocks. Because of that, the Dow gives more emphasis to higher-priced stocks than to lower-priced stocks. "In the Dow, the only thing that matters is the price," says Mr. Birinyi.

So a stock such as United Technologies Corp. constituted only 0.25% of the S&P 500 as of December 31, 1998, yet it accounted for 4.9% of the Dow Jones industrials because it was one of the more expensive stocks in the Dow.

Why is the Dow price-weighted rather than market-weighted? The answer lies partly in the technology of Charles Dow's day. He needed an indication that was easy to figure with paper and pencil; in fact, he probably

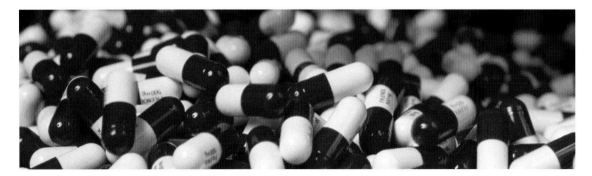

Left: Tylenol capsules on the production line at Johnson & Johnson
Opposite page: A traveling businessman using an early battery-powered laptop computer from Hewlett-Packard

and 500 stocks in the Standard & Poor's (S&P) index but it is the weighting that makes them track closely," says Mr. Dickey of Dain Rauscher. Because the S&P 500 is weighted by market capitalization, "A large part of the movement is determined by the biggest companies," he explains. And a number of the big companies that drive the S&P are invariably also found in the Dow.

In the end, although some indexes may be more closely watched by professionals, the Dow Jones Industrial Average has retained its position as the most popular measure, if for no other reason than that it has stood the test of time. As the oldest continuing barometer of the U.S. stock market, with a century of market history and market lore attached to it, the Dow average tells us where we came from, which helps us understand where we are.

Indeed, when the market plunged 554 points, or 7.2%, on October 27, 1997, and 512 points, or 6.4%, on August 31, 1998, many investors perhaps took it a little more in stride because they had lived through October 19, 1987, when the Dow plummeted 508 points, a 22.6% drop at the time.

"Every adult in this country has heard of the Dow Jones Industrial Average," says Mr. Rekenthaler of Morningstar. "They can relate to that."

never imagined a market-weighted index because there was no readily available way to make the calculations required. And the *Journal*'s editors today feel there's no reason to tinker with the formula because, oddly enough, the seemingly simple method actually works.

Despite the weighting difference, the Dow, by and large, tracks other major-market indexes fairly closely. That's because the stocks in the industrial average generally do an adequate job of representing their industries. So when a stock like J.P. Morgan is rallying, there's a good chance that other banks are doing the same thing. In addition, the indexes' differences tend to balance out in the end.

"There are only 30 stocks in the Dow

THE ORIGINAL DOW DOZEN AND WHAT BECAME OF THEM

When Charles Dow created the Dow Jones Industrial Average (DJIA), first published on May 26, 1896, it consisted of a dozen stocks.

Only one of the original twelve, General Electric, is in the average today. And even GE dropped out for a while. It was deleted in 1898 but back nine years later as a replacement for Tennessee Coal & Iron.

U.S. Steel, run by tycoon J.P. Morgan, swallowed Tennessee Coal in a unique power play, according to historian Robert Sobel. In the panic of 1907, Mr. Morgan agreed to rescue the economy; President Theodore Roosevelt agreed not to object to the acquisition.

Several companies in the 1896 average are ancestors of companies active today (see table). American Tobacco was broken up in 1911 but was the progenitor of such companies

as American Brands and R.J. Reynolds Tobacco. Distilling & Cattle Feeding Co. became Distilling Co. of America and later Quantum Chemical and then Millennium Chemical.

One original listing, U.S. Leather, was a preferred stock — a hybrid of a stock and a bond. Back in 1896, common stocks were considered highly speculative, Mr. Sobel says. Leather, incidentally, wasn't used just for clothing back then; thick leather bands were used for power transmission in factories.

The 30 stocks in the average today were added gradually over the decades. General Motors joined in 1915, Sears Roebuck in 1924, and International Business Machines in 1979. Walt Disney entered the Dow's magic kingdom in 1991.

COMPANY	WHAT BECAME OF IT
American Cotton Oil	Distant ancestor of Bestfoods
American Sugar	Evolved into Amstar Holdings
American Tobacco	Broken up in 1911 antitrust action
Chicago Gas	Absorbed by Peoples Gas in 1897
Distilling & Cattle Feeding	Whiskey trust evolved into Millennium Chemical
General Electric	Going strong and still in the DJIA
Laclede Gas	Active, removed from DJIA in 1899
National Lead	Today's NL Industries, removed from DJIA in 1916
North American	Utility combine broken up in 1940s
Tennessee Coal & Iron	Absorbed by U.S. Steel in 1907
U.S. Leather (preferred)	Dissolved in 1952
U.S. Rubber	Became Uniroyal, now part of Michelin

INDUSTRY COMPOSITION OF THE DOW AVERAGE
MIRRORS CHANGES IN THE UNITED STATES

In the century since it was established, the Dow Jones Industrial Average has become more than merely a chart of stock prices. It is also a biography of American business, chronicling the shift from a nation of farmers and fledgling industrialists to a nation with an economy dominated by service and technology companies.

Even though Charles H. Dow called his list an industrial average, many of the original twelve stocks he chose paint the picture of an agrarian economy. The companies grew cotton, sugar and tobacco and provided cattle feed. To be sure, the original list also included gas, electric and chemical companies, along with streetcar and railroad companies.

Rope and leather figured prominently in the industrial average in its early days. At various times between 1896 and 1915, the average included U.S. Leather, U.S. Cordage, Standard Rope & Twine and Central Leather.

Changing modes of transportation can be traced in the industrial average's history. Pacific Mail Steamship was an early component.

American Locomotive and Baldwin Locomotive Works both joined in 1916 and went out during the 1920s.

The rising power of the auto industry was reflected in listings for American Car Foundry (1901), General Motors (1915), Studebaker (1916), Mack Trucks (1924), Nash Motors (1926), Chrysler (1928) and Hudson Motor Car (1930). In 1928, the first aerospace firm, Wright Aeronautical, was listed.

Despite rapid changes in the economy during and after World War II, the industrial average had no changes in makeup between 1939 and 1956. Since then, the substitutions have reflected the rising importance of the technology, entertainment and service industries.

For example, American Express was added in 1982, McDonald's in 1985 and J.P. Morgan in 1991. Hewlett-Packard joined in 1997.

Left: Farmers and buyers gathered around samples at a tobacco auction in Danville, Va., 1940
Opposite page: "Smokers' Corner" cigar box label with a color lithograph depicting men in a smoking lounge being shown cigars

GAUGING THE INDEX'S ALTITUDE

As the Dow Jones Industrial Average plowed ahead to record after record in the beginning of its second century, people were asking how to tell when stock prices get too high.

Unfortunately, there is no infallible gauge. However, it is certainly possible to say when the average is high or low by historical standards. Three of the yardsticks most commonly used are dividends, book value and earnings.

When the industrial average was created in 1896, detailed records weren't kept on those factors. But Ned Davis Research Inc. of Venice, Fla., has assembled data going back to 1905.

From February 1905 through December 1998, the research firm found, the industrial average has traded, on average, for about 25 times the collective dividends of the stocks that constitute it. Until recently, the record was 43 times the dividends, set in January 1906. The low was 6 times the dividends in May 1932. In April 1998, the price/dividend ratio reached a record of 64.5.

Book value is, in essence, corporate net worth. To determine book value per share, one sums up a company's assets, subtracts its liabilities, and divides by the number of shares outstanding.

The book value data go back only to 1924. Since then, the Dow industrial stocks have sold, on average, for 1.6 times book. The old record, reached in August 1929, two months before the historic crash, was 4.2 times book, and the low was 0.5 times book in June 1932. In 1996, the price/book ratio broke the old high, reaching 4.3 times book. In April 1998, it reached 5.4 times book.

Earnings are simply profits. The typical valuation for the industrial average has been 14 times trailing earnings (earnings for the four quarters preceding the measurement). The highest price/earnings ratio was 931 in August 1933, during the Great Depression. That wasn't because stock prices were especially high, but because earnings had all but dried up. The low was 6 in October 1979. At the end of 1998, the price/earnings ratio was 24. That's higher than usual, but unlike the two other measures, it isn't in the stratosphere.

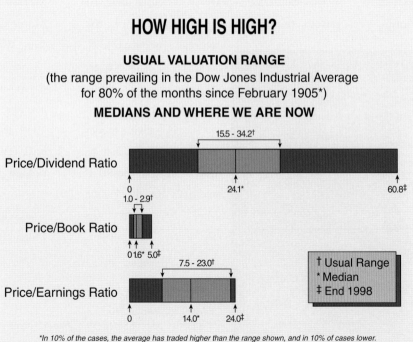

HOW HIGH IS HIGH?

USUAL VALUATION RANGE
(the range prevailing in the Dow Jones Industrial Average for 80% of the months since February 1905*)
MEDIANS AND WHERE WE ARE NOW

Price/Dividend Ratio — 15.5 - 34.2† | 0 | 24.1* | 60.8‡

Price/Book Ratio — 1.0 - 2.9† | 0 1.6* 5.0‡

Price/Earnings Ratio — 7.5 - 23.0† | 0 | 14.0* | 24.0‡

† Usual Range
* Median
‡ End 1998

*In 10% of the cases, the average has traded higher than the range shown, and in 10% of cases lower.
Source: Ned Davis Research Inc.

THE WAY IT WORKS

For as long as people have been investing in the stock market, they have been trying to figure out how it works.

A little more than a century ago, when buying stock was a lot like placing a bet at the racetrack, science had little to do with what we now know as market analysis. If there was anything close to a market theory, it was that a company was worth the net value of its visible assets. Any amount that its stock price rose above that level was somehow illegitimate. The difference between a stock's market price and the value of its underlying assets was considered "water," a term used with derision.

"Depriving a corporation of its stock-watering feature is almost the same as depriving a venomous serpent of its fangs," declared Kentucky Senator William Lindsay, an avowed enemy of these newfangled vehicles called industrial stocks. Senator Lindsay and like-minded people of a century ago considered most common stocks little more than scams.

This was the unruly world upon which Charles Dow in 1896 endeavored to impose the laws of science. Mr. Dow studied the inchoate equity markets in the spirit of a social scientist foraging for understanding among an aboriginal tribe, a viewpoint reflected in his newspaper, *The Wall Street Journal.* "Speculation is not at its best a simple and easy road to wealth," he wrote, "but speculation through people who advertise guaranteed profits and who call for participation in blind pools is as certain a method of losing as could possibly be discovered."

Analysts began speculating on what moves the market about a century ago. They didn't agree then, either.

A crowd of stock traders at the Curb Exchange on Wall Street in 1916. This market was eventually to move indoors and be renamed the American Stock Exchange.

29

From his observations, Mr. Dow discerned three types of movement in the stock market. The first is the daily action; the second, short swings of two weeks to a month or more. The former reflects speculators' activities, he said, and the latter reflects strategies of large investment pools. Both may be outright manipulations. But the third type of movement, roughly four years in duration, is different, he said, deriving from economic forces beyond the control of individuals.

Mr. Dow thought that expectations for the national economy were translated into market orders that caused stocks to rise or fall over the long term — usually in advance of actual economic developments. Thus, he likened the market's relationship to the broader economy to the function of a barometer, rather than that of a thermometer.

To quantify his theories, Mr. Dow developed the Dow Jones Industrial Average. Like most good ideas, it seems obvious in retrospect: How might anyone ponder market behavior without a means of measurement? Mr. Dow knew the average he created in 1896 had flaws, though at the time it was more representative of the market as a whole than it would seem later. There were so few industrial stocks then, that it was still possible to talk about their aggregate market.

Mr. Dow never ventured to give his name to a specific theory, but it happened anyway. What is now known as the Dow Theory was in fact developed by other market watchers who took Mr. Dow's observations of market cycles and spun them into sometimes intricate methods for predicting future price movements based on current trends. This is the heart of so-called technical analysis.

In Mr. Dow's time, the main rivals of the technical analysts, besides the tipsters, were analysts who later became known as fundamentalists. They interpreted economic statistics and, later, corporations' financial results, rather than market action itself. They watched commodity prices, currency exchange rates and the like. The market, in their view, was moved by the economy.

A drought in Europe, for instance, would require exports of grain, which would raise demand for, and thus prices of, agricultural products, and the railroads would gain business — a bullish outcome. They watched the balance of supply and demand in both the economy and the market; a buildup of "undigested securities" — stocks that were traded frequently rather than held — was, in their view, a sure indication of a market decline in the making. They investigated the business cycle, in the belief that the market and the economy moved in tandem.

Top left: Wheat field
Left: A metal grain elevator in Minnesota
Opposite page, top right: A pig-iron ladle pours hot liquid steel into a steel mold
Opposite page, bottom: U. S. Steel Company's Gary, Ind., steel mill

Over the years, fundamental analysts would focus on one or another statistic they considered paramount. In the 1920s, it was freight-car loadings. In the 1930s, it was the operating rate of steel plants and the production of paperboard. For a while in the 1950s, the output of sulfuric acid had its devotees. Then it was the money supply, as monetary economics enjoyed a vogue. By the 1980s, trade and budget deficits were much scrutinized. Through it all, interest rates remained a key indicator, and fads such as the length of women's skirts and the Super Bowl outcome had their day.

The Great Crash of 1929 and the Great Depression that followed not only damped the public's mania for stocks, they also gave rise to a new fundamentalist theory that perfectly suited the times. In 1934, academicians Benjamin Graham and David Dodd published the first of many editions of "Security Analysis," in which they set forth concepts of value investing.

They posited that a stock's price should reflect its underlying value — shades of

1896 attitudes dusted off and modernized. Most important, they said, was a stock's return to the investor. "The price paid for an investment in common stock would be determined chiefly by the amount of the dividend," they wrote.

One offshoot of the Graham-Dodd value theory was that of the risk/reward ratio, which held that the greater the risk, the greater should be the reward. By this reasoning, corporate bonds should yield more than government debt, and stocks more than bonds. Prices came to reflect this insight. In 1950, for example, the dividend yield on the Dow industrials averaged 6.9%, while triple-A corporate bonds offered 2.7% and long-term U.S. government bonds averaged 2.3%.

Out-and-out speculators remained in the market throughout the Great Depression and afterward, so they eventually came to share the market with conservative investors of the

Graham-Dodd variety. This dichotomy showed up on the most-active list. In 1950, the most active issues included Dow industrials such as U.S. Steel Corp. and General Motors Corp. as well as speculative issues selling for less than $10 a share, such as the companies now known as Benguet Corp., PepsiCo Inc. and AMR Corp.

As the 1950s progressed and Depression psychology faded, attitudes toward stocks mutated once more. Gradually, investors were drawn to securities that offered capital gains rather than income. This development

recalled the attitudes of the 1920s, but with a difference: These newcomers to the market had longer time horizons.

Investors and speculators alike sought growth from the next Control Data Corp. (now Ceridian Corp.) or Polaroid Corp. — flashy market performers, yes, but with solid companies behind them. This growing faith in the long-term allure of stocks expanded in the 1960s to include what are today considered the market's major players: pension funds and mutual funds. In 1949, institutions owned $11 billion worth of stocks; by 1971 they held $219

billion, mostly blue-chip, high-capitalization stocks like the Dow industrials.

By the early 1970s, indeed, institutional investors had amassed large holdings of stocks in General Electric Co., Exxon Corp., Procter & Gamble Co. and the like. These large commitments couldn't be liquidated easily, so the issues were dubbed "one-decision stocks." You bought them, period. Thus was born the "nifty fifty" — stocks that went up only because institutions, and those who followed them, just bought more and more, and for the most part held on to what they owned.

Clockwise from top left: Installing a TV antenna, 1951; fins of a 1957 Chevrolet; 1957 model GE steam iron; classic Oldsmobile; 1950 television set; rear light of a 1959 Cadillac
Opposite page: Exxon oil refinery at night

That helped to create a two-tiered market: When stock prices as a whole wobbled, the nifty fifty generally held up. But the bear market of 1973–1974 changed everything. By late 1974, after the Dow had nearly halved itself, the Dow industrials and the overall market were again synchronized, albeit on the downside.

What had happened was that the long-standing inverse relationship between stock and bond prices had dissolved. According to the old rationale, good economic times suggested higher corporate earnings but also higher interest rates. The former would help stocks; the latter would depress bonds. Likewise, during a recession, earnings would decline as would stocks, while falling interest rates and the search for safety would lift bond prices.

The stagflation of the 1970s — stalled economic growth coupled with high inflation — shook this postulate. Higher interest rates and inflation hit both stocks and bonds, and after it was over, the two types of securities tended to move together. As usual, Wall Street produced a reason to explain the change. Higher interest rates hurt business, so declines in the bond market would carry over into stocks. By the same logic, lower interest rates would stimulate the economy and lead to higher earnings and stock prices.

This change, and the public's willing-

A ticker-tape parade on New York's lower Broadway honoring Army General Douglas MacArthur, April 20, 1951. Police estimated that seven million people came to see and cheer the soldier, then the biggest turnout ever for such an event.

ness to pay relatively high prices for "growth" stocks, dismayed Benjamin Graham, among other theorists of the old days. The market, it seemed, betrayed efforts to explain its behavior.

He threw in the towel in 1976, saying, "I am no longer an advocate of elaborate techniques of security analysis in order to find superior value opportunities."

WHY CHARLES DOW WOULD PROBABLY DISCLAIM
ANY ALLEGIANCE TO THE THEORY THAT BEARS HIS NAME

Commentators like to speak of the stock market as though it were one of us — a live, up-and-about creature, occasionally down on its heels, but with a will and temperament all its own. We hear and read almost daily that the market is "trying to rally" or "laboring to overcome a barrier" and, indeed, are routinely apprised of some urgent bit of information that the market "is trying to tell us." So common is this exercise in anthropomorphism that newspaper readers and nightly news addicts barely notice it; probably, few of the commentators have thought about its implications, either.

The unspoken premise is that stock prices, rather than merely recording the past, are also a guide to the future. The evening anchorperson declaims that traders are bullish because on that day the Dow Jones Industrial Average rose. But we take the implicit meaning to be that the bullishness may well continue tomorrow and perhaps for a few tomorrows. Just so, "technical analysts" up and down Wall Street make a living from gazing at price charts.

These modern Merlins claim as their patriarch none other than Charles H. Dow, the inventor of the familiar stock averages, founder of *The Wall Street Journal* and the Dow of the famous Dow Theory of stock-market analysis. Yet if Mr. Dow could return, nearly a century after the phrase "Dow's Theory" first appeared in print, it's possible that he would disclaim any allegiance to it. Indeed, it's arguable that the vast and dubious field of technical analysis — that is, divining the market via chart reading — got its thrust from the distortion and selective editing of Mr. Dow's ideas.

Dow Theory, as it has long been understood, attempts to forecast the market, and also the economy, based on two strands of data — the paths of the industrial average and of its sister index, the Dow Jones Transportation Average (the "rails," in Mr. Dow's day). Although its adherents acknowledge that the theory isn't perfect, they make an oracular claim: All that a forecaster need consider is contained in those two averages. As Richard Russell, a Dow

Theory popularizer, wrote in *Barron's* in 1959, "The closing prices of the Dow Jones rail and industrial averages give us a complete index of everything known by anybody that can possibly affect the economy and corporate profits (excluding acts of God)."

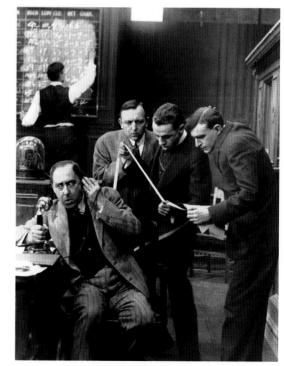

A scene from the 1914 film Queer Quarantine *with Wallace Beery*

Not corporate reports or economic statistics or anything else merits even a look.

The details of how Dow Theorists interpret the averages need not detain us. Suffice it to say that if both averages make higher highs, a bull market is thought to be alive and well, but if one lags behind, its failure to "confirm" is said to jeopardize the rally. In crude summary, if the two averages have been rising, it's time to buy; when both are hitting new lows, sell.

Mr. Dow, a modest man, never affixed his name to that theory or any other. Yet his ideas on investing, set out in hundreds of *Wall Street Journal* editorials, are clear enough.

Certainly, he believed that markets move in cycles; he was undeniably a chartist in the narrow sense that he believed that price patterns recur. Indeed, he devoted much study to the history and trends of recorded prices. But for Mr. Dow, market cycles were inextricably linked to business cycles. He was immensely interested in his stock averages, but no more so than he was in the prices of pig iron, cotton goods, woolens and shoes. He scrutinized the level of bank clearings, wages and railroad profits.

Born in 1851, Mr. Dow worked a great number of odd jobs when he was young, and he cut his journalistic teeth covering topics such as steamship traffic between New York and Providence and the silver strike in Leadville, Colo. By the time he turned to financial reporting, he had seen too much of the dynamism of that rapidly industrializing era to satisfy himself with a mystical faith in stock averages. Moreover, as opposed to Dow Theory, which would see the world through the lifeless prism of the ticker tape, Mr. Dow was ever conscious of the role human actors play in economic affairs. Certainly, no chart could explain the rhythm of the business cycle as vividly as he did.

In a depression, he wrote in 1900, the keeper of a country store buys only enough goods to meet current needs. Someday — perhaps the local farmers have a good crop — he finds his business improving and increases orders from wholesalers.

"Presently," Mr. Dow wrote, "he finds himself unable to get as good prices from the wholesaler as before, because other retailers are increasing their demands. This happens three or four times, and each time the retailer regrets that he did not buy more when prices were lower. Under the influence of this feeling, he buys for future requirements as well as present needs. This goes on all over the country."

And so the cycle turns.

The Dow Theorist — and any purely technical analyst — ignores the store clerks, because everything knowable about them is already reflected, or "discounted," in stock prices. But Mr. Dow thought the picture more complex. Stock prices might discount the future, he wrote, but they discount "shadows as well as substances and often anticipate that which does not occur."

Thus, they were of little help in forecasting. In his 1960 book, *Charles H. Dow and the Dow Theory,* financial historian George W. Bishop, Jr., observed, "There is no evidence that Dow looked upon the averages as containing anything more than an indication of a statistical nature of the trend." Mr. Dow didn't try to call tops and bottoms of markets, and he warned others that it was futile.

Instead, he urged the public to invest on the basis of underlying corporate value. That is, he advised people to value stocks according to their dividends, earnings, soundness of balance sheets and prospects, and to buy those issues trading well below their values. "Values determine prices in the long run," he often reminded readers. In this, he sounded remarkably like Benjamin Graham, the "father" of value investing a generation later. And value investing and Dow Theory are not merely dissimilar; as investment strategies, they are 180 degrees apart.

Mr. Dow's name became associated with the antipodal philosophy through the work of a series of Wall Street writers. The first was Samuel Armstrong Nelson, whose book *The ABC of Stock Speculation,* published in 1902, the year of Mr. Dow's death, referred in footnotes to "Dow's Theory."

Mr. Nelson was faithful in describing Mr. Dow's ideas but focused on only a few of them — namely, his market observations. A subsequent *Journal* editor, William Peter Hamilton, took the revisionism further, both in editorials and in a 1926 book, *The Stock Market Barometer.* Mr. Hamilton claimed to have had theoretical discussions with his mentor, but their relationship was apparently that of editor and cub reporter. As Mr. Hamilton described in the *Journal* in 1922, Mr. Dow "would call me up for a sort of police third degree on my previous day's work."

Once free of Mr. Dow's grilling, Mr. Hamilton reckoned that "Dow's theory in practice develops many implications." Under this umbrella, he adopted the full catechism of modern chart reading, including how to interpret such stock-chart configurations as "double

dips," "double tops" and so forth. Most important, he attributed to Mr. Dow the notion that it was of great predictive importance whether or not the industrial and rail averages moved in tandem (that is, confirmed each other).

Right: Ralph Ince is jubilant over the ticker tape in a scene from the film Wall Street
Opposite page: From the film Chancey on Wall Street, *an undated still shot*

Indeed, Mr. Hamilton regarded stock prices with reverence. Mr. Dow, who was for several years a stock-exchange member and knew its excesses firsthand, was skeptical of short-term stock-price moves. But Mr. Hamilton urged investors to ignore commodities markets, bank clearings, the price of tea or anything else. "Wall Street considers all these things," he argued. What's more, Wall Street's verdict — crystallized in the market — "is always right." No shadows for him.

Thus, whereas Mr. Dow preached a value strategy of buying on dips, Mr. Hamilton, his protégé, espoused the opposite, trend-following tactic of adding to holdings as prices rose. Prices themselves were seen as predictive of future prices.

It was impossible "to reconcile the writings of Dow with [much of] Hamilton," Mr. Bishop would note later. Nonetheless, market writer Robert Rhea, who did more than anyone else to spread the gospel, canonized the Hamilton version in a 1932 book, *The Dow Theory,* and in his 1930s market letters. Later writers such as E. George Schaefer occasionally pointed out that Messrs. Hamilton and Rhea had "steered away from Dow," but the critics were swimming upstream. Mr. Hamilton's ideas, as fiddled with by Mr. Rhea, became "Dow Theory," which "remains the basis for all technical analysis," Mr. Russell says.

The trouble with Dow Theory, and with all chart reading, is the intellectual vacuum at its core. What gives the market substance is that prices (eventually) approach value. By refusing to consider what securities are worth, by instead speculating on the basis of pictures, the chart readers are less investors than astrologers. As Mr. Dow realized more than one hundred years ago, it doesn't work.

With his market barometer in its second century, what better honor to Charles H. Dow than to remove his name from the first theory of chart readers? Perhaps, then, his name could be reclaimed for what he was: creator of the index, newspaperman — and value investor.

> *Mr. Hamilton's ideas, as fiddled with by Mr. Rhea, became "Dow Theory," which "remains the basis for all technical analysis."*

USE OF DOW THEORY IS DEBATED

In its most common form, Dow Theory holds that the Dow Jones Transportation Average must confirm the industrials' movement for a market trend to have staying power. One makes and the other takes, the thinking goes, so both should gain in a healthy market. If they diverge, watch out!

Today, people debate how well Dow Theory works.

Richard Evans, a Flossmoor, Ill., money manager, declares that it "works better than ever," predicting both the 1987 crash and the tepid 1994 market. But he says it isn't as useful in long-running bull markets as in times of sharp market swings.

Tim Hayes of Ned Davis Research Inc. in Venice, Fla., says that declines in trading volume, which Dow Theorists also track, are better warning signals than declines in the transports.

Dow Theory "isn't an exact technique," says Richard Russell, who writes a publication called "Dow Theory Letters" in La Jolla, Calif. Mr. Russell advocates a broad reading of the theory, taking into account many factors in addition to the two averages' interaction.

Fortune telling: Predicting the future by studying the sediments in a tea cup (undated engraving)

REVIEW & OUTLOOK
MR. DOW'S BAROMETER

"The stock market is in the nature of a barometer which reflects the rise and fall of general conditions," Charles Dow wrote in May 1899, in one of the first columns to bear the "Review and Outlook" title that continues on *The Wall Street Journal* editorial page. The Dow Jones Industrial Average has persisted for more than a century precisely because it symbolizes not merely 30 blue-chip stocks, but also the general health of the economy if not, indeed, our civilization. If Mr. Dow were alive today, surely he would be proud to see his average commanding attention daily, if not minute-by-minute, throughout the world.

What the market may be telling us is, of course, still debated among its adepts. Is it "efficient," in the economist's sense of digesting all information available at any given moment, and therefore sounder than even the wisest single sage? Or to the contrary, is it driven by "popular delusions and the madness of crowds"? Our own prejudice is toward the former, though even mere madness would be important as a reflection of the passing times.

As a barometer of the times, the Dow average has the great strength of continuity. Other averages may be mathematically more sophisticated, but the Dow has been tended with

"In The Hands of His Philanthropic Friends," political cartoon by C.J. Taylor, published in 1897

great care for over a hundred years now. So only the Dow Jones Industrial Average shows the sweep of a century, reflecting not only the market but economic and social history, as well.

Considering the variety of opinions, we ask, What is the market telling us? The clear and by no means trivial lesson is that by and large, for all the bumps on the road, history is progress. In little more than a century, the average moved from 40.94 on May 26, 1896, to 10006.78 on March 29, 1999. The market's rise also tracks, even allowing for the vagaries of inflation, the well-being of society and people not only in the United States but throughout the world.

Charles Dow produced his first industrial average at the intersection of two eras. In the years since the Civil War, five great intercontinental railroads had been laid. The 1890 census had measured the closing of the frontier. By 1895, the United States was producing more steel than Great Britain. Indeed, the development of the American continent had been the great project of humankind, with the world's capital and energies brought to bear through such international institutions as the gold standard and British free trade policies.

By the year 1896, British dominance of

the world economy was already ebbing, and in the United States the robber barons were losing sway. The era then budding, today still in bloom, if perhaps starting to fade, is an era of American global dominance and of governmental intrusion to soften the harsh edges of the market.

This era has been economically successful, the average shows, despite the enormous traumas of two world wars, the cold war and the Great Depression. Within the sweep of success, the stock market also shows us the era's fits and starts. Allowing for other interpretations of the charts, a few speculations: The market thrives on sound money and sours on prohibitive tax rates. We live in a global economy; world events repeatedly intrude, particularly in monetary matters.

America was slow to pick up the world economic leadership Great Britain had been forced to relinquish. The period after World War I was affected by the war debts the United States insisted on collecting from its allies and by the reparations the Allies insisted on extracting from Germany. These proved to be unsustainable policies, as John Maynard Keynes had predicted in his most prescient book, *The Economic Consequences of the Peace*, especially after the Smoot-Hawley tariff precluded the trading profits other nations needed in order to earn money to service their American debts.

After World War II, America displayed firm leadership in establishing the Bretton Woods system, thus facilitating the ensuing brilliant quarter-century. It tried to opt out of leadership in August 1971, when the United States abandoned the gold standard, and an era of world inflation began. Gradually, the Federal Reserve Board restored stability to the dollar, and thus to the world economy and this, too, was reflected by Mr. Dow's barometer.

The wars of the century produced big government and high taxes. Stripping away wartime tax rates, as Andrew Mellon and Calvin Coolidge did in the 1920s, Douglas Dillon and John Kennedy did in the 1960s, and Ronald Reagan did in the 1980s, contributed to booms in the markets and

growth in the economy. We can hope that with the fall of the Berlin Wall in 1989, an era of large wars has ended and we are in a new trend toward lower taxes and smaller government.

Indeed, if at its centenary the Dow average happened also to mark a new era, it bids to be one ruled less by nation-state politicians than by impersonal international markets. If so, we can also hope that this will be bullish for the market, promising for international prosperity and empowering for men and women around the globe.

"Uncle Sam Collects Income Tax," an 1895 cartoon by F. Opper

INDEX ROARED TO FAME IN THE 1920s

Try talking about the stock market without mentioning the Dow Jones Industrial Average. It is a little like talking about the weather without mentioning the temperature.

It wasn't always that way. For the first twenty-five years or so of its existence, the industrial average was absent, for the most part, from headlines in the financial press.

In the late 19th century and early 20th century, investors focused mainly on the action of individual stock issues rather than on the market as a whole. When they did look at market averages, they were more likely to look at railroad stocks, the blue chips of the day, than at industrial stocks, which were considered speculations.

It was in the Roaring Twenties that many investors first became intimately acquainted with the industrial average. That was when masses of average citizens began buying stocks by the bundle. Their enthusiasm carried the industrial average from around 100 in 1924 to nearly 400 by mid-1929.

Then the crash of 1929 thrust the Dow industrials into true prominence. Investors were hungry for a way to gauge the overall damage, so the Dow industrials made front-page headlines.

On October 28, 1929, *The Wall Street Journal*'s main headline announced that the "Industrials" were "off 38.33." The next day, they fell another 30.57 points. (Those two plunges, of 12.82% and 11.73%, respectively, remain the second highest and third highest of all time, in percentage terms, behind the record 22.61% crash on Black Monday, October 19, 1987.) In six days, the industrial average lost more than 96 points, nearly 30% of its value.

The Dow industrials began to be faced with competition in the mid-1920s. For example, the forerunner of Standard & Poor's 500 Index began compiling the performance of 90 stocks on a regular basis in 1926.

Today, there are several indexes that are more sophisticated. But the public has long since adopted the Dow Jones Industrial Average as its stock-market standard. If you ask the average investor what "the market" did today, you can bet that he or she will answer with the performance of the Dow industrials.

October 24, 1929, New York, N.Y.: thousands near the New York Stock Exchange as the market experienced the most hectic day of trading in financial history

NOTHING IS PERFECT

Sure, the Dow Jones Industrial Average is the granddaddy of stock-market measures. But it isn't perfect, and there are some on Wall Street who aren't fans of the measure at all.

The detractors argue that the Dow Jones Industrial Average has too few stocks. That it doesn't have all the right stocks. That it has a funny way of giving more weight to some stocks than others.

To a certain extent, they are right on all counts.

Certainly, there are plenty of more sophisticated indexes to chart the market's gyrations. In fact, the Dow can look downright old-fashioned, with its roster of only 30 blue-chip stocks, compared with such broader indexes as Standard & Poor's 500-stock index or the nearly 7,000 stocks in the imprecisely named

Board game manufactured by McLoughlin Brothers, New York, N.Y., 1883

Wilshire 5000. There are also the New York Stock Exchange Composite, the Nasdaq Composite and the Russell 2000 indexes. Dow Jones & Co. itself has a broader market gauge in the U.S. component of the Dow Jones

Global Index, which was rolled out in 1988 as the Dow Jones Equity Market Index and now has more than 700 stocks.

Because the Dow industrial average is selective, with many industries represented by just one or two stocks, it doesn't always accurately reflect what has happened in a particular sector. Just look at some examples in 1998. Exxon Corp., one of the Dow Jones components, posted a 19.5% gain for the year, compared with a 2% decline for energy stocks in general, according to industry-group data from the Dow Jones Global Index - U.S. Another Dow stock, Sears, Roebuck & Co., was off 6.1% for the year, whereas industry-group data showed that the consumer (cyclical) group as a whole gained nearly 40%, and broadline retailers rose 60.9%.

For as long as the Dow Jones Industrial Average has been around, there have been complaints about it.

Thus, most equity money managers don't use the Dow Jones industrials as a benchmark, preferring broader indexes such as the S&P 500, or specialized indexes that focus on such areas as small-capitalization, health care or foreign stocks.

Similarly, the industrial average can't tell investors whether their particular strategy is working. "If you use it as a measure by which to hire and fire your portfolio managers, you're going to be in a lot of trouble," says John Rekenthaler, publisher of "Morningstar Mutual Funds," a Chicago newsletter. "You need a more precise measurement."

But the Dow Jones Industrial Average has always been intended to be more of a general indicator for the public of where the market is going, rather than a microscope for money managers. "There is no index anywhere that satisfies all investors under all circumstances," says John Prestbo, markets editor of *The Wall Street Journal*. "That's why there are so many of them."

The Dow's guardians at the *Journal* have made many substitutions in the industrial average over the years. But, says Norman Fosback, editor of "Market Logic," a newsletter in Deerfield Beach, Fla., although the Dow's caretakers have made some wise changes — such as removing USX Corp. and adding Walt

Disney Co. in 1991 — they have also made some classic blunders.

His favorite example: the 1939 ejection of International Business Machines Corp. (IBM) to make room for AT&T Corp. Over the

next four decades, AT&T's share price slightly more than doubled, a laggardly performance. During the same period, IBM's stock split 29 times and racked up a cumulative price gain of 22,000%, Mr. Fosback says. IBM was brought

An old IBM computer at IBM's Watson Laboratory in 1954

back into the Dow fold in 1979, but by then its banner years were behind it, he says. "When the 20th century's greatest company experienced its greatest growth . . . it did not get credit" in the Dow Jones average.

Certainly, there are always anywhere from about sixty to one hundred twenty companies that would make perfectly good members of the Dow club. But often, "Changing things is just going to rearrange the furniture," says Mr. Prestbo. "It's not going to make any difference in the trend" that the Dow aims to show. Moreover, even though the Dow usually has some poor performers at any given time, it isn't supposed to serve as a model portfolio. In other words, the stocks are supposed to be representative of entire industries, rather than be the highest fliers within their industries at any given time.

Some say the Dow's biggest fault lies in its nature as a price-weighted measure. That means higher-priced stocks hold more sway over the industrial average's movements than lower-priced ones. A 5% move in IBM, for example, at the end of 1998 meant about a 38-point swing in the average, whereas a 5% move in International Paper would budge the average a little more than 9 points.

"It is a completely arbitrary and, many people would say, utterly irrational way to com-

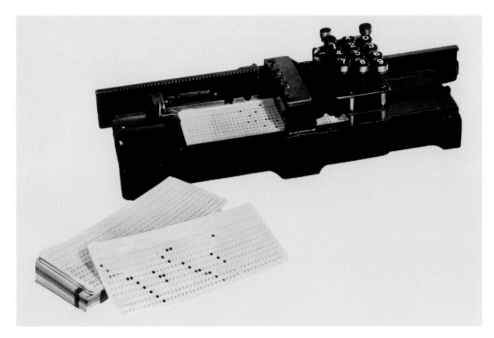

The first IBM key punch, manufactured in 1901

pute a market average," Mr. Fosback says.

Most newer indexes, such as the S&P 500, are weighted by market capitalization, which means they give more weight to bigger companies. Yet, because the industrial average's stocks usually do serve as reasonable proxies for their industries, the Dow generally tracks other indexes.

Of course, there are exceptions. Robert Dickey, technical stock analyst at Dain Rauscher in Minneapolis, Minn., recalls that in the first half of 1995, the S&P 500 outperformed the Dow Jones industrials because of the

strength of technology stocks, which are more widely represented in the S&P. But when the technology stocks started to flag in the second half of the year, the Dow outperformed the S&P.

Sometimes, people simply expect too much from the Dow. It doesn't predict the future, nor can it tell how your particular stock should have performed on a given day.

"People say, 'Gee, how come my stock didn't go up when the others went up?'" says Richard J. Stillman, professor emeritus at the University of New Orleans. "Frankly, they don't understand what the hell the Dow is."

Traders cheer on the floor of the New York Stock Exchange on March 18, 1999, as the Dow Jones Industrial Average hit the 10000-point mark at the closing bell. When the final transactions were tallied up after the closing bell, the market was found to have finished at a record 9997.62, up 118.21 points for the day. The market had hit the 10000 level twice during the day before dropping back. It finally closed above 10000 eleven days later.

THE GAUGE HAS STOOD THE TEST OF TIME

Like any classic, the Dow Jones Industrial Average has stood the test of time as a measure of the stock market's health.

"When we do historical research, we use the Dow," says Timothy Hayes at Ned Davis Research Inc. in Venice, Fla. "People criticize the Dow, saying it's too narrow, but if you want to compare what's happening today with what happened yesterday, it's the best measure."

The Dow Jones Industrial Average does seem, at first blush, like an archaic way to take the temperature of the stock market. To include just 30 stocks seems skimpy in a universe of some 12,000 public companies. Moreover, the average's arithmetic is unsophisticated. It gives more weight to a high-priced stock (such as International Business Machines) than to a low-priced one (such as Wal-Mart).

But for all the carping and complaining, the truth of the matter is that the Dow and other market gauges often move in concert. For

---

"The Dow's success is really more of a cultural phenomenon than anything else. It's something everyone understands."

---

example, the vast Wilshire 5000, an index of nearly 7,000 stocks compiled by computer, and the simple Dow diverged by just 0.05 percentage point in the year ended December 31, 1995. Although the difference was greater in subsequent years, for the five years ended December 31, 1998, they were less than two percentage points apart.

And it's still the Dow Jones Industrial Average that the public uses to measure the market. "The Dow's success is really more of a cultural phenomenon than anything else," says Richard Bernstein, director of quantitative strategy at Merrill Lynch. "It's something everyone understands."

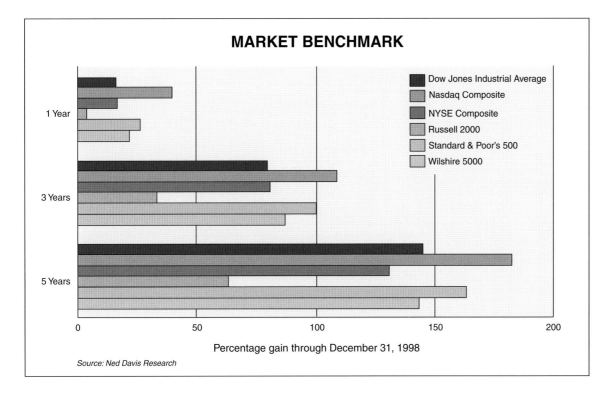

MARKET BENCHMARK

Legend:
- Dow Jones Industrial Average
- Nasdaq Composite
- NYSE Composite
- Russell 2000
- Standard & Poor's 500
- Wilshire 5000

Categories: 1 Year, 3 Years, 5 Years

Percentage gain through December 31, 1998

Source: Ned Davis Research

PART III

THE FIRST HUNDRED YEARS

A Union Pacific locomotive at the railyard in Salt Lake City, Utah

TRANSPORT INDEX: THE OLDEST GAUGE

The Dow Jones Industrial Average is the nation's best-known stock index, but it is not the oldest. The Dow Jones Transportation Average holds that honor.

The first Dow Jones stock index, assembled in 1884 by Charles Dow, cofounder of Dow Jones & Co., was composed of nine railroads, including the New York Central and Union Pacific, and two nonrails, Pacific Mail Steamship and Western Union. That was the ancestor of today's transportation average.

The iron horse powered the U.S. economy in the late 19th century. "The really strong companies at that time were primarily railroads," says Richard Stillman, professor emeritus of business administration at the University of New Orleans.

It wasn't until 1896 that the Dow Jones Industrial Average appeared. The same year, Mr. Dow published a list of twenty "active" stocks, eighteen of which were rails — the direct predecessor of the transportation average. On September 8, 1896, it stood at 48.55. At the end of 1998, the transportation average was just under 3150.

Over the years, railroads such as the Union Pacific (the only remaining original stock) have been joined in the average by the likes of Delta Air Lines, Federal Express and Ryder System.

The story of the rails in this century is one of pride, fall and partial revival. In 1916, 254,000 miles of rail lines crisscrossed the country, nearly twice the current figure. But regulation of prices and featherbedding by unions stunted railroads, says Richard Sylla, an economic historian at New York University. The stagnant industry was pounded by competition from trucks, revitalized waterways and, finally, airplanes.

According to Professor Sylla, the Pennsylvania Railroad was the country's biggest corporation in the 1870s. A century later, its descendant, Penn Central, filed for bankruptcy.

Since 1980, deregulation has brought a revival of sorts. Railroad employment has fallen nearly 60%, but the number of ton-miles shipped and the industry's net income have soared.

The Western Union Co. operating room in New York (undated engraving)

EASY BUT SLEAZY

A century or so ago, stockbrokers led lives many today would envy. When trading ended at 3 p.m., there still was plenty of time to visit the club.

That's what S.S. Pratt reports in his 1903 primer *The Work of Wall Street*, a tome that shows how far life on the Street then was from today's fast-paced financial world of split-second technology and round-the-clock marketplaces.

But although the life of a stockbroker in 1896, the year the Dow Jones Industrial Average was born, may have been one of comparative ease, it wasn't one that garnered much respect. After all, his clients weren't exactly the cream of society, either. "Stockbrokers tended to be sleazy," says Robert Sobel, a business historian at Hofstra University in Hempstead, N.Y. "Bond brokers were not. They catered to a much higher class of people."

If an investor did want to make a trade, he (or she — Hettie Green, renowned as a female speculator, made a fortune from railroad stocks and mortgage bonds) would rarely set foot in a stockbroker's office, leaving that to family retainers such as attorneys.

Those who did venture into the broker's world would find an office that looked like the library of a private home, complete with Oriental rugs and wall etchings. From their perches on comfortable sofas, clients could peruse financial journals and the day's newspapers. Or they could stroll to a buffet and pick at some food or watch the "board boys" manip-

The brokers of 1896 may have led lives of leisure, but they didn't get much respect.

ulate blocks of figures on the huge, wall-sized quote board that listed the latest prices.

Information for the board, organized industry by industry, came from a clacking stock ticker. Introduced in 1867, the ticker was by then old technology. (Before tickers, quotes were carried from office to office by runners.) In addition to stock prices, tickers also carried the big news of the day, such as the assassination of President William McKinley in 1901.

More progressive brokers had newer

An artist's rendition of the fatal shooting of President William McKinley, September 6, 1901, at the Pan-American Exposition at Buffalo, N.Y.

technology, such as the telephone. By 1900, Manhattan had 75,000 phones, used primarily for business. About 20% of them were located south of City Hall, most likely in the financial district.

The better-appointed brokers also had private, rather than public, telegraph lines; one company leased twelve private wires at the then outrageous sum of $55,000 a year. That network of private wires ultimately carried the ability to buy stocks to the rest of the nation.

A trade would commonly start in one of these offices, where an order would be given to a telegraph operator who would wire it to the stock exchange. At the Exchange, a floor broker would make the sale or purchase. He, in turn, would hand a memo of the trade to his telephone boy, who would then wire it back to the office, which would notify the customer.

On an average day, a trade could be executed in minutes. After the stock exchange began a central clearing operation in 1892, armies of runners would enter the street twice a day, carrying securities back and forth between the clearinghouse and the brokerage firms. Such jobs were the Wall Street equivalent of working in the mail room, but they provided starts for such Wall Street notables as E.H. Harriman and Bernard Baruch.

And runners weren't at the very bottom of the financial scene. That distinction went to the scourge of Wall Street — the "bucket shops." "Pests of speculation," wrote Mr. Pratt, "foul excrescences on the stock market." Bucket shops catered to low-end clients who bought stock with all the sophistication that goes into buying a lottery ticket.

There were about two hundred bucket shops located in the Wall Street area around 1900, and an additional eight hundred or so across the nation. They were mostly fly-by-night operations, frequently shutting their doors and moving their offices with no notice, especially in bull markets. That's because bucket shops couldn't make money when the market was going their customers' way for too long.

Bucket shops solicited clients through direct mail and Sunday newspaper advertisements, using such come-ons as "Confidential clerk to prominent operator knows of good dividend paying stock that will yield good profits." Or "Wanted: Party with capital to take advantage of my reliable information on the stock market."

"There was this wild speculation," says Richard Stillman. The bucket shops, he adds, were "the Wild West of the stock-market community," which itself wasn't very tame.

Operators at a telephone switchboard in 1895

Again Stock Quotations were VITAL . . .

Dow Jones Tickers

Flashed *Floor Prices* Yesterday Every 10 Minutes

10/29/29

AGAIN yesterday, as on last Thursday, the Dow Jones Electric Page News Tickers gave their brokerage-house and other subscribers the news of stock prices *which were prevailing on the floors* of the New York Stock Exchange and the New York Curb Exchange.

Every 10 minutes, Dow Jones News Tickers flashed the up-to-the-minute prices of the leading stocks.

Dow Jones News Tickers are located in all the principal financial offices of 98 American and Canadian centers, in 26 states and provinces.

Through the Dow Jones News Tickers the entire continent now obtains immediate news of Wall Street and all financial developments.

They give America the important news of finance, simultaneously with Wall Street.

• • •

Dow Jones Electric Page News Tickers are operated in

ALABAMA
Birmingham

CALIFORNIA
Beverly Hills
Hollywood
Long Beach
Los Angeles
Oakland
Pasadena
San Francisco
Santa Monica

CONNECTICUT
Bridgeport
Greenwich
Hartford
New Haven
Stamford
Waterbury

DELAWARE
Wilmington

DISTRICT OF COLUMBIA
Washington

GEORGIA
Atlanta

ILLINOIS
Chicago

KENTUCKY
Louisville

LOUISIANA
New Orleans

MAINE
Portland

MASSACHUSETTS
Boston
New Bedford
Springfield
Worcester

MICHIGAN
Detroit

MINNESOTA
Minneapolis
St. Paul

MISSOURI
St. Louis

NEW JERSEY
Asbury Park
Atlantic City
Bayonne
Elizabeth
Jersey City
Newark
New Brunswick
Perth Amboy
Spring Lake
Trenton
Union City
Westfield

NEW YORK
Albany
Auburn
Binghamton
Buffalo
Cedarhurst
Flushing

NEW YORK (cont'd.)
Glen Cove
Huntington
Kingston
Long Island City
Long Beach
Mount Vernon
New York
Portchester
Poughkeepsie
Rochester
Schenectady
Southampton
Staten Island
Syracuse
Troy
Utica
Watertown
Yonkers

OHIO
Akron
Canton

OHIO (cont'd.)
Cincinnati
Cleveland
Dayton
Toledo

OREGON
Portland

PENNSYLVANIA
Allentown
Bethlehem
Easton
Harrisburg
Hazleton
Lancaster
Philadelphia
Pittsburgh
Pottsville
Reading
Scranton
Washington
Williamsport

PENNSYLVANIA (cont'd.)
Wilkes Barre
York

QUEBEC
Montreal

RHODE ISLAND
Pawtucket
Providence

TENNESSEE
Memphis
Nashville

VIRGINIA
Richmond

WASHINGTON
Seattle
Tacoma

WEST VIRGINIA
Wheeling

WISCONSIN
Milwaukee

The Dow Jones News Ticker Service is being extended to other cities.
Inquiries are invited.

DOW, JONES & CO.

44 Broad Street, New York • *Publishers of* The Wall Street Journal

---

SENDING NEWS OVER BROAD TAPE

For years, the clatter of Dow Jones "broad tape" machines brought word of the Dow Jones Industrial Average's ups and downs to the nation's investors.

When Charles Dow and Edward Jones first launched their business-news enterprise in 1882, they disseminated the news on "flimsies," essentially sheets of carbon paper with handwritten news on them. A clerk pressing hard on the paper could generate up to twenty-four flimsies at a time; runners carried them to businessmen and speculators eager for the latest business gossip.

By 1883, the pair were labeling their output the "Customer's Afternoon Letter." In 1889, the letter metamorphosed into *The Wall Street Journal,* and in 1896, the Dow Jones Industrial Average was launched.

Just one year later, in 1897, Dow Jones & Co. started disseminating financial news via teletype on the broad tape, so called to distinguish it from the narrow "ticker" tape on which the stock exchanges disseminated stock quotes.

Despite this distinction, many people over the years have informally referred to the Dow Jones News Service as "the ticker," and some do so to this day.

Many of the early machines "looked like upright coffins," recalls Robert N. Williams, an executive with the news service. They were noisy, too. In 1971, Dow Jones began offering a quieter printer, manufactured by General Electric.

But brokerage houses didn't necessarily think silence was golden. "Most of the older brokers objected to not having the printer noise," Mr. Williams says. "They thought it kept the brokers and customers energized."

At one time, more than five thousand printers churned out financial news in brokerage and corporate offices around the nation. Some even projected the news on a giant screen for customers to gawk at. But today the news service no longer disseminates the Dow Jones averages on tape, broad or otherwise. The last broad-tape machines were phased out in 1995. In their place is the quiet hum of computers.

Right: An early Dow Jones ticker machine
Opposite page, left: Advertisement for Dow Jones stock tickers that appeared just after the market crashed in 1929
Opposite page, right: Dow Jones Financial News Bulletin Slip, 1939; like the "Customer's Afternoon Letter" that gave Charles Dow and Edward Jones their start in the 1880s, it provided intraday market news

NO ONE NOTICED THE 100-POINT MARK

On January 12, 1906, the Dow Jones Industrial Average surged above 100 for the first time.

Nobody paid any attention.

In a striking contrast to later milestones, the industrial average's first major benchmark — which occured ten years after the index was launched — occasioned no hoopla or analytical scrutiny.

That day, *The Wall Street Journal* quietly noted the closing level of the Dow industrials — 100.25 — in a table. The day's lead article was about currency reform. The stock-market report talked about a "continuing bullish move" but made no mention of the industrial average.

Why the silence? Well, stocks were still considered speculative investments, industrial stocks particularly so. The blue chips of the day were railroads, and the industrial average, which began life in 1896 at the level of 40.94, hadn't yet caught on as the public's favorite stock-market barometer.

The stock market was extremely strong in late 1905, with the industrial average rising 17% in the fourth quarter as it approached the 100 mark. According to historian Robert Sobel, "The economy was going great guns," President Teddy Roosevelt was avidly probusiness, and the United States had won a ringing victory in the Spanish-American War. The economic boom was spurred partly by strong expansion in railroads, autos and steel and partly by the lingering stimulative effects of big gold discoveries in the Yukon and elsewhere.

Despite all of that, the Dow Jones industrials declined 2% for all of 1906, reflecting the effects the San Francisco earthquake, the major investigation of the life-insurance

industry by New York state, and the anticipation of a 1907 recession.

Incidentally, although the Dow industrials didn't make page one of the *Journal* on January 13, 1906, a situation-wanted ad placed by a stenographer did. She was seeking a position with an established business at a salary of $12 to $15 a week.

Left: Theodore Roosevelt, who later became President of the United States, leading the Rough Riders cavalry regiment to victory at the Battle of San Juan Hill in Cuba during the Spanish-American War
Above: Theodore Roosevelt campaigning for the presidency

DJIA MILESTONE 100
FRIDAY, JANUARY 12, 1906

REVIEW AND OUTLOOK

SWADDLING CLOTHES

Mr. Schiff's recent epigram that New York, while still in swaddling clothes, was trying to play the role of a financial giant is, to say the least, very suggestive. There is unquestionably a certain measure of truth in it.

The idea that Mr. Schiff clearly intends to convey is that Wall Street is attempting to carry on financial transactions of tremendous magnitude without the facilities that are necessary for them. A giant wears armor and wields a battle-axe. But Wall Street, striving to do a giant's work, is still wrapped in baby clothes.

What is there lacking in the financial equipment of Wall Street which justifies this type of speech? Wall Street has banks which in capitalization and deposits rival those of Europe. Wall Street has a great stock exchange. It possesses clearing houses. It has the machinery of a financial first-class market. Why then does Mr. Schiff say that it is still wrapped in swaddling clothes?

He says this because from time to time Wall Street discloses an inability to carry on at once a great speculation and to facilitate the operations of legitimate trade. Its credit facilities seem to be inadequate to furnish at the same time the means for conducting properly both speculation and business. Either the necessities of business reduce the allowance upon which speculation may draw, or the demands of speculation cut short the allowance for trade. As speculators are usually better able and more willing to pay higher rates for money than merchants, it is usually trade that suffers most from this condition of things.

Copying information from a bulletin board inside the New York Stock Exchange, 1905

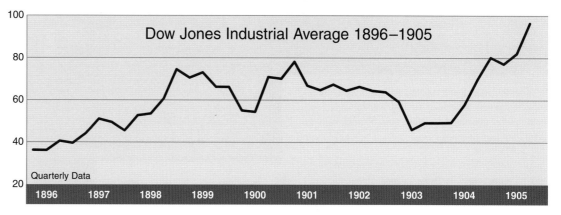

Dow Jones Industrial Average 1896–1905

Quarterly Data

100 80 60 40 20

1896 1897 1898 1899 1900 1901 1902 1903 1904 1905

Left: The wounded are treated in a bombed-out church in Meuse, France, during World War I

Center: A recruitment poster from World War I, designed by Laura Brey

Right: Soldiers at war

Opposite page: Newspaper sellers in London advertise their wares with headlines about the stock exchange and martial law in Germany at the start of World War I

ENLIST

On Which Side of the Window are YOU?

LAURA BREY

BIG BOARD'S 1914 SHUTDOWN

For more than one hundred years, the Dow Jones Industrial Average has been published almost every business day. One big exception ocurred during World War I, when the New York Stock Exchange shut down for four and a half months.

The shutdown began just after the war started in July 1914, as the Big Board followed the lead of European exchanges and closed. The move was unusual because the Exchange has rarely suspended trading for more than a day. Since World War I, the Exchange has remained open through wars, natural disasters and economic crises.

Historians attribute the unusual 1914 decision to the economic theories of British economist Norman Angell. A year earlier, Mr. Angell had written *The Great Illusion*, predicting that a major world war would cause a global financial meltdown. The theory: Businesses and governments would liquidate investments and flee to the haven of gold bullion when such a conflict erupted.

Robert Sobel says the Exchange's board of governors bought this story of doom and gloom. On July 31, the group decided to close the Exchange. Trading in all stocks didn't reopen until December 15, and then under restrictions that specified minimum prices. Unrestricted trading resumed in April of 1915.

Of course, stock traders abhor a vacuum. Within days of the shutdown, traders and speculators had set up shop outside the Exchange's Wall Street headquarters. Despite threats of reprisals from the Exchange, business was conducted in an open-air black market.

When partial trading resumed in December, stocks moved above their late-July levels. Foreigners did, in fact, dump stocks on the Exchange, but they were snapped up by American investors.

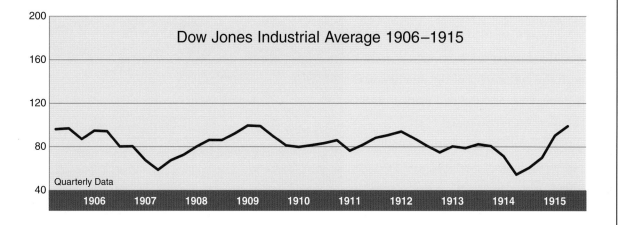

EUPHORIA REIGNED IN '27 MARKET

America was in a cocky mood in 1927.

Charles Lindbergh flew across the Atlantic alone. Babe Ruth hit sixty home runs. Flappers flaunted skirts that rose to goodness-knows-where. And on December 19, the Dow Jones Industrial Average passed 200 for the first time.

It had been more than twenty years since the industrial average had hit the 100 mark in early 1906. For those two decades, the compound average annual gain in the index was an unexciting 3.2%. World War I and a fierce flu epidemic were among the factors that held down stocks in the early part of the century.

But in the Roaring Twenties, the stock market rocketed. The industrial average set a record in each of six consecutive years from 1924 through 1929. That was the longest such string on record until the bull market of the nineties, and by some measures, the bull market of the twenties was the strongest ever.

Give part of the credit to President Calvin Coolidge, known as Silent Cal. When Mr. Coolidge said, "The business of America is business," he meant it. His hands-off, or laissez faire, policies contributed to the economic and stock-market booms of the time.

"Everything was going well" in 1927, says historian Robert Sobel. "There was full employment. There was [almost] no inflation. The [national] debt was being paid off. And there were three tax cuts under Coolidge. People today don't realize how popular Coolidge was at the time."

Inspired by the Lindbergh flight, investors piled into aviation stocks in 1927, Mr. Sobel says, much as they piled into Internet stocks seven decades later. Curtiss-Wright, United Aviation and Boeing were among the beneficiaries.

Of course, the boom didn't reach everyone. "The primary beneficiaries of the prosperity were white males," says Richard Stillman. "Neither females nor blacks were welcome" in the big businesses of the day, or even in the business schools.

Charles Lindbergh in the Spirit of St. Louis, arriving at Croydon Airport outside London after completing the world's first solo transatlantic flight

DJIA MILESTONE 200
MONDAY, DECEMBER 19, 1927

REVIEW *and* OUTLOOK

Credit Confidence

At the beginning of the year businessmen were mostly cautious as to immediate commitments. Bankers were also hesitant. Back of many people's minds was a vague idea that having had a fairly long spell of prosperity some sort of setback was necessarily due. They called this the end of a cycle. The fact that next year is a presidential year was also a deterring factor.

Why the election should make its influence felt a full eighteen months ahead is open to question. It is not as if there is any momentous issue ahead affecting the fundamental welfare of the nation, such as there was for instance, in the 90's when Bryan's silver campaign menaced business enterprise. Happily there is no danger of communism in this country. Labor is itself enjoying prosperity. No movement is under way inimical to "big business." Barring unforeseen events, there is nothing worse ahead than the ordinary domestic problems inherent in a republican form of government, the effects of which this country should now be pretty well inured against. As the national conventions and elections draw nearer these problems will naturally come to the fore in more or less accentuated form.

Flappers dancing on the edge of a rooftop

A PROSPEROUS '28 CLOSES AT 300

It took nearly twenty-two years for the Dow Jones Industrial Average to rise from 100 to 200. But it took barely more than a year for it to vault to the next 100-point mark.

The industrial average hit precisely 300 on the last day of 1928. It had soared 48% that year, making 1928 one of the best in history. (The only better years have been 1915 and 1933.)

"I call it the final fling upward," says Richard Stillman, who has written a book on the DJIA. "This was a great era of euphoria. Prosperity was an explosion: Automobiles were in mass production, radios were in mass production," and the telephone and aerospace industries were taking off.

Professor Stillman thinks that Herbert Hoover's victory over New York Governor Al Smith in the 1928 presidential race also helped the Dow industrials surmount 300. "The political climate continued to be highly favorable to business," he says. Mr. Hoover favored "rugged individualism," and the less interference in business, the better.

A few weeks before the DJIA hit 300, the editors of The Wall Street Journal, who determine how the industrial average is calculated, made major changes. They increased the number of listed stocks to 30 from 20. Today, the industrial average still lists 30 stocks, despite periodic replacements.

The 1928 shift paid homage to the growing power of the auto industry. Chrysler Corp. and Nash Motors were both added, as was Bethlehem Steel Corp., which provided metal for the cars, and Texas Corp., which later became Texaco Inc. Other additions were Postum, which made a then-popular beverage, Victor Talking Machines, a phonograph maker, and Radio Corp. of America.

After hitting 300, the Dow industrials would soar higher in 1929, peaking at 381.17 in September. But in the crash of 1929 and the Depression, they would plummet. It would take a quarter of a century — until 1954 — for them to surmount the 300 barrier again.

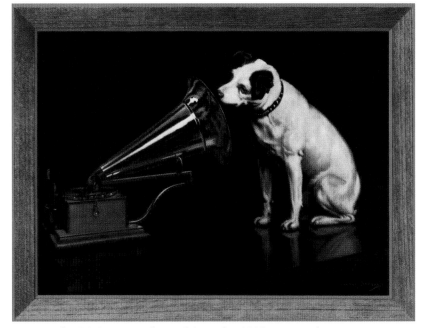

Nipper, the RCA mascot, began life in this 1898 painting by Francis Barraud of a dog looking down the horn of an early phonograph. It was entitled "His Master's Voice."

DJIA MILESTONE 300
MONDAY, DECEMBER 31, 1928

U.S.-PANAMA AIR MAIL LINE

Pan American Airways, Inc., Plans to Inaugurate
New Service on January 11, Next

Air mail service between the United States and the Panama Canal Zone, more than 2,000 miles, linking seven countries with the United States and clipping 5 to 20 days from best previous travel time through Central America, will be opened on January 11, 1929, by Pan American Airways, Inc., the operating company for Aviation Corp. of the Americas.

The new air line will operate from Miami to Havana, Cuba; Belize, British Honduras; Tela, Honduras; Corinto and Managua, Nicaragua; Puerto Arenas, San Jose, Costa Rica; Panama City, David and Cristobal, in the Canal Zone, with overnight stops at Belize and Managua.

Before opening of the Miami-Panama route, Pan American Airways, Inc., will inaugurate regular mail and passenger service over three additional routes, to Havana direct, to Nassau, in the Bahamas and through Cuba, Haiti, San Domingo, to San Juan, at the far tip of the West Indies.

This plane, seen over a ship hundreds of miles from shore, was used in early passenger and mail flights between the United States and points in the Caribbean

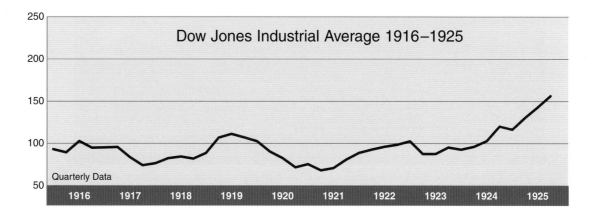

Dow Jones Industrial Average 1916–1925

Quarterly Data

50 100 150 200 250

1916 1917 1918 1919 1920 1921 1922 1923 1924 1925

A LESSON FROM THE CRASH OF 1929

Since the crash of October 1987 and the "minicrash" of October 1989, conventional wisdom has ordained that stocks should be bought after a big market decline. But a look back at another October long ago shows that the stock market can be brutal even to investors who try to get in at bargain levels by "buying on the dips."

In 1987, investors certainly did get a big payoff for buying stocks right after October 19's heart-pounding 22.6% drop in the Dow Jones Industrial Average. That one-day debacle turned out to be the final downswing of a two-month bear market. In less than two years, the Dow returned to its precrash peak, en route to a series of record closes until it reached 10000 in 1999.

The minicrash of 1989 was the same story. The industrial average fell 6.9% in a single frightening day, but seven months later, it was higher than it had been before. After the Dow plunged 7.2% on October 27, 1997, it took less than a month to recover.

But before people turn buying on the dip into a secular religion, they should consider the very different result of the Dow's 23% decline in the famous crash of October 28 and 29, 1929.

From 230, the industrial average zigzagged, heading south to 199 in November, then north to nearly 300 the next spring. But then it began a long, sickening slide that saw it bottom at just 41 on July 8, 1932.

A bargain-hunter who bought on November 30, 1929, and didn't sell in the 1930 rally, had to wait until July 1936 to show a profit, according to Ned Davis Research Inc. in Venice, Fla. And that's assuming all stock dividends were reinvested.

Looking at stock price alone, an investor who bought in 1929 had to wait until 1954 to see the Dow industrials claw their way back to their October 1929 highs.

"Buying on the dips would be a great strategy," says Todd Jaycox of Chicago consultants Ibbotson Associates Inc., "if we only knew what point on the dip was the lowest."

Above: Investor Walter Thornton tries to raise cash by selling his luxury roadster after the 1929 stock market crash. Opposite page: Young men from the Civilian Conservation Corps clear rocks from a truck trail in Snoqualmie National Forest, Wash., August 1933

VOLATILE STOCKS MARKED THE '30s

Most investors know that the Dow Jones Industrial Average did miserably during the Depression of the 1930s. It began the decade at 248.48, down from a high of 381.17 before the crash of 1929. By July 1932, the depths of the Depression, the industrial average was crawling at 41.22. It ended 1939 at 150.24.

What many investors don't know is that the decade of the 1930s was also the most volatile decade on record for stock prices. Investors, their nerves rubbed raw by the Depression, were prone to fits of euphoria and despair.

Thus, the industrial average plunged 52.7% in 1931 and 32.8% in 1937, but it rose 66.7% in 1933 and 38.5% in 1935. Daily volatility was also intense. Strange as it may seem, seven of the ten biggest up days in history, on a percentage basis, occurred during the 1930s.

Franklin Delano Roosevelt took office in 1933, instituted social programs and put people to work constructing roads and public buildings. The history of his administration could serve as a political Rorschach test. Peering at the inky lines, some see Demon Roosevelt, others Savior Roosevelt.

The stock market generally seemed to like FDR's measures. The Dow industrials rose 39 points in 1933, 6 points in 1934, 40 points in 1935 and 36 points in 1936.

Richard Stillman says the launch of the Civilian Conservation Corps, the Securities and Exchange Commission and Social Security helped to turn the Dow around.

Phooey, says Robert Sobel. The market was rebounding anyway, he points out, and the New Deal provided a psychological, not an economic, boost.

By 1938, the Dow had fallen below 100 again. Mr. Sobel blames Mr. Roosevelt, because he raised taxes. Mr. Stillman says overseas demand for U.S. goods was weak, as other countries were embroiled in their own miseries.

The two historians agree that World War II was the spark that finally ended the agony. Says Mr. Sobel, "The war took the country out of the Depression, not Roosevelt. You have Hitler to thank."

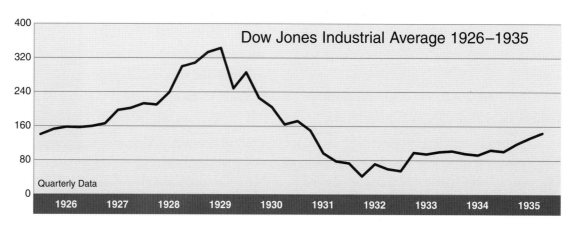

Dow Jones Industrial Average 1926–1935

Quarterly Data

400 — 320 — 240 — 160 — 80 — 0

1926 1927 1928 1929 1930 1931 1932 1933 1934 1935

HITLER AND THE PANIC OF 1940

In early 1940, Adolf Hitler's armies were on the march, sending the Dow Jones Industrial Average into one of the steepest tailspins in its history.

In the panic of 1940, the average declined more than 23% in just two weeks.

From a monthly high of 148.17 on May 9, the average fell to 113.94 on May 24. The market, which had been strong, turned nervous after the Nazi army invaded Denmark

and Norway in April 1940, several months after Germany had overwhelmed Poland. *The Wall Street Journal* noted that "the current stock market is well-charged with psychological dynamite."

On May 9, the *Journal* stated that an invasion of Holland "would awaken fears that England was about to be attacked." The next day, Hitler's armies swarmed into the Low Countries of Holland, Belgium and Luxembourg, and were on their way to a quick victory in France.

In the middle of the decline, the *Journal*'s column "Abreast of the Market" reported that "while numerous practical-minded individuals in Wall Street take the view that more intense warfare will be stimulating to our industries . . . they recognize the dangers inherent in a swift German victory."

By June 11, after the German invasion of France was under way and the British had been forced to abandon their defense of northwestern France

and Belgium at historic Dunkirk, the Dow changed course and stayed largely on an upward trend for the remainder of the year.

"Once the initial shock of the fall of the Maginot Line was over, you had a recovery," says historian Robert Sobel. Economic historian Richard Sylla adds that as the battle of Britain was waged, it became clearer that the Royal Air Force would be able to defend Britain, so American investors felt "they weren't going to wake up the next day and find that Britain had fallen."

Top left: Joseph Goebbels, Nazi minister for propaganda, speaking to members of Hitler Youth in Berlin, 1935
Above: The Blitz bombing of London in September 1940; smoke pours from a building near St. Paul's Cathedral

AN INFAMOUS DAY FOR STOCKS

On December 7, 1941, Japanese planes bombed the U.S. naval base at Pearl Harbor in Hawaii, dragging the United States into World War II.

President Franklin D. Roosevelt called it "a date which will live in infamy," and the stock market certainly agreed. The Dow Jones Industrial Average fell 3.5% on December 8 to a 112.52 close from 116.60, and stayed on a downward trend for five months.

Until Pearl Harbor, many Americans had hoped the United States would avoid direct military involvement in World War II, but the Japanese attack made that impossible.

The attack, which took U.S. forces by surprise, also took the stock market by surprise. Here's how *The Wall Street Journal*'s column "Abreast of the Market" described the situation: "The outbreak of hostilities between Japan and the United States came after the close of a week in which stocks had scored the most vigorous advances witnessed in several months. While tension existed in U.S.-Japanese relations, the Street had felt that negotiations between Tokyo and Washington were likely to proceed for some time before the matter came to a head."

One of the market's big worries was how the war would be financed. It was obvious that the Roosevelt administration would have to raise taxes, borrow heavily or both. This unpleasant situation was described in the *Journal* as a "shadow . . . overhanging the landscape."

On the plus side, however, entrance into the war meant "reshaping the productive machine to assure maximum output for the enemy's defeat," as the *Journal* put it in a front-page article. Some economists believe it was the war effort that finally pulled the United States out of the economic doldrums that had begun in the early 1930s.

The industrial average continued to drift downward until it hit bottom in late April 1942 at 92.92. Then it began to recover and chug upward. By year-end 1942, it was at 119.40, and by the end of 1945, the year the war ended, it stood at 192.91. Over the years, that pattern — an initial drop followed by a rebound — has been the typical pattern to occur when the United States gets involved in military conflicts.

Sailors scramble to escape the sinking battleship U.S.S. California after the surprise attack on Pearl Harbor by the Japanese, December 7, 1941

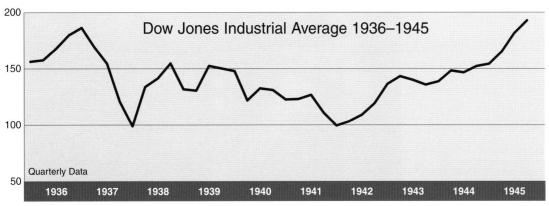

Dow Jones Industrial Average 1936–1945

Quarterly Data

200

150

100

50

1936 1937 1938 1939 1940 1941 1942 1943 1944 1945

Top left: A U.S. Marine on Peleliu Island, Palau Islands, waits for reinforcements before advancing, March 19, 1945
Top right: A poster promoting Victory Gardens as part of the war effort during World War II
Opposite page: An operation on a wounded soldier at the 8209th Mobile Army Surgical Hospital, twenty miles from the front lines of the Korean War in August 1952

DOW REACTED GRIMLY TO WAR

The outbreak of the Korean War sent the Dow Jones Industrial Average into a tailspin.

North Korean forces attacked South Korea on June 25, 1950. The industrial average had begun to decline three days earlier, on June 22.

The confrontation had been building since the splitting of Korea along the 38th parallel after World War II. The North fell under the influence of the Soviet Union, the South under the watch of the United States.

When the 38th parallel was crossed, the United States seemed uncertain how to respond. In just under three weeks, the industrial average fell 12%, to 197.46 on July 13.

By July, Geneneral Douglas MacArthur had taken command of the United Nations forces assisting the South Koreans, and military supplies were being shipped to the troops. As the number of General MacArthur's victories mounted and his men marched northward, so did the Dow. The industrial average ended the year up 17.6%, and it tacked on another 14.4% in 1951.

"The Korean War was a good period for the Dow, but not necessarily all due to the War," says historian Richard Sylla. "The defense stocks did very well and the rails did even better because a lot of supplies needed to be transported."

The Dow industrials dipped again later in 1950, when Chinese forces entered the war on North Korea's side. Fighting continued into 1951 with little hope of a military victory for either side.

Disagreements over U.S. policy toward China spurred President Harry Truman to fire Geneneral MacArthur in April 1951. The stock market rose on the news, reflecting the reluctance of Americans to risk a war with China and, potentially, with the Soviet Union, according to Mr. Sylla.

A truce in July 1953 ended the fighting, after 33,651 American soldiers had died. The following year, 1954, the Dow finally reached and passed the levels it had attained before the great crash of 1929.

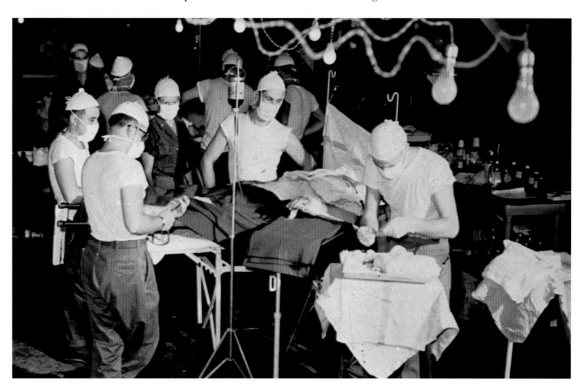

ELVIS, IKE AND DOW JONES 400

In the mid-1990s, the Dow Jones Industrial Average rolled through 100-point milestones like a steamroller plowing through whipped cream. It wasn't always so easy. It took twenty-five years for the industrial average to move from 300 to 400.

The Dow industrials finally cleared the 400 barrier on December 29, 1954. Dwight D. Eisenhower was in the White House that year, *On the Waterfront* was a hit in the movie theaters and Elvis Presley was just starting out on his climb to the top.

The index's breaking 400 was the lead story in *The Wall Street Journal* on December 30. In other articles that day, Henry Ford II said Ford Motor Co. earnings were "way up," NATO was preparing to admit West Germany, and a steel executive predicted record production for the year ahead.

For the Dow industrials, crossing the 400 milestone was only one bright spot in a great decade. The 1950s were the best decade ever for the industrial average, up 239.5% over the ten-year span. (At the end of 1998, it looked like the 1990s would top that record.)

The industrial average had first hit 300 on the last day of 1928, during the great Roaring Twenties bull market. In 1929, it flirted with 400, rising as high as 381.17 at the peak in September.

Then came the great crash of October 1929 and the Depression. In July 1932, the industrial average fell to 41.89, about a point above where it had begun, back in 1896. It didn't make it back up to 300 until March 1954, only nine months before the 400 barrier was shattered.

When the 1950s began, investors were worried about Russia, the chance of another world war, and the prospect of recession. But the country gained confidence as the decade wore on. The United States was a superpower, inflation was low and economic growth was robust. Cars sprouted tailfins and the market sprouted wings.

President Eisenhower's two terms were a bonanza for the already strong stock market, with the industrial average climbing from 291.90 at the end of 1952 to 615.89 at the end of 1960, a gain of 111%. Investors could truly say, "I like Ike."

Even the mike must rock and roll as the volcanic Elvis Presley whips into a hectic finale. Go, man, go!

DJIA MILESTONE 400
WEDNESDAY, DECEMBER 29, 1954

Comics Adopting Dior Look for Their Ladies In Clean-Up Campaign

* * *

Many Will Drop Gap-Tooth Hags, Details of Crime as Well, Industry Censor Says

By a THE WALL STREET JOURNAL *Staff Reporter*

NEW YORK — The "Dior Look" is coming to comic books.

Full-blown feminine curves have been de-emphasized in the comics that will begin appearing on newsstands in January with the seal of the Comics Code Authority, says Charles F. Murphy, the industry's censor. The books will also omit gap-toothed hags, pools of blood, and detailed illustrations of how crimes were committed, he adds.

In his first press conference since the industry's self-regulatory code to clean up crime, horror and sex in the comics was adopted on October 27, Mr. Murphy, a former New York City municipal judge, reviewed the work his office had done. His five reviewers had rejected entirely 126 comic-book stories of 2,640 submitted for review; eliminated 5,656 drawings, and caused revision of many others, he said.

About 25% of the material banned, he asserted, had concerned exaggerated female curves. These have been "restored to more natural dimensions," and the ladies are more fully covered, he said.

Judge Charles F. Murphy, code administrator for the Comics Magazine Association of America, holding a selection of approved comic books

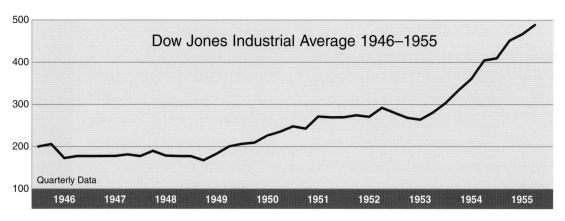

Dow Jones Industrial Average 1946–1955

Quarterly Data

1946 1947 1948 1949 1950 1951 1952 1953 1954 1955

DOW CRUISED TO 500 IN THE NIFTY FIFTIES

It took a quarter century for the Dow Jones Industrial Average to crawl from 300 to 400. But in little more than a year, the average sped through the next barrier, 500.

The 500 milestone was reached on March 12, 1956. It was one manifestation of the power of the long-lasting stock-market rally of the 1950s and its record-breaking climb of 239.5% during those ten years.

Low inflation and low interest rates provided an ideal backdrop for stocks to thrive. The spanking new interstate highway system helped to zip goods from place to place, and the new medium of television helped to create an appetite for those goods. President Eisenhower was popular, and the country, for the most part, was in a good mood.

Jeffrey Rubin, an analyst at Birinyi Associates in Greenwich, Conn., says that good news about Mr. Eisenhower's health was important in propelling the Dow industrials to a strong month in March 1956. The president had suffered a heart attack the previous fall, and people were wondering whether he would run for reelection. In February, Ike announced that he would, indeed, run.

The 500 level was breached on a day when the headlines told Americans about not just one, but two international crises. In the Middle East, tensions were running high between Egypt and Israel. The situation would erupt into outright warfare later that year during the Suez crisis. Meanwhile, in Cyprus, a general strike was under way, protesting Britain's deportation of Archbishop Makarios, who had led a movement to unite Cyprus with Greece.

Such crises often spook the stock market, at least for a short time. But in March 1956, the bull market shrugged off those crises.

Some investors active today remember 1956. The DeSoto was still a popular car. "Hound Dog," by Elvis Presley, was a red-hot hit song. In baseball, Mickey Mantle was the most valuable player in the American League. And on television, Robert Young was starring in "Father Knows Best."

Robert Young and Jane Wyatt with their TV family from "Father Knows Best": Billy Gray, Lauren Chapin and Elinor Donahue

DJIA MILESTONE 500
MONDAY, MARCH 12, 1956

HOW GALBRAITH MOVED THE MARKET

In 1955, a gangly Harvard economics professor named John Kenneth Galbraith briefly sent the Dow industrials swooning by means of a few hours of Senate testimony.

It was less than a year after the industrials had finally pushed back past their old 1929 highs. The crash had been a quarter-century earlier. But with the market up 50% since 1953, fears of another crash became so widespread that Senate Banking Committee Chairman J. William Fulbright opened hearings.

Enter Professor Galbraith, armed with galleys of his new book about 1929, called *The Great Crash*. On March 8, he appeared at the highly publicized hearings and sometimes compared 1955 with 1929.

Although he minimized the risk of another crash imminently, he warned of "a substantial element of speculation in the market" and proposed that margin requirements be boosted to 100% from 60%. (The margin is the proportion of a stock purchase an investor must pay for in cash; the rest can be borrowed from the broker. Rampant speculation on skimpy 10% margins is widely believed to have contributed to the crash of 1929.)

The industrials began to drop while the professor was talking, eventually losing 1.85%. With selling pressure heavy, the New York Stock Exchange's ticker ran nine minutes late. News of the decline spread, and the hearing filled with senators.

Mr. Galbraith, who turned 90 in 1998, said it was the memory of 1929 more than his remarks that sent down the market, but "I got more mail that week than any time in my life. One man mailed me four letters from Florida to say he was coming up to knock me off." When Mr. Galbraith broke his leg skiing in Vermont that same week and newspapers carried pictures, "I got letters from people saying their prayers had been answered."

Whether spurred by his accident or not, the market recovered late that week.

Pressure Politics
Lobbyists' Activities Spark New Inquiry But Tighter Curbs Unlikely

---

"Crude" Vote-Buying Trys Rare, Solon Says; Most Use "Grass Roots" Way

---

Some Sugar Bill Sweetening

By Alan L. Otten
Staff Reporter of The Wall Street Journal

WASHINGTON—"Someone working against the bill you're for is a lobbyist. If he's on your side, he's a public-spirited citizen exercising his constitutional right to petition Congress."

That definition, coming from a Capitol Hill veteran, capsules the dilemma now rising to confront Congress: what, if anything, to do about tighter control of lobbying. The Washington consensus is that the special bipartisan Senate committee tackling the topic—now that it's past last week's organizing troubles—will turn a searching spotlight on lobbying by the gas industry, labor unions and other groups, and that proposed remedies for abuses may get plentiful publicity. But it's widely agreed that few if any basic changes in existing curbs will result.

If this seems surprising, the explanation is simple. A slow but fundamental shift in the nature of influence pressures on Congress has made them harder and harder to control or, many lawmakers agree, less and less in need of control.

Today, more than ever, Washington lobbyists simply give the signal for the real "lobbying" pressures—letters, telegrams, phone calls and even visits from the folks back home. This pressure, most congressmen find, is more effective than anything half a dozen Capitol Hill influence men could do, and the lawmakers couldn't curb it if they wanted to.

SPUTNIK LAUNCH SPOOKED STOCKS

The space shot that launched humankind's first Earth-orbiting satellite on October 4, 1957, was achieved by the Soviet Union, at the time the archenemy of the United States. As a result, it was a shot that wounded the U.S. stock market.

The Dow Jones Industrial Average stood at 465.82 on October 3, 1957, the day before Sputnik was launched. By October 22, it had fallen to 419.79, nearly a 10% drop in just three weeks. A feeble recovery ensued, but at year-end, the industrials remained 30 points below their early-October level.

The selling reflected decreased confidence among U.S. investors, as the Soviets seemed to have captured the technological lead in the space race — and, people feared, in other areas too.

But the selling wasn't across the board. Aircraft and missile stocks showed some strength, as investors surmised that the United States would commit greater resources to those industries. As the *Journal*'s column "Abreast of the Market" put it, "Some of the aircraft stocks [were] lifted by the Soviet moon."

On October 10, 1957, the Dow industrials fell 9.69 points, the biggest decline stocks had suffered since President Eisenhower's 1955 heart attack had jolted the market two years before. That drop also left the industrials at their lowest point in two years.

Then, on October 21, the stocks took an even worse tumble, with a 10.77-point decline. Brokers and traders blamed the drop partly on U.S. government complacency in the wake of Sputnik; the Pentagon announced plans to cut aircraft procurement, which struck many people as unwise, given the technological prowess the Soviets had just displayed.

Tensions between Syria and Turkey also contributed to the October 1957 declines. Not until May 1958 did the Dow industrials climb back to their pre-Sputnik level.

Fears that the United States was losing its technological preeminence sparked the post-Sputnik decline, but the opposite was happening in the nineties. Increasing confidence that U.S. companies were the world's technology leaders fueled the strong stock-market performance of the 1990s.

Technicians at the Moscow Planetarium trace the orbit of Sputnik, the Soviet Earth satellite, on a huge globe, October 6, 1957

DJIA MILESTONE 600
FRIDAY, FEBRUARY 20, 1959

Above: Surrounded by models of various types of missiles, Army missile expert Wernher von Braun (left) explains their functions to Chairman Overton Brooks (D.-La.) and James G. Fulton (R.-Pa.), ranking minority member of the House Space Committee, February 5, 1959

Right: Governor Nelson Rockefeller gets a hug and kiss from four-and-a-half-year-old Susan Wolk after a speech in May 1959

Who Else But Nels?

Grass-Roots Drive On But Rockefeller Shuns Presidential Push Now

He Aims to Build Record as Governor, Look Carefully Before Making a '60 Leap

His Assets—and His Problem

By ALAN L. OTTEN
Staff Reporter of THE WALL STREET JOURNAL

ALBANY, N.Y.—Nelson Rockefeller has settled on a political strategy that leaves him free to challenge Vice President Richard Nixon for the GOP presidential nomination—or to remain content as governor of New York.

As of now, there's no doubt that Mr. Rockefeller is a White House candidate. His upset victory last fall over Democrat Averell Harriman makes that a fact. But there's considerable doubt, indeed, as to whether he'll still be a candidate when the Republicans meet next year to pick their standard-bearer.

Much as Dwight D. Eisenhower became a presidential aspirant seven years ago, the New York governor now is running in the only way he can—by trying to appear not to be. Political authorities figure that by becoming an avowed candidate now, Mr. Rockefeller would lessen his chances in the long run. But he and his aides are stopping short of taking any step that might nip in the bud the Rockefeller boomlet that's now getting started.

DJIA MILESTONE 700
WEDNESDAY, MAY 17, 1961

Red Farming

Drought Follows Floods In China; Planting Lags Behind Plans in Russia

———

Peiping Taps Gold Reserves To Buy Grain; Soviet Cuts Wheat Sales to Satellites

———

Private Plots vs. Collectives

———

By Joe Western
Staff Reporter of The Wall Street Journal

WASHINGTON—Eavesdropping at the Iron Curtain, U.S. officials are getting an earful about hard times down on the old collective farm.

What they hear amounts to a tale of bungling, waste, ignorance, self-delusion, often-blind subservience to Marxist doctrine and natural misfortune. To Free World listeners, the obvious conclusions are that agriculture seems likely to re-main Communism's greatest economic problem, and that Nikita Khrushchev's boast of overtaking the U.S. in farm abundance remains, at best, years away from fulfillment.

Consider these nuggets of Communist-admitted fact from behind the Iron Curtain:

Red China's masses, already grappling with starvation, are threatened with the third straight year of lean production from their rural communes. Drought is gripping vast areas of farmland, including parts of at least nine provinces, after earlier buffeting by floods elsewhere. China's Red rulers are tapping precious gold reserves to buy $500 million worth of grain from Australia and Canada. Previously the gold had gone almost entirely for purchase of goods for buildup of heavy industry.

President John F. Kennedy with U.S. Army officials during the Cuban Missile Crisis of October-November 1962

CUBAN MISSILE CRISIS SHOOK INDEX

For a while, it seemed that Chicken Little might finally be right.

News of the Soviet Union's move to install offensive nuclear missiles in Cuba jolted the Dow Jones Industrial Average in late October 1962. The missile crisis shifted into high gear on October 22, when President John F. Kennedy warned that all ships bound for Cuba, from whatever nation or port, "will, if found to contain cargoes of offensive weapons, be turned back."

As Soviet ships steamed toward Cuba, fears mounted that Armageddon was near. The president's brother, Attorney General Robert F. Kennedy, called it the worst crisis since World War II. The tension cast a cloud over the stock market, frightening investors who were already unnerved by stocks' poor performance that year. (President Kennedy's confrontation with steel companies accounted for part of the earlier drop.)

Rumors of Soviet activity in Cuba spread as early as August, but the gravity of the situation didn't emerge until October. On the day after President Kennedy's grim October 22 speech, the industrials closed at 558.06, down nearly 2% from the previous day's close — and down 24% from the levels reached at the beginning of the year.

With hindsight, it can be seen that that chilling week was a remarkable buying opportunity. Before the month was over, Soviet leader Nikita Khrushchev had agreed to withdraw the missiles, and the Dow industrials began a long upward march.

A year later, at the end of October 1963, less than a month before President Kennedy's assassination, the index stood at 755.23, a stunning 35% increase.

"Both superpowers realized, after looking down that nuclear gun barrel at each other, there had to be better ways of resolving their differences," says former JFK aide Ted Sorensen. One result: the 1963 nuclear test-ban treaty. But the crisis also brings to mind a wisecrack someone once made: The reason life is extinct on other planets is that their scientists were more advanced than ours.

MRBM LAUNCH SITE 1
SAN CRISTOBAL, CUBA
23 OCTOBER 1962

MISSILE ERECTOR

CABLE

MISSILE SHELTER TENT

TRACKED PRIME MOVERS

FUEL TANK TRAILERS

OXIDIZER TANK TRAILERS

An aerial intelligence photograph taken during the Cuban Missile Crisis in October 1962 of MRBM Launch Site 1 in San Cristobal, Cuba, showing missile erectors, fuel tank trailers and oxidizer tank trailers

DJIA MILESTONE 800
FRIDAY, FEBRUARY 28, 1964

Education & Race
School Integration Stirs Mounting Controversy In Some Northern Cities

---

Civil Rights Leaders Split Over Boycotts; Whites Balk At Mass Pupil Transfers

---

Spotlight Swings off Dixie

By STANLEY PENN
Staff Reporter of THE WALL STREET JOURNAL

NEW YORK—The focus of the school integration controversy has shifted from the South to the North for the present.

Here in New York, where a massive boycott of public schools was staged by pupils Feb. 3 to protest de facto classroom segregation, a militant Negro leader this week called for another walkout March 16. This Tuesday thousands of youngsters in Chicago stayed out of school in a similar protest. The same thing happened in Boston Wednesday. In Milwaukee civil rights leaders will meet Sunday to consider a school boycott unless officials yield to demands to improve racial balance in classrooms.

The push for more school integration in the North is touching off bitter controversies. Within the ranks of civil rights leaders there are sharp splits over tactics. The boycott backers insist such demonstrations are the only way to dramatize their cause and force action. But some rights advocates question whether any significant progress can be made in the heated atmosphere created by the boycotts.

Top left: Martin Luther King delivering his "I Have a Dream" speech at the Lincoln Memorial, August 28, 1963
Top right: Police lead youths from the campus of Collinwood School in Cleveland, scene of racial clashes in March 1965, after the boys refused to obey an order to attend classes or go home
Left: Three mothers and a grandmother arrested for trespassing after a three-week sit-in at a Queens, N.Y., public school to protest redistricting in 1963

DJIA MILESTONE 900
THURSDAY, JANUARY 28, 1965

President Looks Ahead To 5,000 mph Plane; 2,000 mph Craft Nearing Prototype Stage

Staff Reporter of **THE WALL STREET JOURNAL**

WASHINGTON—President Johnson stirred visions of a 5,000-mile-an-hour hypersonic plane flying from New York to Paris in less than an hour just as indications are growing that the administration soon will issue orders to move ahead with the construction of prototype models of a 2,000-mile-an-hour supersonic plane.

One possible sign that a go-ahead on the supersonic transport is near came in this statement by William M. Allen, president of Boeing Co.: "In the past few months, the prospects for this airplane have come forward rather spectacularly... particularly with respect to operating economics."

It was, apparently, a coincidence that on the same day the President topped Mr. Allen's comments on a spectacular supersonic plane with visions of a superspectacular hypersonic plane. There isn't any real competition, according to the National Aeronautics and Space Administration. A hypersonic plane is "at least 25 years away," a NASA spokesman said.

The president brought up the hypersonic craft in his report to Congress on aeronautical and space progress during 1964. He said NASA is building two models "embodying design concepts applicable to the fuselage of a hydrogen-fueled hypersonic aircraft." A NASA spokesman, to deflate any notion that these are flying models, said they are strictly for wind-tunnel testing.

Supersonic Concorde No. 002 rolls out at British Aircraft Corp.'s works in England in September 1968; thirty years later, there's still no prospect of a 5,000-mile-an-hour plane

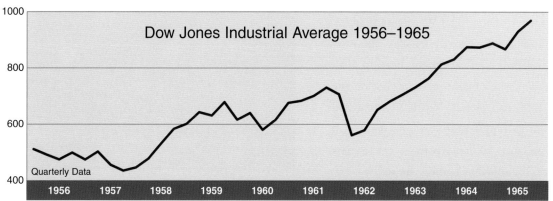

Dow Jones Industrial Average 1956–1965

Quarterly Data

1956 1957 1958 1959 1960 1961 1962 1963 1964 1965

DOW 1000: FINALLY IN '72

Cheers rang out on the floor of the New York Stock Exchange when the Dow Jones Industrial Average crossed the 1000 mark on November 14, 1972.

If ever there was a psychological barrier for the Dow industrials, "Dow 1000" was it. The industrial average had knocked on the door of 1000 repeatedly for six years, but never had been able to close above that magic level.

For example, the industrials closed at 995.15 on February 9, 1966, and at 985.21 on December 3, 1968. There were also close calls in May 1969. But no cigar — until the euphoria of 1972.

Many investors active today remember 1972. Richard Nixon was president, *The Godfather* was packing them in at the movies, and Americans were tuned to "All in the Family" on television. The Watergate scandal, which later destroyed the Nixon administration, was only a cloud on the horizon. The Vietnam War was a major problem, but on the day the 1000 barrier fell, North Vietnam had agreed that its representative would meet with U.S. negotiator Henry Kissinger for a new round of talks aimed at ending the war.

The reelection of Mr. Nixon over George McGovern had occurred a week earlier. And the economy was doing well. Economic growth was unusually strong, inflation was moderate and interest rates were low.

In the stock market, it was the heyday of the "Nifty Fifty," stocks that were so popular that it was said they were "one-decision" stocks: Buy them, and never worry about selling. Among the most popular stocks of the day were Xerox, Avon, IBM and McDonald's.

Not long after the industrial average punctured the 1000 barrier, a recession occurred and the brutal bear market of 1973 to 1974 set in, pushing the industrial average all the way down to 577.60 in December 1974. It would be late 1982, a full decade after the 1000 milestone was first passed, before the industrials rose above 1000 to stay.

"All in the Family": A scene from the TV series, with Carol O'Connor, Jean Stapleton, Sally Struthers and Rob Reiner

DJIA MILESTONE 1000
TUESDAY, NOVEMBER 14, 1972

Shape of 'Peace'

Vietnam Accord Seems Likely but May Lead To a New Kind of War

---

Bombing, Main-Force Actions Will Stop, but Both Sides May Push Low-Level Fight

---

Needed: Cheaper Ways to Kill

By PETER KANN
Staff Reporter of THE WALL STREET JOURNAL

SAIGON—In this lengthening limbo between the announcement of a peace agreement and the signing of a peace agreement, three things may be said with a fair degree of confidence:

1) The movement toward a peace agreement has gone too far to be reversed, despite the continuing objections of Saigon, some gamesmanship by Hanoi, some second thoughts among elements of U.S. officialdom and perhaps some doubts among the Viet Cong. An agreement substantially like the one announced by Hanoi Oct. 26 will be signed.

2) The agreement, which involves some significant concessions on all sides, appears to be a considerably better deal for Washington than for either Saigon or Hanoi. As one senior Saigon official says: "It certainly gets you [America] off the hook."

3) The agreement won't usher in an era of real peace in Vietman but rather will set some ground rules for a new-albeit far less destructive and fully Vietnamese-sort of conflict. The political future of South Vietnam is unlikely to look much clearer after an agreement is signed than it looks today.

An interpreter stands between White House Advisor Henry Kissinger and Hanoi's senior representative, Le Duc Tho, in the garden of a villa in Gif-sur-Yvette, France

1973-1974: A BAD TIME FOR STOCKS

It was a long, slow grind.

The 1973–1974 bear market, from peak to trough, racked up losses of 45% over the course of nearly two years. It was one of the biggest declines in the history of the Dow Jones Industrial Average.

The Arab oil embargo, which began in the fall of 1973, aggravated both the stock market's slide and the recession that accompanied it. But the market's skittishness had begun in January, months before Arab states launched a surprise attack on Israel on the Yom Kippur holiday, October 6. And stocks stayed weak even after the embargo ended in March 1974.

The industrial average had broken 1000 in 1972 and had peaked on January 11, 1973, at 1051.70. It then took ten years to reach 1100.

Even before the war hit, rising oil prices, a weakening dollar and accelerating inflation began to wear on stock prices. So did the brewing Watergate scandal surrounding President Richard M. Nixon. In March 1973, Mr. Nixon imposed price controls on oil, and in the summer, he instituted general wage and price controls. Meanwhile, the dollar was floating against gold — floating down mostly, which added to the pressure from foreign oil producers that were getting paid in cheapening dollars.

"Everything was falling apart," says historian Robert Sobel. "The golden years of the '60s were over."

After the Arab attack on Israel, the

A gas station during the gasoline shortage and energy crisis of the 1970s, when sales were limited to ten gallons per customer

stock market actually edged up a bit initially. But then, in mid-October, the Organization of Petroleum Exporting Countries barred the sale of oil to the United States, ushering in the era of excruciating lines at gas stations and double-digit inflation.

Gasoline prices shot sky-high. In August 1974, President Nixon resigned. The industrial average slid during the entire year of 1974 and hit a low of 577.60 on December 6.

"Although the oil embargo was a major economic factor in the dramatic drop in the Dow industrials, there were other significant factors," says Richard Stillman. "It was a depressing time for the country."

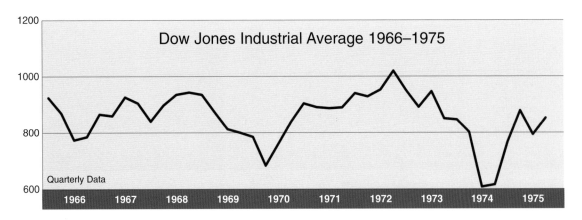

Dow Jones Industrial Average 1966–1975

Quarterly Data

1966 1967 1968 1969 1970 1971 1972 1973 1974 1975

COMPARE AND CONTRAST

The bear market of 1973–1974 nearly halved the Dow Jones Industrial Average, sending it spiraling down from a January 1973 peak of 1051.70 to 577.60 in December 1974. It was a slide that permanently changed the way people judge investment performance.

Before the fall, institutional and individual investors often didn't bother to measure the returns their money managers produced against a benchmark index. Instead, they innocently turned over their money to bank trust departments and insurance companies, never doubting that they would get results that handily outpaced the Dow Jones Industrial Average.

What's more, when performance comparisons were made in the 1950s and 1960s, they weren't very meaningful. Money managers often looked just at the price change for the industrial average, says Peter Bernstein, an economic consultant and former money manager in New York. What about dividends, which historically have accounted for almost half of the market's total return? They were ignored.

"Any sort of performance measurement, as we think of it today, was extremely primitive," Mr. Bernstein recalls. "We had portfolios in which everybody owned bonds, and we compared them to the Dow Jones average, which was ridiculous. But nobody told us it was ridiculous."

The 1973–1974 bear market changed all that. Investors, burned by the plunge, vowed to keep closer tabs on their portfolio managers by comparing each manager's performance with a benchmark. For many managers, the comparison didn't prove flattering. That, in turn, prompted some investors to use investments that removed the manager from the decision making: index funds.

Before the bear market, "Managers were expected to regularly beat the market by 20%," recalls Stephen Rogers, chairman of pension consultants Rogers, Casey & Associates in Darien, Conn. "Most investors just relied on what their managers told them [about performance]. It was only with the 1973–1974 [plunge] that things got torn apart."

The unflattering comparisons shouldn't have been a huge surprise. Earlier academic studies had compared mutual-fund performance with the major indexes and found the funds lacking. Many money managers didn't disclose their individual track records, but mutual-fund performance figures were readily available, and the data cast doubt on the notion that hiring an active portfolio manager ensured market-beating results.

Still, investors reacted strongly to the slide, largely because many of the stocks favored by professional money managers had fared far worse than the overall market. A portfolio that contained the hugely popular "nifty fifty" growth companies, which included such members of the Dow Jones Industrial Average as General Electric Co., Sears, Roebuck & Co. and Eastman Kodak Co., would have tumbled 54%, calculates Jeremy J. Siegel, a finance professor at the University of Pennsylvania's Wharton School. With one dreadful blow, money managers had lost their aura of invincibility.

> *The bear market of 1973–1974 changed the way people judged investment performance — much to the chagrin of many money managers.*

Many of the burned investors were large corporate clients. "Pension plans became underfunded, which had implications for reported earnings," says Michael Stolper, president of Stolper & Co., a San Diego consulting firm. "That got management's attention."

Some companies quickly ditched their money managers and hired pension consultants to root out stock pickers who had fared better through the slump. There "was a huge shift in assets from banks and insurance companies to these independent money-management firms," which generally hadn't invested as heavily in the nifty fifty, Mr. Stolper says. "That really fueled the growth of these boutique firms through the 1970s and 1980s."

The most obvious result of this upheaval was widespread benchmarking. More large investors started comparing their money managers' returns with benchmark indexes. Meanwhile, up-and-coming money-management firms began comparing their returns with an index to lure clients, a practice that became common in the investment community.

Benchmarking also became a way for institutional investors to set investment policy, says Charles Ellis, managing partner of Greenwich Associates, a Greenwich, Conn., pension consultant. For instance, if an investor tells a small-stock portfolio manager that his results will be measured against the Russell 2000 index of smaller-company stocks, the manager probably won't stray far from his specialty by, say, investing in foreign or blue-chip stocks.

Moreover, as investors began paying closer attention to indexes, the number of indexes themselves exploded. In the early 1970s, few looked at anything other than the Dow Jones average and Standard & Poor's (S&P) 500-stock index. But today, investors draw on a host of specialized indexes that cover everything from value stocks to bonds to small-capitalization issues.

The 1973–1974 plunge in the Dow — and little investor confi-

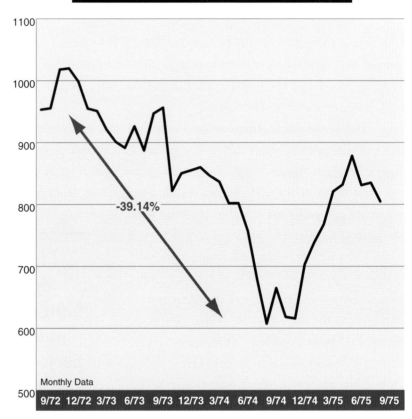

The Bear Market of 1973-1974

-39.14%

Monthly Data

9/72 12/72 3/73 6/73 9/73 12/73 3/74 6/74 9/74 12/74 3/75 6/75 9/75

dence in money managers — also fueled the growth of index investing, the strategy of buying the securities that constitute an index in an effort to replicate the index's performance.

The idea was first tried out in July 1971, according to Mr. Bernstein, a consultant. A fund started by Wells Fargo & Co. as part of luggage maker Samsonite Corp.'s pension plan invested an equal amount in a sampling of the stocks listed on the New York Stock Exchange. Two years later, Wells Fargo (whose institutional money-management business is now a unit of London's Barclays Bank PLC) brought out an institutional index fund based on the S&P 500.

Other corporations, including AT&T Corp., Exxon Corp. and Ford Motor Co., soon followed Wells Fargo's move toward indexing in their pension plans. But these companies tended to hedge their bets, indexing a portion of their pension funds and leaving the rest with conventional money managers.

The idea of indexing, previously confined to academic periodicals and publications devoted to professional money management, also started cropping up in the mainstream press. "Index Funds — An Idea Whose Time Is Coming" shouted the headline on a major story in the June 1976 issue of the magazine *Fortune*. The article noted that from 1966 to 1975, managed pension-fund stock portfolios returned just 1.6% a year, well behind the S&P 500's 3.3% annual gain.

Even so, "Indexing had a very slow start," says Budge Collins, president of Collins Associates, a pension consulting firm in Newport Beach, Calif. "There were few supporters for it in the early years." Opponents argued that it was imprudent to buy stocks in an index "blindly," with no eye to their quality.

Even today's largest index mutual fund, Vanguard Group's 500 Index Fund, which had more than $70 billion in assets at the end of 1998, had a shaky beginning. When it was introduced in 1976, an index fund for small investors was still a novelty. The fund pulled in just $11 million in its initial offering period, not even enough to buy meaningful amounts of all five hundred stocks in the Standard & Poor's index. "It took three years before we stopped sampling and started buying the whole five hundred," says Vanguard Senior Chairman John Bogle. "[The fund] was very slow to take off. It was called communistic, un-American, settling for mediocrity."

"That," he adds, "is when I knew it was going to be big."

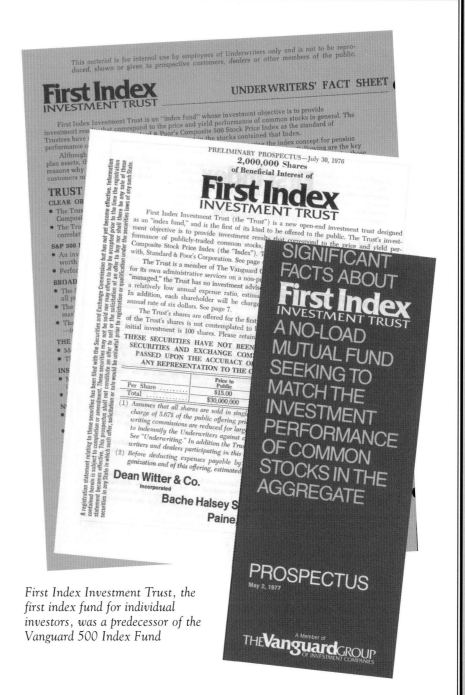

First Index Investment Trust, the first index fund for individual investors, was a predecessor of the Vanguard 500 Index Fund

THE INDEX'S DARK DAYS IN 1980

In March 1980, the Dow Jones Industrial Average began one of its most rapid slides in history, falling 16% in just two months.

According to most stock-market observers, the Panic of 1980 was touched off by an abortive effort on the part of the Hunt brothers of Texas to corner the world market in silver. "It was the only time I can ever recall seeing the price of any commodity fall by 50% in a single day," said Jeffrey Christian, principal of CPM Group Ltd., a New York precious-metal consulting firm. "It was a nerve-racking ordeal."

The price of silver fell to $10.80 an ounce from $21.62 on March 27, 1980, a far cry from its peak of $52 that January. The silver catastrophe was triggered by rule changes made by commodities exchanges that were aimed at driving speculators like the Hunts out of the market. "Since the Hunts, and the firms that they'd been dealing through, had big positions in the stock market as well, the stock market was pulled into the fray," Mr. Christian said. Some people sold stocks to cover silver losses.

The silver crisis was the final straw for a stock market under siege by worries as diverse as the Iranian hostage crisis, the Russian invasion of Afghanistan and soaring interest rates.

"The Iranian hostages were on TV every night, the prime lending rate soared to 22% and everyone was predicting disaster," said Robert Stovall, president of Stovall/Twenty First Advisers Inc. in New York.

In April, the Dow average hit its low for the year, 759.13, down from 903.84 at the February peak. But like a thunderstorm on a summer day, the whole decline was almost forgotten by the year's end. "There was a lot of euphoria surrounding the elections, which swept Ronald Reagan and the Republicans into office," said Richard Stillman. The Dow industrials ended 1980 at 963.99, up 12% for the year.

President Jimmy Carter, about to sign a document freezing all official Iranian monies in U.S. banks, a move intended to pressure Iranian terrorists to release American citizens held hostage at the U.S. embassy in Tehran

DJIA MILESTONE 1500
WEDNESDAY, DECEMBER 11, 1985

Judgment of $11.1 Billion for Pennzoil Co. Is Upheld, But Texaco Gets Concession After Hasty Discussion

The Agreement is Intended To Help Texaco Avoid Bankruptcy-Law Filing

HOUSTON—A state judge upheld an $11.1 billion judgement for Pennzoil Co. against Texaco Inc., a figure that includes interest on the award, after Texaco won a last minute concession intended to keep the oil giant out of bankruptcy-law proceedings for at least 60 days.

The ruling erases Texaco's hope of a quick escape from the largest legal judgement in history and casts a cloud of insolvency over the nation's fifth-largest company. Despite the temporary reprieve from a Chapter 11 Bankruptcy Code filing that Texaco obtained late yesterday, the ruling by Judge Solomon Casseb to affirm a jury's Nov. 19 judgement puts a stamp of legal credibility on a verdict that many had dismissed as a fluke. The jury awarded Pennzoil $10.53 billion after finding that Texaco improperly wrested control of Getty Oil Co. from Pennzoil last year.

Judge Casseb's action is certain to spread deep anxiety among Texaco's suppliers, business partners, employees, stockholders and others for the foreseeable future.

Texaco's only apparent means of quickly resolving the greatest crisis in its 83-year history is a settlement with Pennzoil, and that possibility was unexpectedly disclosed by the company in open court. "We had discussed the possibility of a transfer of assets to settle the entire matter," David Boies, one of Texaco's chief attorneys, told reporters later during a recess. Mr. Boies added that the talks were "nothing formal, nothing substantive, at this point."

Ronald Reagan reaches into a sea of hands during his 1980 campaign for the presidency

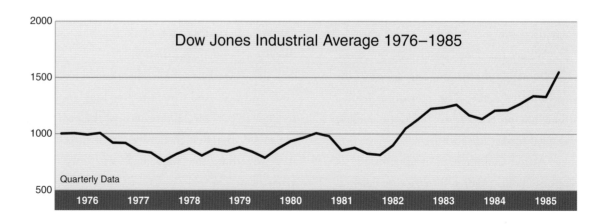

Dow Jones Industrial Average 1976–1985

Quarterly Data

WHERE WERE YOU AT DOW 2000?

It may seem hard to believe, with the Dow Jones Industrial Average passing both the 7000 and the 8000 marks in 1997, but it had been only about ten years earlier, on January 8, 1987, that the average had first hit 2000.

You remember 1987. Michael Douglas starred that year in the movie *Wall Street*, portraying the greedy Gordon Gekko.

But the real fireworks in 1987 took place on the real Wall Street. The industrial average started the year at 1895.95, then staged one of the most impressive advances in history, surging nearly 44%, and peaking at 2722.42 on August 25. In the fall it turned around and suffered one of the biggest declines on record, dropping nearly 1,000 points in two months. The selling crescendo peaked on October 19, with a 508-point, nearly 23%, crash, the worst one-day drop ever.

When the Dow industrials surpassed the 2000 mark, almost no one foresaw the pyrotechnics to come. The prevailing feeling was that, having climbed to 2000, the average would need to rest for a while.

Alfred Goldman of A.G. Edwards & Sons in St. Louis predicted "a victory celebra-tion and then a headache." Robert Stovall pre-dicted a "groundhog day" effect in which the market would "see its shadow, and promptly duck down again." Mary Farrell of Paine Webber predicted a trading-range market hovering between 1800 and 2200.

Nor did many people guess at the time that six additional millenary milestones would occur over the course of a decade. After all, it had taken the industrial average about seventy-six years to reach 1000, in 1973. Then it took nearly fourteen years for the average to climb to 2000.

Of course, it's easier and easier to hit each 1,000-point milestone, because each point gain becomes smaller on a percentage basis as the index rises.

"I'm excited. This is history," exclaimed trader Jack Baker, then with Shearson Lehman Brothers in New York, the day the 2000 barrier was snapped. "I caught 1000 and 2000 and I hope to live long enough to catch 3000." Mr. Baker captured the prevail-ing mood. But though hardly a soul suspected it at the time, the 3000 mark was only four years away.

"The Floor of the New York Stock Exchange,"
acrylic on paper by Franklin McMahon, 1984

DJIA MILESTONE 2000
THURDSAY, JANUARY 8, 1987

Myopic Managers?
Trying to Streamline, Some Firms May Hurt Long-Term Prospects

---

They Are Cutting Research, Investment and Products; U.S. Growth May Suffer

---

But Lower Costs Are a Help

By Ralph E. Winter
Staff Reporter of The Wall Street Journal

Streamline.

In more and more corporate boardrooms, that has become the buzzword.

Gone is the talk of balanced, long-term growth; impatient shareholders and well-heeled corporate raiders have seen to that. Now, anxious executives, fearing for their jobs or their companies, are focusing their efforts on trimming operations and shuffling assets to improve near-term profits, often at the expense of both balance and growth.

Michael R. Milken, Drexel Burnham Lambert's junk-bond king, speaking to a forum in California in June 1989, when he urged the United States to forgive Latin debt and forge trade partnerships. Indicted on ninety-eight counts of fraud and racketeering, Mr. Milken later pleaded guilty to six felony charges and spent nearly two years in prison for securities-law violations. He is now involved in various educational ventures and funds prostate-cancer research.

News of the 1987 crash, reported by the Dow Jones News Service as it was happening

DJIA DOWN 119 POINTS

NEW YORK -DJ- THE STOCK MARKET ROUT IS
CONTINUING WITH A VENGENCE AMID WIDESPREAD
INVESTOR PANIC, BORNE OUT BY HEAVY
FUTURES-RELATED ARBITRAGE AND PORTFOLIO
INSURANCE SELLING, PLUNGING BOND PRICES AND A
WEAK DOLLAR.
THE DOW JONES INDUSTRIAL AVERAGE IS DOWN
MORE THAN 119 POINTS AT THE 2,127 LEVEL AFTER
DROPPING A RECORD 108 POINTS ON FRIDAY.
-- 10 42 AM EDT 10-19-87

-- 12 53 PM EDT 10-19-87

N.Y. STOCKS SINKING TOWARD
MORNING LOWS: DJIA DOWN 189

NEW YORK -DJ- STOCK PRICES CONTINUE TO SHOW
HUGE LOSSES IN RECORD HEAVY TRADING AND ARE
HEADING BACK TOWARD THEIR SESSION LOWS AFTER A
LATE-MORNING BOUNCE.
THE DOW JONES INDUSTRIAL AVERAGE IS DOWN
ABOUT 189 POINTS AT THE 2,057 LEVEL. IT WAS OFF
ABOUT 211 POINTS EARLIER TODAY, THEN BOUNCED TO
A 108-POINT DEFICIT BEFORE HEADING LOWER AGAIN.

-- 2 04 PM EDT 10-19-87

DJIA DOWN 274 AT 1,972 LEVEL
AS ROUT CONTINUES

NEW YORK -DJ- STOCK PRICES CONTINUE TO
CRUMBLE IN RECORD TRADING.
THE DOW JONES INDUSTRIAL AVERAGE IS DOWN
ABOUT 274 POINTS, OR 12.06 PC, AT THE 1,972
LEVEL.
BIG BOARD VOLUME TOPS 422 MILLION SHARES.
THE DOW AVERAGE HASN'T CLOSED WITH A
ONE-DAY PERCENTAGE LOSS EXCEEDING 12 PC SINCE
OCT. 28, 1929, WHEN THE INDEX LOST 12.82 PC.
-0- 2 05 PM EDT 10-19-87

N.Y. STOCKS POSTING MASSIVE
LOSSES: BUT DJIA FIRMS

NEW YORK -DJ- STOCK PRICES ARE POSTING
MASSIVE LOSSES AS WIDESPREAD PANIC SELLING
CONTINUES ON WALL STREET.
THE DOW JONES INDUSTRIAL AVERAGE IS DOWN
264 POINTS AT THE 1,982 LEVEL, BUT HAS RECOVERED
SOMEWHAT FROM A 302-POINT LOSS IT WAS POSTING
EARLIER.
NEVERTHELESS, THE DECLINE REPRESENTS ABOUT
A 11.75 PC DROP FOR THE DAY. THE DOW HASN'T
DROPPED MORE THAN 12 PC SINCE OCT. 28, 1929,
WHEN IT DROPPED 12.82 PC.
THE DOW JONES TRANSPORTATION AVERAGE IS
DOWN ABOUT 118 POINTS AND THE UTILITY INDEX IS
DOWN ABOUT 24 POINTS.
DECLINING STOCKS OUTNUMBER ADVANCERS BY
NEARLY A 40-TO-1 MARGIN ON THE NYSE, WHERE ABOUT
471 MILLION SHARES HAVE CHANGED HANDS.
-0- 2 40 PM EDT 10-19-87

DJIA IN HISTORIC 508-POINT
PLUNGE AS MARKET COLLAPSES

BY JIM STOREY
DOW JONES STAFF REPORTER

NEW YORK -DJ- THE STOCK MARKET SUFFERED AN
HISTORIC COLLAPSE UNDER THE WEIGHT OF WIDESPREAD
PANIC SELLING.
THE DOW JONES
A RECORD 508.32
1,738.74, WIPING
YEAR AND CLOSING
7, 1986.
IN PERCENTAGE
BIGGEST SINCE TH
STOCKS OCT. 1, 1
12.82 PC DECLINE
COMMONLY REFERRE
GREAT DEPRESSSIO
TODAY'S LOSS
108-POINT, 4.6 P
NEW YORK STOC
604.4 MILLION SH
338.5 MILLION.
ADVANCERS BY ABO
THE HECTIC TR
STOCK EXCHANGE T
SAME TIME AS THE
ANALYSTS AND
SNOWBALLING INVE
IS DEAD, A VIEW
WORRIES OVER THE
RATES AND AN APP
IN THE REAGAN AD
WITH THE NATION'
THE EMOTIONAL
CHARACTERIZED BY
INSTITUTIONS AND
DOMESTIC; MUTUAL
AND SELLING ASSO
ARBITRAGE AND PO
''IT'S BEEN C
DORR, A BLOCK TR
MARKETPLAC
ACROSS-THE
''ABOUT THE O
ABOUT THE DAY IS
COMMISSIONS,'' F
''ANYBODY WHO TH
GOING TO END IS
ANOTHER TRADE
SAID MARGIN CALL
FIST,'' ADDING T
CALLS ALL WEEKEN
-- 4 18 PM EDT

LATE N.Y. MARKET COMMENT -3-

NEW YORK -DJ- TODAY'S 508-POINT, 22.62 PC
COLLAPSE IN THE DOW JONES INDUSTRIAL AVERAGE WAS
NOT ONLY THE SINGLE WORST DAY FOR THE MARKET
SINCE BEFORE THE GREAT DEPRESSION. IT ALSO
EXCEEDS THE BIGGEST WEEKLY PERCENTAGE LOSS.
THAT LOSS OCCURRED THE WEEK ENDING JULY 21,
1933, WHEN THE DOW FELL 15.55 PC.
SINCE THE BLUE CHIP AVERAGE PEAKED AT A
RECORD 2,722.42 AUG. 25, IT HAS PLUMMETED 984
POINTS, OR 36.14 PC. THE DECLINE OF THE PAST
FOUR SESSIONS ALONE TOTALS OVER 769 POINTS, OR
30.69 PC.
IN TERMS OF BOTH PERCENTAGE AND POINTS, THE
EIGHT-WEEK DROP NOW IS THE LARGEST STOCK MARKET
SETBACK SINCE THE END OF WORLD WAR II.
''THE SELLING SEEMED TO FEED ON ITSELF,''
SAID JOHN BURNETT, A SENIOR TRADER AT DONALDSON,
LUFKIN & JENRETTE. ''I DON'T KNOW WHAT THE
SUPPORT LI
THING IS (
DALE T
EQUITIES I
& CO., CAL
''ABSOLUTE
''THE F
CHANGED.
THE REST (
BECAUSE OF
PSYCHOLOGY
TILLS 9
HE SAID TH
HUGE NUMBE
MARKETPLA
ACROSS-TH
''I'D L
YOU'D MAKI
VALUE OF 1
IT'S JUST
STOCKHOLDE
''IT'S
GERALD SI
LISTED TR
UPHAM & CO
TO HAVE TH
WHEN. IT
IT STILL (
AFTER 1
EXCHANGE C
CONFERENCE
USUAL TOMORROW.
THE NYSE COMPOSITE TAPE WAS RUNNING MORE
THAN TWO HOURS LATE AT THE CLOSE TODAY.
-- 4 58 PM EDT 10-19-87

LATE N.Y. MARKET COMMENT -4-

NEW YORK -DJ- AMONG THE BIGGEST LOSERS IN
THE DOW JONES INDUSTRIAL AVERAGE, INTERNATIONAL
BUSINESS MACHINES FELL 33 TO 102; EASTMAN KODAK
LOST 27 1-4 TO 62 7-8; MERCK PLUNGED 33 TO 151;
PROCTER & GAMBLE COLLAPSED 23 1-4 TO 61 AND
PHILIP MORRIS FELL 14 5-8 TO 88 1-8.
ELSEWHERE, DIGITAL EQUIPMENT PLUNGED 42 1-4
TO 130; CBS SANK 42 1-8 TO 152 1-2; CITICORP
LOST 16 1-8 TO 37 AND ATLANTIC RICHFIELD FELL
23 1-2 TO 65.
OF THE TOP 10 BIGGEST PRICE GAINERS ON THE
BIG BOARD IN TERMS OF POINTS, ONLY THREE GAINED
MORE THAN A POINT.
ABOUT THE ONLY GAINERS FOR THE DAY WERE
SOME GOLD-RELATED STOCKS, WHICH BENEFITED FROM A
SHARP RISE IN PRECIOUS METALS PRICES. NEWMONT
GOLD ROSE 3 3-8 TO 39 1-8 AND CALLAHAN MINING
GAINED 2 1-4 TO 32 1-2.
DALLAS CORP. ROSE 3-4 TO 12 1-2. THE
COMPANY REPORTED THIRD-QUARTER EARNINGS ROSE TO
30 CENTS A SHARE FROM 12 CENTS A YEAR EARLIER.
THE AMERICAN STOCK EXCHANGE INDEX PLUNGED
41.05 TO 282.50.
THE WASHOUT ALSO WAS REFLECTED IN
OVER-THE-COUNTER TRADING, WHERE THE NASDAQ
COMPOSITE INDEX DROPPED 46.12 TO 360.21.
DECLINING ISSUES OUTNUMBERED ADVANCERS BY ABOUT
3,573 TO 139.
-- 5 17 PM EDT 10-19-87

THE BIG TOP: SUMMER OF 1987

On August 25, 1987, the Dow Jones Industrial Average hit a historic peak that marked the end of a great bull market.

This was the bull market of the mid-1980s that pulled the Dow industrials up to a dizzying peak of 2722.42 from a trough of 776.92 in August 1982.

> ## "It's pretty much being taken for granted now that the market is going to go up."

Ronald Reagan was president during the entire bull run. His big budget deficits fueled the economy, even as they worsened the national debt. His free-market stance was also popular with investors. "It's pretty much being taken for granted now that the market is going to go up," said one trader, who turned out to be speaking on the very day of the top.

In retrospect, there were some danger signs. Stock valuations were extremely high. The dollar was weak. Perhaps most ominously, interest rates had been rising steadily.

Between March and October, the yield on the benchmark thirty-year Treasury bond climbed to more than 10% from about 7.5%. The gap between the yields on long-term bonds and the miserly 3% dividend offered by many stocks became too great to ignore. And the threat that rising rates would pinch economic growth also scared investors.

A scant two months after the August peak, the Dow industrials had dropped about 1,000 points. More than 500 of those points were lost in a single day's plunge — the crash of October 19, 1987.

If interest rates brought the stock market down, they had also nudged it to life five years earlier. The bull market of the mid-1980s gave off its first exuberant snort in August 1982, in a climate of falling rates. On August 17, 1982, the Dow industrials jumped 38.81, almost the equivalent of a 300-point rally today.

The spark was Henry Kaufman, Salomon Brothers' chief economist, predicting a further drop in rates. "The markets could no longer ignore the rapidly falling interest rates," observed one analyst. "The new stance by Mr. Kaufman was the icing on the cake."

A Texas longhorn bull walks down Wall Street in New York during the filming of a commercial for Merrill Lynch & Co., the big brokerage firm

CRASH COURSES:

HOW THE TWO GREAT STOCK-MARKET CRASHES COMPARE

The two great stock-market crashes of the 20th century offer a terrific lesson in how hard it is for anyone — no matter how famous in politics, business or punditry — to predict the future.

In 1929, after the Dow Jones Industrial Average plunged to 230 from 381, business and government leaders rushed to proclaim that everything was fine. A joint press release by thirty-five brokerage houses declared that the economy and the stock market were "fundamentally sound." President Hoover remarked that "the fundamental business of the country . . . is on a sound and prosperous basis."

Despite these "incantations," as John Kenneth Galbraith calls them in *The Great Crash*, the country soon fell into the worst depression in its history. It took until 1954 — a full quarter-century — for the industrial average to regain its 1929 peak.

In 1987, after the Dow plummeted to 1738 from 2722, many pundits recalled the false optimism of their predecessors. Fearing that history would repeat itself, they veered toward pessimism, only to prove, in the end, equally wrong.

For example, Robert Prechter, then an influential newsletter writer, predicted the worst financial shakeout since the industrial revolution. Martin Zweig, a respected money manager and commentator, noted that all similar drops during the market's history, except those that occurred in wartime, had been followed by a recession or depression. And televised pundit Dan Dorfman predicted that it would be a long time before people would ever "look at the stock market again."

As it turned out, however, business stayed good, recession stayed away for three years, and when one came, it proved mild. The industrial average had regained all of its lost ground by August 1989 and stood at about 8200 at the end of 1997, or more than triple the level at which the 1987 decline had begun.

Above: The crowd across the street from the New York Stock Exchange on the day of the 1929 crash
Opposite page: A trader on the floor of the New York Stock Exchange reading about the 1987 crash

Here are some other things the two great crashes did — and didn't — have in common.

Magnitude. On the Richter scale of stock-market earthquakes, the two big ones had remarkable similarities. To start with, both crashes occurred in October, a month that has seen a number of other wrenching market declines.

In 1929, the industrial average fell 12.8% on Monday, October 28, and an additional 11.7% on Tuesday. Together, the two-day decline clipped 23% from the value of investors' portfolios. The October 1987 crash saw a 22.6% swoon in a single day. So the two crashes were within 0.4 percentage point of each other in terms of immediate damage.

And in both cases, the market had already turned downward a few weeks before the crash hit. In 1929, the peak was reached September 3, with a close of 381.17. The industrial average had declined 21.6% in the weeks preceding the crash's two-day tumble. Similarly, in 1987, the market peaked on August 25 at 2722.42. It gradually slid 17.5% to 2246.74 before the blast of October 19.

Causes. Most economic historians agree that heavy speculation on margin by individual investors was a major cause of the 1929 crash. In those days, people could buy stock by putting only 10% of the money down in cash and borrowing the rest from their brokers. That enabled many small investors to load up on stocks they wouldn't otherwise have been able to buy. (Today, as in 1987, the margin requirement is much higher, at 50%.)

Being able to buy stocks without putting much money down is a great convenience when the market is going up. But when the market falls, the system can unravel fast. Investors find themselves faced with "margin calls," demands from their brokers for more collateral.

If the investor doesn't promptly put up the additional money, the broker will sell the stock, whether the customer likes it or not. Such forced sales can cause prices to fall further, triggering a vicious circle of sales and margin calls.

"The 1929 market was powered by massive leverage and the barely controlled use of margin," says Robert Stovall. Among the people wiped out by margin calls, he says, were "my father and my uncle, who both had beautiful houses under construction in the Louisville, Ky., area. They both lost them and had to move in with their in-laws."

The later crash was driven by a different kind of investor, but it also featured a special investing technique that poured gasoline on the fire.

By 1987, institutional investors such as pension funds and insurance companies had become dominant in the marketplace. Many of these large investors used a tool called portfolio insurance, which was portrayed by high-powered investment consultants as almost a guarantee against losses. Needless to say, the "insurance" was misnamed.

The technique involved selling stock-index futures (or sometimes options, or batches of stock) in computer-guided trading whenever the market declined by a certain amount. By triggering a cascade of such sell orders, however, portfolio insurance actually aggravated the disease it was intended to cure.

Aftermath. The two crashes couldn't have been more different in their aftermaths. Harvard University historian Alfred Chandler notes that after the 1929 crash, the country's gross national product (the value of all goods and services produced by the nation) was sliced almost in half within four years. In constant 1958 dollars, the output of the United States amounted to $103 billion in 1929, he says. By 1933, it had fallen to $56 billion.

Some historians blame economic protectionism, and specifically the Smoot-Hawley Tariff Act of 1930, for much of the damage to the economy. But Prof. Chandler says, "I don't buy that at all." He thinks the stock-market crash "was much more important than the tariff" in touching off the Depression. People lost much of their wealth when the market collapsed, he says, making it harder for them to buy goods and services such as cars.

The economic debacle that followed the crash was in large part "a Detroit and Pittsburgh" phenomenon, Prof. Chandler says. Car sales plummeted, dragging the steel industry down with the auto industry. About 4.6 million cars and trucks were sold in 1929; by 1933, sales had fallen to 1.5 million vehicles. This economic fallout spread quickly.

Many economists expected a similar "wealth effect reversal" to punish the economy after the 1987 debacle. That didn't happen, and there were a number of reasons. For one thing, in 1987, many families had placed a bigger chunk of their net worth in real estate and a smaller portion in stocks than they had in 1929.

In addition, the Federal Reserve Board came to the rescue of the economy more vigorously in 1987 than it had fifty-eight years before. Many investors were nervous because the highly respected Paul Volcker had recently stepped down as Fed chairman. His successor, Alan Greenspan, was regarded as untested.

But as it turned out, under Mr. Greenspan's leadership, the Fed opened up the gates and expanded the money supply to keep the economy afloat. Furthermore, President Reagan, unlike Mr. Hoover, stayed silent concerning the crash.

"If Reagan had gone on television to calm the country down," suggests Robert Sobel, "it would have caused a panic."

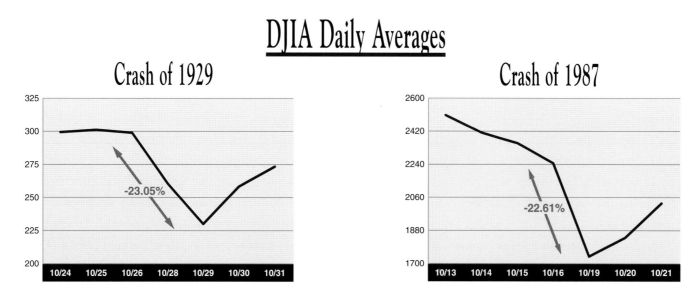

DJIA Daily Averages

Crash of 1929

-23.05%

10/24 10/25 10/26 10/28 10/29 10/30 10/31

Crash of 1987

-22.61%

10/13 10/14 10/15 10/16 10/19 10/20 10/21

WHEN SADDAM UNCAGED A BEAR

Who's afraid of Saddam Hussein?

The stock market was, in 1990. Iraq's invasion of Kuwait along with concern about the Iraqi leader's unpredictable behavior helped to spark a 21% decline in the Dow Jones Industrial Average.

It became known as the Saddam Hussein bear market. Although unusually swift, the decline met the classic definition of a bear market: a 20% decline in major stock indexes.

The average had been knocking on the door of the 3000 mark that summer. It stopped a fraction of a point away, with twin peaks of 2999.75 on July 16 and July 17. Then prices began to slide, ending with an October 11 low of 2365.10.

Iraq invaded Kuwait August 2, and much of the damage to the stock market took place in mid-August, after President George Bush said the invasion "cannot stand" but before it was clear what America would do. Fear that the United States might get involved in a prolonged war or that Mr. Hussein might deploy chemical or biological weapons helped to spook stocks. As it turned out, the war was quickly over and resulted in an overwhelming U.S. victory. On January 17, 1991, after hostilities actu-

A pro-Saddam Hussein rally in Baghdad during the Gulf War, January 1991

ally had begun and the results looked good for U.S. forces, the Dow industrials soared 114 points.

Laszlo Birinyi of Birinyi Associates says the stock market predicted the outcome of the war better than most people did. "The market as early as October had decided that the war was not going to be an event of lasting significance," he says.

Of course, Iraq wasn't the only thing troubling the stock market in 1990. There also was unease about the economic situation. In fact, the United States was in an undeclared recession. Not until 1992 did the National

Bureau of Economic Research officially recognize that the United States had been in a recession from July 1990 to March 1991.

At the end of 1998, many people still considered the 1990 decline the last bear market, although a 19.3% drop in the summer of 1998 came close. The market recovered in less than a month from the 512-point, or 6.4%, plunge in the Dow on August 31, 1998, and soared to a new high in November. Investors shrugged off a new U.S. attack on Iraq in December, and the industrial average ended the year up 16.1%.

TOPPING THE ELUSIVE 3000 MARK

Talk about a tease.

The Dow Jones Industrial Average seemed to be closing in on the 3000 mark in the summer of 1990. It looked as if the Dow would make quick work of the 3000 milestone about three and a half years after it had passed the 2000 mark in January 1987.

On July 17, 1990, the Dow industrials closed just a quarter point shy of the next 1,000-point mark, closing at 2999.75. The next day, the industrial average shot above 3000 in intraday trading, only to close unchanged at the tantalizing level of 2999.75.

Several times during July, the intraday high exceeded 3000, but the industrial average couldn't manage to close above that mark. And for the remainder of 1990, the 3000 mark proved elusive.

The economy was in a recession — albeit one that wasn't declared until it was already over — and worries about Iraqi dictator Saddam Hussein's aggression in the Persian Gulf ran high. The industrial average fell all the way back to 2365.10 in October. Investors saw eerie reminders of 1966, when the Dow industrials broke 1000 intraday, only to wait six years before piercing that level at the closing bell.

Finally, in the spring of 1991, after the United States had overwhelmingly vanquished Saddam Hussein's forces and the recession (still undeclared) was over, the industrial average broke the 3000 barrier, closing at 3004.46. The date was April 17, 1991, a little more than four years after the 2000 barrier had fallen. By contrast, it took the average fourteen years to get from 1000 to 2000 (a larger percentage of movement).

George Bush, who had presided over the Gulf War against Mr. Hussein's forces, was president when the milestone was reached. But the economic weakness of 1990 and early 1991, among other things, weakened his standing with the electorate and he lost the 1992 presidential election to Bill Clinton.

Once the 3000 mark was passed, notes Laszlo Birinyi, the market settled into a remarkably tight trading range, "almost a knot." For eight months, the industrial average spent almost all its time between 2900 and 3100. It was as if the 3000 level had become a magnet. Then in late December, stocks took off again, on their way to the next milestone.

A U.S. battle tank during a training exercise in the Saudi Arabian desert prior to Operation Desert Storm

DJIA MILESTONE 3000
WEDNESDAY, APRIL 17, 1991

Hard Times Trim CEO Pay Raises

By Amanda Bennett
Staff Reporter of **The Wall Street Journal**

For Barry F. Sullivan, chairman of First Chicago Corp., last year's hard times brought both good and bad pay news.

The bad news: a pay cut. Because of slumping profits at the Chicago-based bank holding company, Mr. Sullivan did without a bonus last year, thus cutting his cash compensation by 50%, to $735,632. The good news: Last year, the company gave him 65,000 stock options, as well as 25,000 restricted shares valued at $662,500.

"Our senior people took a significant zap in terms of annual pay," says Paul Knuti, vice president of human-resources policy at First Chicago. But in bad times and good, he adds, "we want to provide them significant long-term opportunities. Then our shareholders will be happy, and we will create some nice wealth for our senior management."

As Mr. Sullivan and others are discovering, hard times cut into many executives' pay last year. Overall, chief executives' salary and bonuses still rose, but the rate of increase slid for the second year in a row, to its lowest rate in five years. Many executives saw annual bonuses slip away altogether as corporate profits faded.

But don't weep for anyone just yet. Behind the scenes, many companies continue to fatten executive stock plans. That may not have boosted pay for 1990, but it set the stage for huge pay gains in the future.

Who Made the Big Bucks

It may not have been the best year in general for chief executives, but 1990 was still a great year for many of them. According to the Towers Perrin survey of chief executives' pay, 1990's highest-paid executives — taking into account salary, bonus and long-term incentive payouts — included:

- Stephen M. Wolf, UAL Corp., with total compensation of $18.3 million. Much of that was due to a $14.8 million stock gain.
- John Sculley, Apple Computer Inc., $16.7 million. Of that amount, $14.5 million came from exercising stock options.
- Paul Fireman, Reebok International Ltd., $14.8 million, all of it cash. This is the last year Mr. Fireman will get such a big cash payout; the company put a $2 million cap on the cash component of his 1991 pay, although it gave him options for 2.5 million shares.
- Dean L. Buntrock, Waste Management Inc., $12.3 million, including $8.1 million from stock-option gains.
- Martin S. Davis, Paramount Communications Inc., $11.3 million.
- Michael D. Eisner, Walt Disney Co., $11.2 million. Mr. Eisner didn't exercise options last year (1990).
- Rand V. Araskog, ITT Corp., $9.7 million.
- Joseph D. Williams, Warner-Lambert Co., $8.5 million, including $6.6 million from options exercised.
- Roberto C. Goizueta, Coca-Cola Co., $8.3 million, including $2.2 million from stock options.
- P. Roy Vagelos, Merck & Co., $7.1 million.

GREENSPAN: "DOW 4000" HERO

For years, the Dow Jones Industrial Average hit new milestones slowly and grudgingly. But 4000 was the first of six 1,000-point marks that fell in rapid-fire succession in just over three years.

The industrial average passed the 4000 level on February 23, 1995. The hero of the day was Alan Greenspan, chairman of the Federal Reserve Board, who remarked to Congress that he saw no need for the Fed to raise interest rates. Indeed, Mr. Greenspan said the Fed stood ready to lower rates at the first sign of a recession.

Mr. Greenspan's comments helped to push the industrial average up 30.28 points. Jack Baker, a veteran trader with Furman Selz, described the atmosphere as "jubilant, boisterous."

Mr. Greenspan "caught people off guard" with his assessment that the economy was slowing down, said Dana Johnson, head of research at First Chicago Capital Markets. That led them to believe that the interest-rate climate would be much friendlier than had been supposed.

Low interest rates were potent fuel for the long bull market that began in 1990. Depending on their political bent, commentators gave part of the credit either to President Clinton or to the Republican Congress for showing fiscal restraint.

After rising above 4000 in the morning of that February day, the industrials crisscrossed the line several times later and looked as if they would fall short. But in the final few seconds of trading, the average made it over the top.

The next day, *The Wall Street Journal* ran a headline that in retrospect looks silly, though it seemed sensible to many people at the time. "Stocks Cross 4000 for First Time, But the Visit There May Be Brief," the headline said. The accompanying "Abreast of the Market" column said that market watchers viewed a correction as "inevitable."

Two days later, the industrials fell below the 4000 level, and stayed mostly in the high 3900s until the second week of March. But then it was off to the races. Surpassing the expectations of almost everyone, even the optimists, the industrial average raced ahead to erase even more 1,000-point barriers.

Federal Reserve Chairman Alan Greenspan (right) listening to Treasury Secretary Robert Rubin

DJIA MILESTONE 4000
THURSDAY, FEBRUARY 23, 1995

Turner, TCI Seek Time Warner's 19.4% Stake in Turner Broadcasting

By ANITA SHARPE
And EBEN SHAPIRO
Staff Reporters of THE WALL STREET JOURNAL

Ted Turner, chairman and president of Turner Broadcasting System Inc., and cable giant Tele-Communications Inc. are negotiating to jointly purchase Time Warner Inc.'s 19.4% stake in Turner Broadcasting, according to people familiar with the talks.

In a shift of strategy, Time Warner has apparently dropped its insistence that it receive a Turner asset, such as the Cartoon Network, in exchange for the Turner stock. If a deal is worked out, Time Warner is expected to receive a premium above Turner's recent stock price of about $18 a share. Time Warner's 19.4% stake in Turner has a current market value of about $1 billion.

The proposal was discussed at Turner's board meeting last Friday, the people close to the situation said. Time Warner, Turner and TCI all declined to comment.

Above: Turner Broadcasting System CEO Ted Turner and Gerard Levin, CEO of Time Warner, attend the press conference announcing the sale of Turner's company to Time Warner, September 22, 1995
Left: CNN Television Studios in Atlanta

U.S. President Bill Clinton speaks with Secretary of State Warren Christopher and U.N. Ambassador Madeleine Albright while Attorney General Janet Reno and National Security Council Advisor Tony Lake look on. The group was at the U.N. General Assembly that day to take part in the organization's fiftieth anniversary celebration, October 1995

DJIA MILESTONE 5000
TUESDAY, NOVEMBER 21, 1995

Gingrich Says Clinton Must Move Right on Budget

By DAVID ROGERS
And CHRISTOPHER GEORGES
Staff Reporters of THE WALL STREET JOURNAL

WASHINGTON—As President Clinton called on Democrats to rally behind him on a balanced budget, Speaker Newt Gingrich said the president must move far to the right of his own party before any agreement can be reached with the GOP.

"The coalition has to start from the right," said the speaker. He scoffed at the idea of a more centrist compromise under which Mr. Clinton might be joined by 100 moderate-to-conservative Democrats in the House.

"It is simply impossible," said Mr. Gingrich. "There aren't 100 moderate and conservative Democrats, if you count the House and Senate together."

The speaker's remarks came as Mr. Clinton met with House Democrats last night at the Capitol to discuss his pledge to begin negotiations with the GOP toward balancing the budget over the next seven years. The agreement, reached Sunday, cleared the way for passage of a stopgap bill last evening to keep the government funded through Dec. 15.

The House Speaker and the President, Newt Gingrich and Bill Clinton

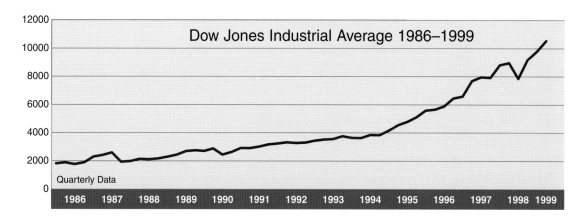

Dow Jones Industrial Average 1986–1999

Quarterly Data

101

PART IV

THE SECOND CENTURY BEGINS

DJIA MILESTONE 6000
MONDAY, OCTOBER 14, 1996

GOP Seeks U.S. Probe Into Lippo Contributions

WASHINGTON—Several Republican lawmakers have called for the appointment of an independent counsel to investigate whether the Democratic Party has received illegal foreign contributions, including nearly $1 million from individuals tied to an Indonesian financial conglomerate, Lippo Group.

Federal regulators and congressional investigators also are examining the ownership structure of Lippo Bank, a California institution that has as some of its major stockholders members of the Riady family of Jakarta, which controls Lippo Group. A former Lippo and DNC official, John Huang, has raised $4 million to $5 million in contributions to the Democratic Party, mainly from the Asian-American business community.

Mr. Huang's fund-raising and the Lippo contributions were the focus of

By Wall Street Journal staff reporters Jill Abramson, Glenn R. Simpson and John R. Wilke.

articles in The Wall Street Journal last week. It is illegal for foreign companies and individuals to contribute to U.S. candidates or parties. However, it is legal for permanent residents and the U.S. subsidiaries of foreign companies to donate to U.S. candidates and political parties.

Attorney General Janet Reno testifies before the House Committee on Government Reform, December 1997

THE MOST POWERFUL BULL MARKET

By many measures, the stock market of the 1990s has been the most powerful bull market in history.

In little more than four years, the Dow Jones Industrial Average sailed past seven 1,000-point marks, crossing 4000 on February 23, 1995, 5000 on November 21, 1995, 6000 on October 14, 1996, 7000 on February 13, 1997 and 8000 on July 16 of the same year. It closed above 9000 for the first time on April 6, 1998 and above 10000 on March 29, 1999. Although it took ninety-five years for the Dow Jones Industrial Average to reach the 3000 plateau (about seventy-three times its starting level of 40.94 in 1896), it was only five years before it tacked on the next 3,000 points, hitting 6000 before the end of its centennial year.

That centennial year, 1996, was the sixth straight year of rises for the industrial average, breaking the old record of five consecutive winning years in 1924–1928 and 1985–1989. Stocks had two more winning years in 1997 and 1998, making it eight in a row.

As 1999 began, the industrial average had risen in thirteen of the pre-vious fourteen years, an unprecedented streak. (The lone down year, 1990, saw a moderate decline of 4.3%, or 0.6% after dividends are considered.)

The big rise put stock valuations at levels never seen before. At the end of 1998, for instance, the 30 stocks in the industrial average were selling for nearly 61.0 times dividends. That's just slightly below the high of 61.1 in July 1997, but way above the earlier high of 38.0 set in August 1987. Stocks sold for about 5.0 times book value (corporate assets minus liabilities) in December 1998, after reaching a record of 5.4 in April. In August 1996, the price/book ratio hit 4.3, breaking the record of 4.2 set in August 1929, just before the Great Crash.

The multiple of corporate earnings was about 24.0 at the end of 1998, high but not a record.

The market's buoyancy made Bill Clinton the only president whose administration has seen the shattering of more than one 1,000-point barrier. He is also the first Democrat to hold office when such a milestone was passed.

Presidents Nixon, Reagan and Bush presided over the crossing of the 1000, 2000 and 3000 marks, respectively. Teddy Roosevelt was in the White House when the industrials charged past 100. President Coolidge held office when the 200 and 300 marks fell, and President Eisenhower was at the helm when the 400 and 500 barriers were crossed. All six men were Republicans.

Fans of Mr. Clinton credit him with trimming the federal budget deficit, helping to keep interest rates low. Detractors say Mr. Clinton was just lucky to occupy the White House in a time of modest inflation and steady economic growth.

The floor of the New York Stock Exchange, October 1995

DJIA MILESTONE 7000
THURSDAY, FEBRUARY 13, 1997

Senate Democratic Whip Ford Backs Capital-Gains Tax Cuts, a 'Hot-Button'

By GREG HITT
Staff Reporter of THE WALL STREET JOURNAL

WASHINGTON -- The move to cut capital-gains taxes picked up a powerful ally as Senate Democratic Whip Wendell Ford of Kentucky endorsed a broad-based reduction in the levy.

Sen. Ford, staking out new ground, proposed a sliding-scale plan that would reward investors with progressively deeper tax cuts the longer they held an asset. Sen. Ford described the proposal as an attempt to set aside partisan advantage on a "hot-button" issue. "I think it's time we moved beyond this stage," he said.

Senate Finance Committee Chairman William Roth immediately signaled his interest. "I'll listen to it," Sen. Roth said. "It shows there is recognition on both sides of the aisle as to the desirability" of a capital-gains tax cut. "It's a very encouraging sign." In fact, Sen. Roth, a Delaware Republican, supported the sliding-scale concept several years ago when advisers to then-President Bush offered a similar proposal in budget negotiations with Congress.

Under Sen. Ford's plan, the top individual capital gains tax, now 28%, would be reduced by two percentage points for each year a stock, bond or other asset was held. Ultimately, an investor could halve the tax to 14% on assets held more than eight years.

Ready to ring the opening bell that begins the day's trading at the New York Stock Exchange

CHANGING WITH THE TIMES

The Dow Jones Industrial Average changes when change is warranted.

The two biggest alterations in the DJIA in roughly forty years occurred in 1997 and 1999. Both instances involved four stocks each.

On March 17, 1997, Hewlett-Packard Co., Johnson & Johnson, Travelers Group and Wal-Mart Stores Inc. replaced Bethlehem Steel Corp., Texaco Inc., Westinghouse Electric Corp. and Woolworth Corp. On November 1, 1999, Home Depot Inc., Intel Corp., Microsoft Corp. and SBC Communications Inc. were substituted for Chevron Corp., Goodyear Tire & Rubber Co., Sears, Roebuck & Co. and Union Carbide Corp.

The 1999 change involved adding Nasdaq stocks (Intel and Microsoft) to the industrial average for the first time. Previously, all stocks in the DJIA had been listed on the New York Stock Exchange, although that wasn't a requirement for admission to this exclusive "club." Nasdaq stocks had been in the Dow Jones Transportation Average since 1991.

The modifications enlarged representation of the technology, finance and health care sectors to better reflect the stock market and the economy. "We've always thought of 'industrials' as meaning more than manufacturing," Paul E. Steiger, managing editor of *The Wall Street Journal*, said. "Nowadays, technological innovation and services of all types are major propellants of the U.S. economy."

The revisions constituted the largest one-time alterations in the 30-stock composition since four were changed in June 1959. In May 1991, three alterations were made. The largest number of changes made at once was eight on May 26, 1932.

The Wall Street Journal editors decide which stocks are in the average. "It's intentional that we don't change the stocks often," said John A. Prestbo, markets editor, who oversees the industrial average and other indexes produced by Dow Jones & Co., publisher of the Journal. "It isn't a 'hot stock' index, after all, and we believe that stability of composition enhances the trust that many people have in the industrial average."

Two of the changes were in anticipation of corporate events. Westinghouse, which had acquired CBS in 1995, was in 1997 about to spin off its industrial operations and become a pure broadcasting company; broadcasting already was well-represented in the industrial average. In 1999, Union Carbide had agreed to be acquired by Dow Chemical Co.

Frequently, such "external" events affecting a DJIA component trigger changes in the industrial average because they prompt a review of all 30 stocks.

Johnson & Johnson expanded the representation of health care. Hewlett-Packard, Intel and Microsoft enlarged the technology

---

"We've always thought of 'industrials' as meaning more than manufacturing."

---

sector. SBC Communications, mainly a local telephone-service company, also has a technology role in moving large data transmissions and providing Internet access.

Wal-Mart had replaced Woolworth as America's general merchandise retailer, and in fact became the largest retailer in the world. Rather than continuing with two broadline retailers in the DJIA, Sears was dropped in 1999 and Home Depot was included to add a specialty retailing dimension to the industry coverage.

Above: Futures traders at the Chicago Board of Trade
Opposite page: The first trading card for futures based on the Dow Jones Industrial Average on October 6, 1997

AT LAST, DOW JONES ALLOWS DJIA DERIVATIVES

After years of saying no, in 1997, Dow Jones & Co. finally said yes to derivatives on its storied industrial average. Investors can choose among three different products — options, futures and options on futures, and an exchange-traded fund — all based on the Dow Jones Industrial Average.

The three products can be used by institutional and individual investors for various purposes, including hedging the performance of existing portfolios, managing a diversified portfolio's exposure to stocks, or speculating on future moves of the 30-stock Dow Jones Industrial Average.

After a fierce competition, Dow Jones awarded the options contract to the Chicago Board Options Exchange (CBOE), the futures and options on the futures contracts to the Chicago Board of Trade (CBOT), and the fund contract to the American Stock Exchange. "This is a historic event for Dow Jones & Co. and for investors everywhere," Peter R. Kann, chairman and chief executive officer of Dow Jones, said when the contracts were announced. "Investors will [now] be able to invest using the tool they use to follow the stock market, the Dow Jones Industrial Average."

Despite the popularity of its average, for many years Dow Jones had steadfastly refused to permit any options, futures or other derivatives to be based on it. In large part, this was because of concern that such financial instruments were inappropriate for many investors and concern over their possible negative effects on the underlying markets. But eventually the company became convinced that experience with such products and safeguards designed by the Exchanges made the time right to consider licensing indexes, said John A. Prestbo.

Derivatives are financial contracts whose value is based on some underlying asset, such as stocks, bonds or commodities. Options give the holder the right but not the obligation to either buy or sell a basket of stocks linked to the underlying index at a predetermined price on a future date. A future is a contract to buy or sell the underlying index at a predetermined price at on future date.

Each of the Dow Jones products works differently and is targeted toward a slightly different audience. The exchange-traded fund, for instance, represents a share in an underlying trust of the 30 Dow stocks. Known as a Diamond, it is, in essence, a mini-mutual fund that trades like a single stock on the American Stock Exchange. It can thus be bought and sold at any time during the trading day by an investor, unlike most mutual funds, which can be traded only at the closing price. It also has tax benefits over mutual funds.

The futures contract, traded at the CBOT, essentially is an obligation to buy or sell the value of the Dow Jones average at a later date. In this way, investors can take a position on where they think the blue chips are going. Futures traders at the CBOT can buy and sell contracts on the industrial average that trade at ten times the value of the Dow average. At the CBOE, options on the Dow average are priced significantly lower, as this Exchange targets a more retail, or individual, customer base.

DJIA MILESTONE 8000
WEDNESDAY, JULY 16, 1997

VA Begins Processing Smoking Claims; Potential Wave Could Cost U.S. Billions

By BRUCE INGERSOLL
Staff Reporter of THE WALL STREET JOURNAL

WASHINGTON — The Veterans Affairs Department has begun processing the first in a potential tidal wave of compensation claims for smoking-related diseases and deaths that could cost the government billions of dollars a year over the next decade.

More than 4,500 veterans already have filed disability claims for tobacco-related diseases and VA officials estimate that 2.5 million veterans and surviving dependents could qualify for compensation under a new interpretation of VA law.

Yesterday, the agency gave guidance to 58 VA benefits offices nationwide on how to determine who qualifies for compensation for smoking-related disabilities and deaths. Veterans who became hooked on tobacco while in the service and continued smoking after their discharge would be eligible.

Meanwhile, in a meeting at the White House yesterday, attorneys representing cigarette companies seemed surprisingly flexible over the terms of the $368.5 billion tobacco settlement, administration officials said. Some of the key lawyers working on the settlement with state attorneys general attended the session, including J. Phil Carlton, the lead tobacco negotiator. The officials said that while the two sides didn't discuss specific changes, the tobacco lawyers said they were open to modifying provisions restricting regulation of nicotine and penalties the tobacco companies would pay if youth smoking doesn't decline to targeted levels.

U.S. Marines wading across a river in Vietnam

MONDAY, BLOODY MONDAY

What is it about Mondays in October?

Ten years after the market plunge of 1987, and within a day of the anniversary of the 1929 crash, the Dow Jones Industrial Average posted its worst one-day point loss ever on October 27, 1997. The industrial average was down 554.26 points to 7161.15, off more than 13% from its high just two months before.

But as grim as the numbers were, it wasn't a crash. By Wall Street standards, it constituted a "correction" — the first drop of more than 10% in seven years. The Dow had dropped 7.2%, the twelfth-worst one-day fall in the history of the industrial average in percentage terms.

The selling avalanche swept almost the entire market. On the New York Stock Exchange, a scant 182 issues rose while 2,937 fell. Trading on the Big Board totaled a record 685.5 million shares. The massive drop occurred despite two shutdowns of stock trading designed to stanch investor panic, "circuit breakers" created after the 1987 crash.

But many small investors saw the turmoil more as a potential buying opportunity than a cause for panic. Hairstylist Mitsuo Kato, for example, having his Mercedes-Benz sedan washed in West Hollywood, Calif., said he still trusted the underlying fundamentals of the market. "It's not like 1987, so I'm not going to sell, and I don't think other people should sell," said Mr. Kato, 43 years old. "This time, the economy is so much stronger."

The reverberations in foreign markets were disheartening. Tokyo fell 1.9%, London 2.6%. Markets plunged 15% in Brazil, 13% in Argentina. The Mexican peso fell to 8.5 pesos per dollar from 7.9 pesos. It was clear that to an extent never seen before, the world's stock markets are interconnected and codependent.

Fund managers trying to lock in the year's profits were widely fingered for the selling. Jack Bouroudjian, a futures broker for Nikko Securities International at the Chicago Mercantile Exchange, said investors, rather than offering to sell at a certain price, were willing to sell at any price.

The roots of the plunge went back to the previous summer, when shakiness in Thailand's currency began to roil markets throughout East Asia. The speculation finally washed ashore in Hong Kong, whose markets had remained relatively unscathed. Less than a week before Bloody Monday, Hong Kong's blue-chip Hang Seng index had plunged 10.4% in a single day. It recovered somewhat, then dropped 5.8% on October 27.

The economic crisis in Asia was enough to convince many investors that the apparent "perfect scenario" of low interest rates

Main Street is increasingly unaffected by gyrations on Wall Street

111

and rising earnings wasn't so perfect anymore. The rout in Hong Kong spread into European markets and then to the United States.

"What would you do if you were up 25% on the year and you saw what was happening around the globe?" said Michael Clark, head of stock trading at Credit Suisse First Boston. "There [was] a reason for people to protect their gains."

By 2:35 p.m. in New York, the industrial average was down more than 350 points, the trigger for the New York Stock Exchange to halt trading for thirty minutes. When trading began again, so did the declines. The Dow fell an additional 200 points, touching off a second mandated trading halt at 3:30 p.m. and ending trading for the day. It was the first time since the 1987 crash that prices had fallen far enough to trigger halts in trading on the New York Stock Exchange.

Stocks' steady climb upward resumed the following day. The DJIA soared 337.17 points to 7498.32, a 4.7% gain. Nearly 1.2 billion shares changed hands on the Big Board, a record. Within six months, the industrial average crossed the 9000 mark, and less than a year after that, it crossed 10000.

Traders at the Hong Kong Futures Exchange

The Dow's Big Drops

LARGEST ONE-DAY PERCENTAGE LOSSES IN THE DJIA

Date	% Change	Point Change
Oct. 19, 1987	-22.6	-508.00
Oct. 28, 1929	-12.8	-38.33
Oct. 29, 1929	-11.7	-30.57
Nov. 6, 1929	-9.9	-25.55
Dec. 18, 1899	-8.7	-5.57
Aug. 12, 1932	-8.4	-5.79
Mar. 14, 1907	-8.3	-6.89
Oct. 26, 1987	-8.0	-156.83
Jul. 21, 1933	-7.8	-7.55
Oct. 18, 1937	-7.7	-10.57
Feb. 1, 1917	-7.2	-6.91
Oct. 27, 1997	-7.2	-554.26

DJIA MILESTONE 9000
MONDAY, APRIL 6, 1998

U.S. Closes In on New Microsoft Case

Officials Think Evidence Supports a Broad Charge On Extending Monopoly

By John R. Wilke
Staff Reporter of The Wall Street Journal

WASHINGTON -- Justice Department investigators believe they have enough evidence to bring a new antitrust case against Microsoft Corp. before the end of the month, people close to the probe said.

The new case, if it goes forward, would allege "illegal maintenance and extension" of Microsoft's control of personal-computer operating software, in violation of the Sherman Antitrust Act, these people said. It also would repeat an existing charge that Microsoft violated a 1995 antitrust settlement by "bundling" Internet software with Windows , extending to Windows 98 last fall's charge that Microsoft uses Windows as a weapon against business rivals.

The investigators are taking final depositions from senior Microsoft officials and issued new civil subpoenas last week to major PC makers, including Compaq Computer Corp., company spokesmen said. They are racing to complete their work before Microsoft's planned May 15 release to computer makers of Windows 98, the next version of its PC operating software, the people close to the probe said.

Restrictions and Sanctions

If the case moves forward, prosecutors are expected to ask a federal court here for immediate temporary restrictions on Microsoft's practices plus unspecified permanent sanctions. The temporary restrictions are likely to include a requirement that Microsoft give PC makers a choice of whether to install Windows 98 with or without Microsoft's Internet software, as well as relief from alleged exclusionary contract terms imposed on PC makers and companies that provide Internet services.

Right: Microsoft CEO Bill Gates testifying before a U.S. Senate panel, June 1999
Below: Bill Gates talking to children at the Seattle Art Museum in October 1997 in connection with an exhibit about the Codex Leicester, the Leonardo Da Vinci manuscript he purchased in 1994

WHAT MOVES MARKETS — NEW FORCES POWER SURGING STOCKS

Where's the market headed? Even better, what stocks are going to be hot today — and not? How about tomorrow?

Not so long ago, information that was whispered over three-martini lunches moved markets. Today, markets often are moved by ordinary people double-clicking their computer mice.

That huge shift in the rules of the game helps to explain why so many experienced professionals have embarrassed themselves by underestimating the bull market's power.

Basic economic forces such as interest rates and earnings still dictate much of the stock market's direction, of course; the market reacts instantly to employment figures because they can signal whether inflation is rising.

But not so long ago, market experts examined arcane factors such as money supply, corporate price-to-book ratios, dividend yields, and the trade deficit. Few bother with such quaint indicators today. The investors themselves, the information they seek, the ways they exchange it and the public figures they look to for guidance about it have changed radically since the days when bigwigs drank vodka over lunch.

What moves stocks today are the Internet, instant television analysis and the explosion of electronic means of moving money. They aren't necessarily improvements; all seem to have created greater market volatility. But theory has it that more information is better than less. Regardless, these market accelerators are replacing reasoned analysts' reports, brokers' recommendations and the private, inside scoop that once set market-movers above ordinary Joes.

In fact, the "dumb money" — the mass of individual investors who once were viewed as putty in the hands of stockbrokers — today often can get information almost as soon as the "smart money." Even conference calls with corporate chieftains, once the reserve of selected analysts, today are being opened to the general public, at least on a listen-only basis. That helps to explain why the stock market has become so volatile and also why the "dumb" individual sometimes has looked more adept than the "smart" pro.

"When I first got into the business in the early 1970s, good information was hard even for institutions to obtain," said J. Thomas Madden, chief investment officer at Federated Investors in Pittsburgh. "Now it is presented to market-savvy grandmas in small towns in Arkansas first thing in the morning."

When Federal Reserve Chairman Alan Greenspan tells a Senate committee that he is worried about inflation, when Prudential Securities technical analyst Ralph Acampora turns bullish or bearish, when Merrill Lynch Internet analyst Henry Blodget revises targets for Amazon.com, the news flashes across television screens and the Internet before it hits many pros' desks. Millions of ordinary investors, including small-time "day traders" who sit at computer terminals buying and selling stocks, can react faster than the pros did ten or twenty years ago.

Now it is the pros who can be taken by surprise. "The structure of the marketplace has changed," says Robert Morris, chief investment officer at New York money manager Lord Abbett & Co. "But as yet, no one really understands how."

One of the biggest changes is that the agonizingly simple concept of momentum has replaced elaborate investment models as a driver of stocks. Stocks rise because as long as they look strong, investors pile in. As soon as a stock looks weak, investors pile out. And professionals, who try to foresee a trend by examining price-to-earnings history and other once useful barometers, can get burned.

Momentum-based investing, which has taken the market up, down and sideways in recent months, is just the most prominent of the new market drivers. There are others.

Liquidity

When you see "liquidity," think "savings." During the 1990s, individuals and their employers pumped retirement savings into stocks at historic rates. For some analysts, that, in a nutshell, is what has been pushing stocks upward. "Individual stocks may be driven by earnings, but markets are driven by liquidity," maintains investment strategist John Manley of Salomon Smith Barney.

How do you know what's happening to liquidity? One key source: data on mutual-fund inflows that is released every month by the Investment Company Institute (ICI), a trade organization. Two private data services update customers on their estimates of the flows every few days.

Although some experts doubt the importance of mutual-fund flows, with the stock market's overall value near $14 trillion and billions of dollars in money from pension funds, foreign investors, private funds, and day traders also hitting the market, the numbers are startling. The ICI says stock mutual funds pulled in just $5.9 billion in net new money in 1984. A decade later, in 1994, they sucked in a remarkable $119 billion. By 1997, the figure had nearly doubled to $227 billion. That's a powerful shift.

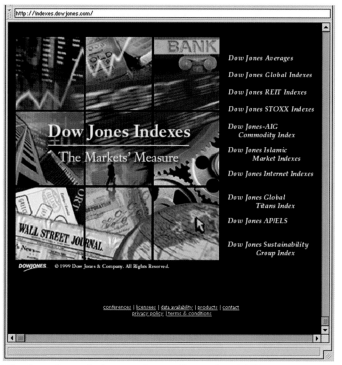

The Dow Jones Indexes web site, September 1999

In 1998, a year in which stocks suffered from sharp, painful swings, net new money put into mutual funds fell back to $159 billion. For the first year since 1986, more money went into money-market funds — cash — than into stock funds. To liquidity devotees, that was a clear indication that individual investors were turning more cautious and that a big prop for stocks could be weakening.

The Internet

It may be the "World Wide Wait," but it is driving stocks.

"I remember in the 1970s, I was visiting a fund company and asked them where they got their stock quotes," says PaineWebber investment strategist Edward Kerschner. "They said, 'The Wall Street Journal.' They didn't even have any quote machines."

Today, the *Journal* and others offer Internet-based news and information services. Many individuals receive electronic price quotes on their favorite stocks at home. Many execute trades electronically, although plenty of people complain that their trades aren't executed fast enough. Gossip from Internet chat rooms and message boards threatens to become as important as analysts' comments. Stockbrokers certainly aren't as important to many investors as they used to be.

Mr. Madden of Federated worries that confidence gained from using the Internet also encourages investors to "surf the wave and ride in and out of the market. It can lead to assuming levels of risk that later events may prove inappropriate."

Television

The pros keep an eye not just on their banks of quote machines, but also on television screens. "In my fixed-income trading room and my stock trading room, CNBC is on all during the day," says Henry Herrmann, chief investment officer at Overland Park, Kan., mutual-fund group Waddell & Reed. He put in television sets in 1997 when he was upgrading the bond trading room. "It is just another tool but it is a tool," he says. When Prudential's Mr. Acampora turned bearish in August 1998 and CNBC relayed his warning of a sharp market drop, the prediction proved self-ful-

CNBC's David Faber, Mark Haines and Joe Kernan discuss the market with Joseph V. Battipaglia (second from left), chief investment officer of Gruntal & Co., on "Squawk Box," July 15, 1999

filling and helped to push stocks down. The experience indicated that, at the right time, television appearances by any of a variety of market players can hit the market just as hard as a warning from the Fed's Mr. Greenspan. And television can turn once unknown analysts such as Merrill's Mr. Blodget into instant celebrities. (Dow Jones & Co. is a co-owner of CNBC television operations in Asia and Europe, and provides news content to CNBC in the United States.)

Individuals and pros alike probably get more instant information from television than they do from the slow Internet. Competing channels abound, offering live stock information for hours before, during and after the trading day.

Indexing

Perhaps the single greatest change in the mutual-fund world in recent years was the willingness of investors to quit trying to beat the market and, instead, join it.

Index funds, most of which try simply to duplicate the performance of the S&P 500 by holding most of the 500 stocks, have been the fastest-growing single fund category since the end of 1993.

The simple fact of being added to the S&P 500 can mean a 5% boost in a stock's value, as index funds line up to buy. It helps to explain momentum: The more money that goes into index funds, the more the same big stocks move upward, and the more investors, who don't necessarily own index funds, decide to keep buying the big stocks for their own accounts so they don't miss out.

"The driver in the '80s was greed. The driver in the '90s is fear," says Mr. Manley of Salomon Smith Barney.

DJIA MILESTONE 10000
MONDAY, MARCH 29, 1999

NATO Is Set to Target Sites in Belgrade

Escalation Comes as Allies Fear That Serb Forces Could Destroy Kosovo

By Carla Anne Robbins
And Thomas E. Ricks
Staff Reporters of The Wall Street Journal

WASHINGTON – In a sharp escalation of its air war against Serbia, NATO plans to bomb military targets in the center of the Serb capital of Belgrade in coming days, U.S. officials said.

Meanwhile, the Pentagon is expected to announce soon that the U.S. is sending dozens more bombers to Europe as part of a stepped-up air campaign.

The escalation reflects a growing fear among the Western allies that Serb forces in Kosovo could destroy the province before NATO forces accomplish their goal of "significantly degrading" the Serbs' military.

The strikes against downtown Belgrade, which until now the alliance has considered off limits, carry considerable risks of civilian casualties. But they are intended to boost political pressure against President Slobodan Milosevic and his top generals in hopes of getting them to halt their offensive in Kosovo and accept a peace settlement.

At a gut level, officials say, the message of bombing Belgrade is that there is no sanctuary for the Serb leadership, which has waged war on its neighbors for seven years without ever feeling the sting at home.

"You have to... increase the level of pain to Milosevic," said a NATO official.

Left: A US F-15C Eagle flies a mission over the former Yugoslavia, April 8, 1999
Below: Flames and smoke rise from an electric power plant in a Belgrade suburb, May 28, 1999, the day after the plant was hit by a NATO missile

THE FIRST 10,000 POINTS

Amid a mixture of exhilaration and relief, the Dow Jones Industrial Average leapt the historic 10000 hurdle on March 29, 1999.

On the floor of the New York Stock Exchange, traders cheered and a few threw paper into the air. Exchange Chairman Richard Grasso and New York Mayor Rudolph Giuliani gaveled the trading session to a close and then tossed blue hats emblazoned with "Dow 10000" to eager traders.

Nearly one hundred and three years after its creation by cofounder Charles Dow, the venerable industrial average had surged 184.54 points, or 1.9%, to close at 10006.78, territory that few analysts had foreseen — much less forecast — as recently as two years before. Enthusiasm on the floor was somewhat tempered because the industrials had broken 10000 during the day on three days earlier in the month, only to fall back by the close.

"It is a testament to the market's strength and the underlying strength in our economy," said Robert Murphy, chief executive of floor-based firm Robb Peck McCooey. "It is exciting that we have come this far this fast."

Reaching the five-digit Dow capped a spectacular recovery by big stocks that just seven months earlier had seemed to be headed for a bear market. Traders said the close above 10000 was a landmark in a bull market that made millions of Americans, especially those nearing retirement, feel more financially comfortable than they had ever imagined possible. But at the same time, the bull was aging, and even its most emphatic supporters believed that it would have to run less rapidly than in the past.

The industrials topped 10000 at 2:29 p.m. Eastern Standard Time, fell back four minutes later, and then, after gyrating above and below the level, finally moved above it just before 3:15 p.m. and stayed there. The day's high was 10040.36. At the end of Big Board trading, twenty-five of the thirty industrials were up, led by International Business Machines, General Electric and Wal-Mart Stores. Declining were AT&T, Boeing, General Motors, International Paper and Union Carbide.

In the end, it was a broad range of large stocks that helped the overall market gain. Technology stocks rose on hope that first-quarter earnings would surpass expectations. Oil stocks climbed on the continuing rise in world oil prices. Retailers advanced on signs of economic strength at home. And banking stocks went up on hope that inflation and interest rates would remain low and that the economy would continue to be strong.

Robert McCooey, president of Griswold Co., a Big Board floor brokerage firm, had watched skeptically as the average mounted its first of several assaults on 10000 during the day. But as it finally closed above the mark, he said, "It's like a burden that's been hanging over the market the last couple weeks and now it's kind of a relief."

James Maguire, Jr., the specialist charged with matching buyers and sellers in the stock of American Express, barely looked up as a dull roar greeted the first crossing of the mark: "That's got to be Dow 10000," he said offhandedly as he busied himself with a burst of orders.

But his father, James Maguire Sr., a floor veteran who remembers Dow 1000, was more reflective. About crossing 1000 in 1972, he said, "For people who were on the periphery, it wasn't an important media event. There is more excitement around 10000." But he noted that in recent years the stock exchange emerged as "not only an important financial institution but a cultural institution. It's part of the evening news."

To floor traders, the relatively light volume of 742.9 million shares seemed incongruous considering the momentous move.

Some special factors helped to account for the industrial average's ability to close above 10000. With optimism spreading about first-quarter earnings and stocks up for the year, professional investors were eager to avoid being caught with cash on their books as they closed out the first quarter, and they were buying big stocks.

In August, worries about Russia and Asia had come within a hair of pulling the industrials into a bear market. On August 31, 1998, the industrials fell 512.61 points in a single day, hitting 7539.07. Then, on the back of a strong consumer-driven economy, the blue-chip index staged a 33% gain, a move of almost 2,500 points. The move past 10000 represented a doubling of the average in little more than three years.

Many market analysts, especially those with enough gray hair to remember past bear markets, worried that Dow 10000 could be remembered as a high point not of investor triumph but of market excess. The Dow industrials, they noted, were trading at an astronomical 25.6 times earnings for the previous twelve months, a level that many market analysts considered excessive. They pointed to Internet stocks, to a fascination with a handful of technology highfliers and, above all, to what they called the "narrowness" of the stock market.

While industrial average and market darlings soared, many other stocks didn't. As the Dow industrials crossed the 10000 mark, forty-six stocks hit new highs on the New York Stock Exchange, but twice as many hit new lows.

Treasury Secretary Robert Rubin, who had tried to avoid saying much of anything about the level of the stock market allowed, a few weeks before the big day, that piercing 10000 has "a kind of symbolism, and that symbolism can have an effect." He went on to caution that investors often err in "good times" because they abandon "rigor" in their decision making.

Traders gather on the floor of the New York Stock Exchange to celebrate the closing of the Dow Jones Industrial Average over 10000 for the first time on March 29, 1999. The market finished at 10006.78, up 184.54 for the day. The Dow index first broke 10000 points on March 16, 1999.

Dow Jones Industrial Average 1896–1999

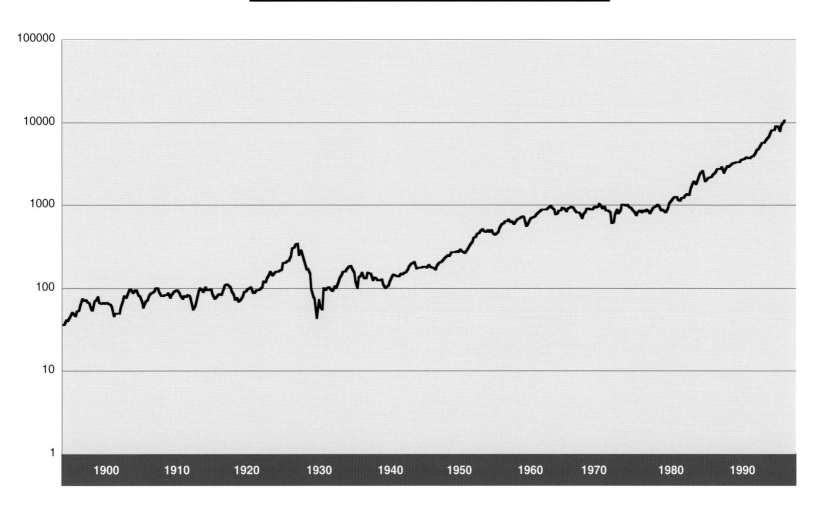

In the most common form of price chart, a change in the Dow from 100 to 200 covers the same vertical distance as a change from 10000 to 10200. Yet the first is a 100% move, and the second only a 2% move, a significant difference to an investor. This logarithmic chart gives equal percentage changes equal vertical distances, whatever the price level. Thus, the distance between 10 and 100 is the same as between 1000 and 10000. This treatment provides a clearer picture of the stock market's impact on investors over the past century.

PART V

DOW TRIVIA

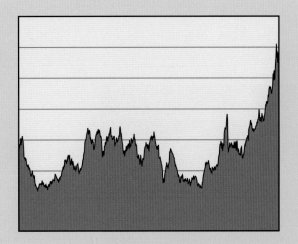

IN BIG GAINS, PERCENTAGE IS KEY

Imagine that the Dow Jones Industrial Average exploded upward tomorrow and rose more than 1,000 points.

Sound impossible? Such surges happened five times during the Dow industrials' first one hundred years. The key is to look at the percentage change in the industrial average, which is more important than the point change. A one-hundred-point move today enriches investors no more than a one-point move did in the mid-1930s.

The table shows the biggest one-day gains, all 10% or more. Most of them came in the early 1930s, when stocks were extraordinarily volatile. Investors' nerves were rubbed raw by the crash of 1929 and by the Depression. Alternating currents of fear and greed pushed the market up and down violently.

The biggest gain ever was 15.34% on March 15, 1933, the day after Franklin D. Roosevelt's bank holiday ended. All trading on the New York Stock Exchange had been suspended since March 3. When it resumed, *The Wall Street Journal* reported a "wave of buying," which "reflected more than anything else the transformation which has occurred in public psychology."

Laszlo Birinyi, who heads a stock-market information firm in Greenwich, Conn., says the March 1933 advance was helped along when people were given extra time to file their tax returns, reducing their need to sell stocks.

Two of the biggest gains were rebounds following the crashes of 1929 and 1987. That's no surprise, says Tim Hayes, of Ned Davis Research Inc. in Venice, Fla. Volatility, he says, is most pronounced near market bottoms.

President Franklin Delano Roosevelt and his wife Eleanor returning to the White House after his third inauguration, January 20, 1941

Biggest Gains in the DJIA

THE FIVE LARGEST ONE-DAY GAINS
IN THE HISTORY OF THE DOW JONES INDUSTRIAL AVERAGE

Date	% Gain	What Was Happening
Mar. 15, 1933	+15.34	Trading resumed after bank holiday
Oct. 6, 1931	+14.87	Hoover offered plan to revive business
Oct. 30, 1929	+12.34	Rebound after crash of Oct. 29
Sept. 21, 1932	+11.36	Railroad loadings hinted at recovery
Oct. 21, 1987	+10.15	Bounceback after crash of 1987

Sources: Wall Street Journal research, Birinyi Associates

MARKET CRASH? WHAT'S THAT!

What does a bad day in the stock market feel like? In a sense, people who started investing in the early 1990s wouldn't know.

Sure, there have been days when the Dow Jones Industrial Average lost a lot of points. But what affects investors' wallets isn't the point change; it's the percentage change. As of year-end 1998, the biggest one-day percentage loss in the industrial average during the 1990s was a 7.2% drop on October 27, 1997.

That decline was spurred by economic woes in Asia that pushed the Hong Kong market down more than 23% in four days. But the drop in the Dow didn't even make the top ten list (it was number twelve).

The fact is, only two of the one hundred greatest percentage losses in the Dow industrials (all 4.29% or more) have occurred in this decade: the October 27, 1997 drop and a 6.4% slide on August 31, 1998.

The accompanying table shows the five biggest one-day percentage losses in history. The biggest was the historic crash that brought the industrials down 22.61% on October 19, 1987. Among the causes of the 1987 crash were rising interest rates, the U.S. bombing of Iranian oil platforms, friction with U.S. trading partners, rampant speculation in the futures markets, and loss of investor confidence after the Dow industrials skidded in September and early October.

The second-worst, third-worst and fourth-worst days occurred within about a week of each other in the crash of 1929. As in 1987, the 1929 crash had been preceded by a boisterous economic and stock-market boom. Speculation by investors who were required to put down only 10% of the purchase price for their stocks fueled the bull market of the Roaring Twenties but also aggravated the crash. When their brokers demanded more collateral, investors were forced to sell shares, producing a downward spiral.

The fifth-worst day was December 18, 1899. According to historian Robert Sobel of Hofstra University, the United States had suffered some casualties in the Philippines, fighting against guerrillas seeking independence, and the British had suffered losses in the Boer War. What's more — as is so often a factor in market declines — interest rates were rising.

The Five Worst Days

THE LARGEST ONE-DAY PERCENTAGE DROPS IN THE DOW JONES INDUSTRIAL AVERAGE

Date	Point Loss	% Loss
Oct. 19, 1987	508.00	-22.6
Oct. 28, 1929	38.33	-12.8
Oct. 29, 1929	30.57	-11.7
Nov. 6, 1929	25.55	-9.9
Dec. 18, 1899	5.57	-8.7

OCTOBER IS A SCARY MONTH FOR STOCKS

Does the stock market care what month it is? It certainly acts as if it does.

For the Dow Jones Industrial Average, October has been the most dangerous month — the month of the great stock-market crashes in 1929 and 1987, plus numerous other jolts over the decades, such as the Cuban missile crisis in 1962, the mini-crash of 1989, and the big sell-off in 1997. Of the twenty largest daily percentage drops in the industrial average, eight have occurred in October, including the three biggest.

Yet October isn't the worst month for average performance. September is. The industrial average has declined, on average, 0.9% in September, according to Ned Davis Research Inc., which has studied monthly returns going back to 1900.

Why September has been so weak remains a mystery, even to academics who study such things. Three other months — February, May and October — also show a negative average return, with May off 0.1%, and February and October down even less. (The figures are price change only, without dividends.)

Since 1900, December has been the king of months for the industrial average, with an average gain of 1.5%, or 18%, annualized. July is the next best, at 1.4%, followed by January (1.2%) and August (1.1%).

The strong performance around Christmastime has been attributed to holiday cheer, but it's more likely to be caused by pension plans. Many corporations contribute to pension or profit-sharing plans at the turn of the year, and much of that money flows to stocks.

The same explanation might also apply to January or July, but it's hard to explain the strength in August. In any event, the monthly returns are consistent with market lore that there is usually a "summer rally."

In the middle of the performance spectrum, showing moderate gains are April with about 1.0%, March with 0.7% and November with 0.9%.

Besides looking at average gains, it's also possible to look at the odds that the industrial average will be up in a given month. In that regard, December again leads the way, with gains about 72% of the time. The worst month is poor old September, when the leaves begin to fall and so do stocks — 58% of the time.

Right: A page from a 19th-century calendar with an illustration depicting two women at the piano
Opposite page: A restaurant in Kalispell, Mont., July 1980

THE DOW'S SIZZLERS AND FIZZLERS

Stock	Dates	Gain or Loss %	DJIA Gain %
HELPED THE AVERAGE			
Sears Roebuck	1924–present	+371,211	+9,343
Exxon	1928–present	+109,090	+3,725
Coca-Cola	1987–present	+1,012	+305
HURT THE AVERAGE			
Colorado Fuel	1901–1912	-74	+16
Johns Manville	1930–1982	-59	+241
Amer. Sugar Refining	1896–1930	-56	+488

In propelling the Dow Jones Industrial Average forward, some stocks have pulled their oars extraordinarily well, but others have been dead weights.

The accompanying table provides some examples. Since it was added to the industrial average in 1924, Sears Roebuck has done particularly well in pulling the average forward. Oil giant Exxon (originally Standard Oil Co. of New Jersey) also has been a big winner over the long haul.

Among stocks added to the average more recently, Coca-Cola has been a star, rising more than 1,000% since 1987, while the overall average was going up 305%. Coca-Cola was also in the average from 1932 to 1935, during which time it rose 1,186% compared with 193% for the overall average. Obviously, for the Dow industrials, things go better with Coke.

What traders call "the two Generals," General Motors and General Electric, also have been strong performers over the years. GE has been in the average almost continuously for the past century, and GM has been in continuously since 1925.

In addition to the losers shown in the table, Anaconda Copper, Chrysler, United Drug and U.S. Rubber were all duds while they were part of the industrial average.

Other stocks gained, but so sluggishly that they were a drag on the average. These companies include Bethlehem Steel, International Harvester, U.S. Steel and Woolworth.

KEEPING "CIRCUIT BREAKERS" IN SYNC

After the Dow Jones Industrial Average plunged 508 points in the October 19, 1987, crash, government officials had a question: What could be done to prevent a replay?

The response was two major new rules, which were implemented in 1988. The first established circuit breakers that would halt trading for an hour if the Dow Jones Industrial Average plunged 250 points, and for two hours if it fell 400 points. The second clamped restrictions on the ability of program traders to dart between stocks and stock index futures when the Dow industrials rose or fell more than 50 points, an effort to reduce the volatility such arbitrage trading was said to cause.

"I've been in markets all my life, and I don't like circuit breakers," John J. Phelan, Jr., then Big Board chairman, said at the time. "But I have to adjust just like everybody else." The Dow was used as the gauge because to the person on the street, it is the measure of the market, and 50 points is a big move, he said.

But less than a decade later, the industrial average had more than tripled, giving rise to criticism that the circuit-breaker trigger points were too low, in percentage terms. In 1996, the halt times were halved and in 1997, the trigger points were raised to 350 and 550 points.

The circuit breakers were activated for the first time when stocks, responding to a plunge in Asian markets, tumbled on October 27, 1997. The first circuit breaker was triggered at 2:35 p.m. Trading resumed at 3:05 and the market immediately plummeted an additional 200 points, closing the market for the day at 3:30, with the Dow industrials down a record 554 points.

The circuit breakers kicked in far too soon, most market participants agreed. They had originally been meant to bring order to the sort of disorderly conditions that accompanied the 22.6% plunge in 1987. But in the 1997 drop, trading, by all accounts, was orderly. The market was down just 7.2% when it closed — not a crash by any standard. In fact, the circuit breakers probably made matters worse. When the first halt ended, desperate sellers rushed to trade, while buyers went on strike. Overseas, news that the world's largest stock exchange had closed prematurely engendered panic the following morning.

In April 1998, the Securities and Exchange Commission approved new circuit breakers. If the Dow Jones Industrial Average falls 10% before 2 p.m. eastern time, trading halts for one hour; if the 10% drop occurs between 2:00 and 2:30 p.m., it stops for thirty minutes, and if the drop occurs after 2:30, trading does not stop. Trading will halt for two hours if the average falls 20% before 1 p.m. eastern time, for one hour if it falls between 1 and 2 p.m., and for the rest of the day if it falls after 2 p.m. A drop of 30% at any time would close the market for the day. The circuit breakers are fixed in Dow industrials points at the end of each quarter for the following three months.

For the first quarter of 1999, the trigger levels were 900, 1,800 and 2,700 points on the Dow industrials. As the Dow average crossed the historic 10000 mark on March 29, 1999, the new circuit breakers had never been triggered.

In February 1999, the Securities and Exchange Commision also approved a new formula for the program-trading collar. The collar is now set quarterly at 2% of the level of the Dow Jones Industrial Average. The collar is lifted when the industrials return to within 1% of their previous close, or at the day's end. The initial collar was set at 180 points.

THE DJIA'S PAST ISN'T PROLOGUE

In the spring of 1951, when his best student was graduating from Columbia Business School, Professor Benjamin Graham, often called the father of value investing, had some advice.

The Dow Jones Industrial Average had traded below 200 at some time during every full year since its inception in 1896, Prof. Graham noted. Because the average, then at about 250, had yet to trade below 200 in 1951, perhaps the student would be better off postponing his investment career, waiting until the average made its usual sojourn below 200.

This advice — singularly bad in retrospect — violated Prof. Graham's own tenet against trying to forecast markets. No matter. The student, Warren E. Buffett, who had received the only A-plus that Prof. Graham had ever awarded, didn't listen to him. Lucky thing, because the industrial average didn't go back to 200 in that year or, indeed, in any year since.

Today, Mr. Buffett is a billionaire and is considered by some people to be the best investor in history. "I had about ten thousand bucks" when Prof. Graham gave his advice, Mr. Buffett recalled. "If I'd taken [the] advice, I'd probably still have about ten thousand bucks."

In retrospect, it is obvious that teacher and pupil were separated by a generational divide. For investors who were nearly wiped out in the 1930s, the Great Crash was formative. Whenever the industrial average got "too" high or the mood on Wall Street too happy, old-timers expected another crash.

Prof. Graham's mistake has been faithfully repeated by investors in each succeeding era. His real error was to ascribe some meaning to an absolute number on the industrial average. In the abstract, neither DJIA 250 nor DJIA 10000 is "high" or "low." It all depends on the earnings and prospects of the underlying stocks in the index. To assume that the index will return to a previous level is like calling a pitch a strike with one's eyes closed, merely because the previous pitch was over the plate.

Left: Professor Benjamin Graham, left, and General Robert E. Wood of Sears, Roebuck Co. as they testified before the Senate Banking Committee about the stock market, March 11, 1955
Above: Warren Buffett, left, makes his way through the crowds during the lunch hour at the annual Berkshire Hathaway stockholders' meeting in Omaha, Neb., on May 3, 1999; about 17,000 stockholders were at the meeting

SHIFTING PERSPECTIVES

Any way you measure it, the DJIA has done pretty well

SMOOTHED-OUT DOW

From month to month and year to year, Wall Street goes through booms and busts. But for investors who want to discern long-term trends, it can help to smooth out the short-term gyrations. Here is a smoothed-out version of the Dow Jones Industrial Average, using a twenty-four-month rolling average.

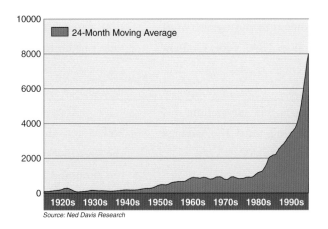

Source: Ned Davis Research

DOW vs. DIVIDENDS

Another yardstick for evaluating a stock is its price/dividend ratio (which mathematically is the reciprocal of its dividend yield). On average, the DJIA has traded at about twenty-four times the dividends of the stocks that compose it. It's more than twice as high now.

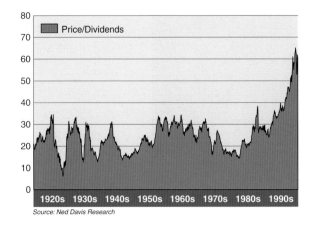

Source: Ned Davis Research

DOW vs. EARNINGS

One tool for judging whether an individual stock is cheap or expensive is to divide its price by per-share earnings (profits for the previous four quarters). The same can be done with the industrial average. Because earnings swing widely, so does the price/earnings ratio. Values below zero or above one hundred are usually considered not meaningful and are not shown.

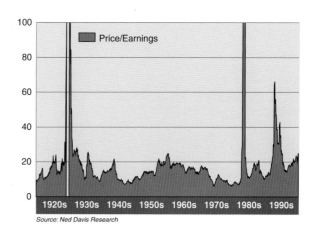

Source: Ned Davis Research

DOW vs. BOOK VALUE

Book value is simply a corporation's net worth — its assets minus its liabilities. The price/book ratio is a stock's price divided by per-share book value. For the Dow Jones industrials, the index reading is divided by the collective book value of the stocks that compose it.

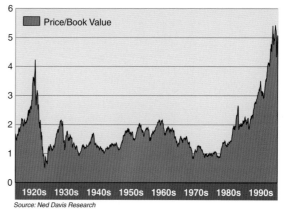

Source: Ned Davis Research

DOW vs. THE WORLD

New York, London and Tokyo stocks performed well in the decades after World War II, with Japan's market reflecting its postwar industrial might. Since 1990, Japanese stocks have lost ground as U.S. and British markets have boomed. Major indexes were reindexed to 100 on January 31, 1924 (plotted on a logarithmic scale).

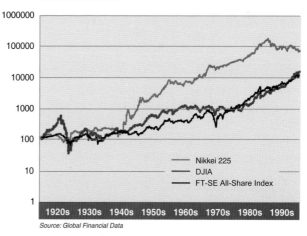

Source: Global Financial Data

PART VI

THE EVOLVING
STOCK MARKET

FROM SPECULATION TO BLUE CHIPS

One hundred years ago, the West wasn't the only thing wild. Up in the East, there was Wall Street.

In the financial district of lower Manhattan, runners, traders, prospectors and speculators peopled an insular hive in which clandestine investment pools manipulated share prices with impunity. This was no place for widows and orphans — or any other investors with an aversion to risk.

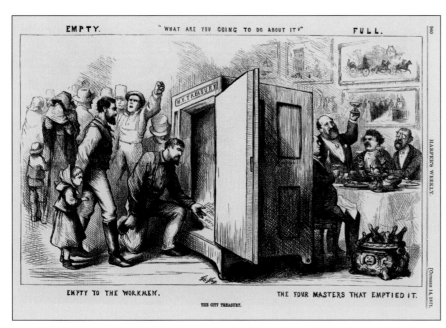

EMPTY.   "WHAT ARE YOU GOING TO DO ABOUT IT?"   FULL.

EMPTY TO THE WORKMEN.   THE FOUR MASTERS THAT EMPTIED IT.

THE CITY TREASURY.

A political cartoon lampoons the corrupt administration in New York, led by Boss Tweed and the Tammany Society (ca. 1871)

"The nouveaux riches might [buy stocks], but it wasn't done" by the average investor, says Prof. Richard J. Stillman.

Indeed, other than in tip sheets and the pages of *The Wall Street Journal,* stocks weren't news. In the spring of 1896, when Charles Dow introduced the Dow Jones Industrial Average, the nation was more concerned with William Jennings Bryan and the Populist battle for the silver standard — ultimately defeated by William McKinley and other supporters of gold's primacy. In New York City itself, the peccadilloes of the Tammany Hall political machine and the impending annexation of Brooklyn, the Bronx and Queens provided much of the grist for the media mill.

"Think of some of the things we take for granted today

as part of market calculations: the Federal Reserve, the federal income tax, the Securities and Exchange Commission," says Hugh Johnson, director of investment strategy at First Albany Corp. in New York. "None of those things existed a hundred years ago."

Now, more than one third of American households have come to own stock, directly or indirectly. Millions of investors across the country receive quarterly earnings reports, watch television channels devoted to the performance of stocks and bonds, and read magazines and best-selling books about how to play the market. Billions of dollars in retirement funds reside not just in savings bonds and money-market accounts, but also in equity mutual funds.

How was stock investing transformed from a ruffian speculators' sport into an investment of choice for millions?

Stock-market historians outline a slow, erratic evolution of the public's attitude toward equities over the past century — from outright revulsion to an ever wider embrace. As in the market itself, the process has had its ups and downs: the Roaring Twenties, when large numbers of Americans discovered Wall Street

One hundred years ago, only gamblers and manipulators dared venture into the stock market. It has been a long, steady climb to the mainstream.

for the first time; the 1929 crash and the Depression that followed, which left the Street deserted; the 1950s, when postwar prosperity brought renewed confidence in stocks; and the wrenching uncertainty of stagflation in the 1970s.

But stock investment has nonetheless traced an obvious progression toward broader public acceptance. Advances in technology have helped by bridging the distance between Wall Street and Main Street. Just as important, the stock market has won the public's trust through its own lengthening record of healthy long-term returns as well as the increasing oversight — within and without — which has taken much of the fear and loathing out of investing.

A hundred years ago, few people cared enough about the stock market to fear, loathe or love it. For those who did care, logistics got in the way. Imagine being a mining prospector in California at the end of the 19th century.

Down from the hills you come to convert a bag of gold dust into cash. Wells Fargo in San Francisco happily obliges. With cash in hand, you might — just might — want to try your hand at the stock market, where, you have heard, fortunes can beget fortunes.

So you telegraph a message to a New York brokerage firm, triggering a series of events involving any number of go-betweens. Eventually, a broker is dispatched to execute your trade. If the stock you want is listed on the New York Stock Exchange, it probably is one of the railroad stocks that dominate the Big Board. It might also be one of the new, largely untested industrials among the stocks traded outside, literally on the curb of Broad Street.

Confirmation of your trade comes perhaps by telegraph a day later, or by post several days later. But that's all assuming you want stock in the first place. Chances are, you would put your money in bank savings or bonds or, like a lot of Californians back then, real estate.

Attitudes remained much the same through the first couple of decades of the 20th century. Bonds were the preferred investment. The 1920s marked the start of America's romance with the stock market.

That decade opened ominously enough when a bomb exploded in front of the New York Stock Exchange, killing thirty people. Newspapers accused Bolsheviks and anarchists, but the crime was never solved. The following year, the curbside market moved indoors and named itself the American Stock Exchange. Edgar Loren Smith, a New York investment banker, laid the groundwork for the broader public's willingness to nibble at the market in his 1924 book *Common Stocks as Long-Term Investments*.

"That was the first book that said stocks were not just speculative, but were actually good long-term investments," says Jeremy J. Siegel, professor of finance at the University of Pennsylvania's Wharton School of Business. "So people started to believe this."

The scene after a bomb exploded on Wall Street in 1920

135

Where belief wavered, margin buying often helped. Through this practice of borrowing from a broker to buy stock, not only did speculators flourish; average Americans partook of the rage, too. By some accounts, more than a million Americans owned stock on margin by 1929, and more than 40% of household assets were involved in stock trading. Small wonder, then, that a stock such as Radio Corp. of America, though it didn't pay a dividend, could zoom from $85 to $428 in 1928.

But popularity didn't always mean admiration. In *The Great Gatsby*, F. Scott Fitzgerald draws few distinctions between the goons who fix the 1919 World Series and the stock jobbers who manipulate share prices. Out of this milieu arose the likes of Jesse Livermore, a real-life Gatsby who amassed a fortune playing the stock market. In the summer of 1929, he went short in the market, betting that prices would drop. They didn't fall soon enough, and he went bust, beginning a downward spiral that ended in poverty and suicide several years later.

Mr. Livermore's fate was portentous. "Wall St. Lays an Egg," screamed the headline in *Variety* after the crash of October 1929.

Faith in stocks as a solid long-term bet was largely destroyed.

The sharp shock of the Great Crash was followed by a slow burn of steadily declining stock prices. By 1932, according to researchers, stock prices had lost 85% to 90% of their pre-Crash values. The Dow Jones Industrial Average, which had peaked at 381.17 in September 1929, fell to 41.22 on July 8, 1932.

As memories of the Crash persisted and the pain of the Great Depression worsened, the stock market receded farther and farther

Above left: The headline on page one of Variety *after the October 29, 1929, stock market crash*
Above right: An employment agency crowded with men seeking work during the Depression
Opposite page: Sen. E. Capehart (R.-Ind.) (left) with Chmn. W. Fulbright (R.-Ark.) of the Senate Banking Committee during a 1955 investigation of the stock market

from the nation's collective conscious-ness. While undertaking high-profile efforts to provide food and jobs to an impoverished citizenry, President Franklin D. Roosevelt's administration also set about reworking the ways Wall Street functioned, crafting tougher securities laws and establishing the Securities and Exchange Commission.

Regulation would ensure a more level playing field for investors in the future, but its immediate impact was to damp trading among the few stalwarts who remained in the market. Daily volume on the New York Stock Exchange fell to fewer than one mil-lion shares a day in the 1930s from four million shares a day in 1929.

As America retooled for World War II, the economy began to revive. Jobs proliferated. Stocks languished. "Japan was knocking on the door in Los Angeles, the world looked like it might be delivered into the hands of fascists, communists, or the extreme likelihood of a New Deal domestic market," says James Grant, editor of "Grant's Interest Rate Observer" in New York. "It was American capitalism's darkest hour. Who could imagine, at that very point, that the great American Century lay ahead?"

Even as the war ended and American industrial preeminence became obvious, the public still shied away from stocks. Certainly, memories of the 1929 crash and the Depression lingered, stoking fears of more hardship to come. In the early 1950s, Senator William J. Fulbright of Arkansas called hearings to inves-tigate the possibility of yet another stock-mar-ket crash. To attract nervous investors, compa-nies paid dividends higher than the yield on the bonds that were considered the safe invest-ment choice.

Slowly, though, with prosperity in the air, confidence in stocks crept back. In 1954, the

Dow Jones Industrial Average finally eclipsed its previous record, reached in the autumn of 1929.

Underscoring the budding enthusiasm for stocks, the New York Stock Exchange start-ed its "own your share of America" program in 1954, in an attempt to educate the public about the benefits of investing in stocks. As part of the program, the Big Board published magazine inserts to explain stock investing and initiated a monthly stock-purchase plan. At the start of the decade, six million individuals owned stocks; by the end, more than twelve and a half million did.

Market experts point to several key

events that lured investors into the market. Among them were Polaroid Corp.'s introduction of the Land Camera, which helped make that company's shareholders rich, and a push among brokerage firms, led by what is now Merrill Lynch & Co., to reach more retail customers. Also, in 1956, common stock in Ford Motor Co. was offered to the public for the first time, an event that, because of its sheer size and the sterling reputation of the company, provided a critical stamp of approval for the maturing market.

"It was like letting the crowd into the palace," says Michael Robbins, a principal with New York Stock Exchange member firm Robbins & Henderson, who recalls the Ford offering from his days as a youthful Wall Street employee. "It was a seminal event in a decade that marked the return of the public to the stock market."

Perhaps more telling, if less dramatic, was the point in 1958 when rising stock prices pushed the dividend yield below the bond-market yield for the first time since the 1929 crash. That trend has continued. At the end of 1998, the average dividend yield on the 30 Dow industrials stood at 1.7%, compared with a 5.1% yield on Treasury bonds.

"This moment, when the yield picture reversed, marked a real watershed for the stock market and the general public," says James M. Griffin, Jr., chief economist at Aeltus Investment Management Inc. in Hartford, Conn. "People had their guts spilled on the floor in the 1930s, and the shift in yields indicated that the public had finally put those demons to rest."

Byron Wien, an investment strategist at Morgan Stanley Dean Witter & Co., adds that 1958 "was the most important date in the history of stock-market investing. People finally realized that bonds can only pay what they can pay you, but stocks could pay you much more."

Another nascent factor in the stock market of the 1950s would come to dominate in subsequent decades: mutual funds, which began to enjoy broad popularity. Gerald Tsai's reputation as a top-flight money manager helped boost the prospects of a modest mutual-fund firm in Boston called Fidelity Investments.

Workers assembling Ford sedans at a factory, 1955

Investor confidence suffered through several jolts in the 1960s, the stagflation and malaise of the 1970s, and the 1987 crash, but it never disappeared as it did after the 1929 crash. Investors had come to accept the notion, bolstered by market studies, that no matter how bumpy the short-term ride, stocks provide the best return in the long haul.

That idea has become almost a market mantra today. Many investors see the 1987 stock-market crash as the greatest buying opportunity of a generation. In fact, "buying on the dips" has become nearly as common as "don't fight the Fed" among Wall Street's phrase masters.

"**P**eople more and more often say they don't care what happens to their stocks in the short term, and even when things get tough they say they will stay with stocks," says Kenneth Safian, president of Safian Investment Research, a money-management firm in White Plains, N.Y. "The investors so heavily involved in the stock market today, most of them haven't been tested like we were in the 1970s. That's a big question. The public is more confident about stocks as a long-term investment, but will they hang in there

when we get the next bear market?"

One factor that may argue for a positive answer is the changing nature of stock investment. Yes, investor confidence is high, but investors' desire to hold individual stocks

A herd of bulls trotting past the New York Stock Exchange on January 4, 1999, the first trading day of the year, part of an annual event to predict the year's outcome on Wall Street

has waned. To many market observers, the bull market of the 1990s more firmly institutionalized the stock market. Not only do institutions play a much larger role in the market, but individuals have, in a sense, become institutionalized as well. Bundled into mutual funds and participating in pension funds, many investors now leave the majority of their investing decisions to professionals.

In fact, even as prices have soared in the past few years, individuals have been net sellers of individual equities. Firms such as Merrill Lynch, the great pioneer of the 1950s, now promote a smorgasbord of mutual funds as much as individual stocks.

"I don't believe these folks investing in mutual funds today are looking for ways to double their money every twelve months," says Professor Siegel. "But it's also important to note that we are at the high tide of American-style capitalism. Will that be the case fifty or a hundred years from now? Just look how different things were a hundred years ago, and you have to wonder how different things will be a hundred years from now. Things don't remain the same."

THE INDUSTRIALS' OFF-TRACK ORIGINS

Forget blue chips. Think poker chips.

The Dow Jones Industrial Average is synonymous with secure, high-quality blue-chip stocks today, but back when it was introduced, most industrial stocks, including the initial Dow dozen, were considered strictly gamblers' material.

Industrial stocks were a newfangled creation in the largely agrarian America of the late

19th century. Before a great wave of incorporations began in the late 1880s, most manufacturers were family-owned businesses or small partnerships. Many were strictly local operations, although that was already changing, thanks to the completion of cross-country railroads.

Moreover, about half of the original Dow stocks had had a somewhat unsavory genesis. They had previously been trusts, joint operations established by several large companies in an industry in an attempt to fix prices and discourage competition. Incorporation offered the trusts access to capital markets as well as a potentially more friendly environment in the wake of the Sherman Antitrust Act of 1890, says historian Robert Sobel.

The New York Stock Exchange was initially so wary of the fledgling industrial stocks that it relegated them to a separate Unlisted Department set up in 1885. By the time the Dow Jones Industrial Average appeared in 1896, the Big Board had relented somewhat. All but three of the twelve stocks in the average were traded on the Big Board's regular floor. The three exceptions were American Sugar, National Lead and U.S. Leather preferred shares.

Charles Dow, the index's inventor, recognized the risks and the potential rewards of industrial stocks. "The industrial market," he declared in a 1901 *Wall Street Journal* editorial, "is destined to be the great speculative market of the United States."

Left: A cartoon depicting Andrew Carnegie as a "Lavish Library Distributor" (undated, photographed 1902)
Above: John Pierpont Morgan as the Field Marshall of Industry; the caption said his hand can be seen in schemes that reach around the globe
Opposite page: A sign at the 1984 Democratic National Convention

OVER AND OVER

A few things come in four-year cycles. Presidential elections. The Olympics. Leap year.

Add to that list the stock market.

At least, that's what Charles Dow thought. After a careful study of market trends, Mr. Dow proclaimed in an 1899 *Wall Street Journal* editorial that "the great swings of the market up or down have in no case been completed in less than four years."

That might sound like a simple notion in today's complex market, and in fact many people have argued persuasively that the market

these days is moving away from such a cycle.

Nevertheless, throughout this century, Mr. Dow's theory of four-year cycles has, for the most part, held up.

According to research by David Poole, a business consultant in New York, the average time between stock-market lows in the past century, as measured by the Dow Jones Industrial Average, has been about four years.

Mr. Dow postulated that the four-year cycle stemmed from several factors. Chief among them was the slow flow of information in his day. Mr. Dow felt that big market swings took at least four years because that's how long it took news of significant shifts in the business world to work its way into the investment community.

But Mr. Dow may have simply stumbled onto the business-cycle pattern that has dominated the country's economy throughout the 20th century, especially since World War II, when the average economic expansion has lasted forty-eight months. And with the Dow Jones industrials stuffed with economically sensitive stocks, the measure inherently reflects attitudes about economic performance.

Mr. Poole, in his research, found that lows in the Dow Jones average have run close to official recession lows as measured by the Commerce Department. But that relationship, while remaining close, can prove tricky. The economy hit a recession low in 1961, but the Dow Jones industrials didn't tumble until mid-1962, when the average fell 27% from its 1961 high.

"The industrials' sensitivity to the economy is very strong, and it tends to precede

---

The stock market seems to move in four-year cycles, although nobody is quite sure why.

---

economic developments and changes by about six months," says Charles Carlson, editor of "Dow Theory Forecasts," an investment newsletter in Hammond, Ind. "But that obviously doesn't always hold true. We just feel that usually the stock market is leading the economy, and the Dow industrials should reflect that."

But what about the effects of progress? Some people say the world has changed so much that Mr. Dow's theory may not hold true in the years to come.

Consider modern technology. The widespread availability of economic data means that sentiment can change in an instant. For example, the moment an economic report is issued from Washington, investors decide whether it has bullish or bearish implications and react accordingly.

The speed with which things can change was illustrated starkly in the autumn of 1987, when stocks experienced a nearly instant bear market. Within months, the market was already showing signs of rebounding.

In addition, analysts believe that the Dow Jones industrials' relationship to economic lows is bound to diminish as financial markets grow more complex.

"Part of the reason that the Dow Jones industrials reflect that attitude toward the economy is that the component stocks, at least initially, were important industrial stocks," says James Solloway, former director of research at Argus Research in New York. "I think the correlation between the general economy and the Dow's movements was better a hundred years ago than today, but a lot of that reflects the increasing diversity of the country's economy."

Not only is the U.S. economy diversi- fying away from industrial production into services, but it is also becoming increasingly enmeshed with other national economies, such as those of Germany and Japan.

"Unless we see synchronous economic growth or recession [in world markets], it's hard to get the kinds of bear markets that Dow wrote about and understood," says Mr. Safian. "Instead, with Japan down and the United States up, or vice versa, we see sharp moves among more specific sectors. So, in the current environment, it gets tougher to have that terrible bear market that drags everyone down."

But some possible explanations for the four-year cycle persist. Mr. Dow's theory grafts nicely onto the popular four-year presidential-cycle explanation of stock-market movements. This theory holds that stocks perform better late in a president's term, when an incumbent tries to goose the economy to help his (and his party's) election prospects. By contrast, early in presidential terms, presidents do the unpopular heavy lifting that can harm stock-market performance.

At the beginning of this century, no president would have dreamed of trying to influence the U.S. economy. But since the New Deal, government has been pushing and pulling the levers of the economy to a consid- erable degree. Presidents (and sometimes cooperative Federal Reserve chairmen) try to see that the economy has some steam in it when presidential election years roll around. If they need to "take a recession," they try to take it early in a presidential term.

From 1900 through 1991, the DJIA averaged about a 7% gain in the first half of presidential terms and better than a 20% gain in the second half. The final six months of presidential election years have been particularly strong, with average gains of around 10%. The pattern held up at least for the first term of the Clinton administration. In 1993 and 1994, the Dow industrials advanced about 15%, but in the second two years, they surged more than 40%.

A delegate at the 1996 Republican National Convention

Cycles in the Dow

LOW		HIGH			SUBSEQUENT LOW			NUMBER OF YEARS FROM LOW TO LOW	OFFICIAL RECESSION LOWS*
YEAR	DJIA	YEAR	DJIA	GAIN	YEAR	DJIA	DROP		
1896	28	1899	77	+175%	1900	53	-31%	4	1900
1900	53	1901	78	+47%	1903	42	-46%	3	1904
1903	42	1906	103	+145%	1907	53	-48%	4	1908
1907	53	1909	100	+88%	1911	73	-27%	4	1912
1911	73	1912	94	+29%	1914	53	-44%	3	1914
1914	53	1916	110	+107%	1917	66	-40%	3	1919
1917	66	1919	119	+80%	1921	64	-46%	4	1924
1921	64	1925	160	+146%	1926	135	-15%	5	1927
1926	135	1929	381	+182%	1929	199	-48%	3	—
1929	199	1930	294	+47%	1932	41	-86%	3	1933
1932	41	1937	194	+373%	1938	99	-49%	6	1938
1938	99	1940	153	+55%	1942	93	-39%	4	—
1942	93	1946	212	+128%	1946	163	-23%	4	1945
1946	163	1948	193	+18%	1949	161	-17%	3	1949
1949	161	1953	294	+83%	1953	255	-13%	4	1954
1953	255	1957	521	+104%	1957	420	-19%	4	1958
1957	420	1961	735	+75%	1962	535	-27%	5	1961
1962	535	1966	995	+86%	1966	745	-25%	4	1967
1966	745	1968	985	+32%	1970	631	-36%	4	1970
1970	631	1973	1052	+67%	1974	577	-45%	4	1975
1974	577	1976	1015	+76%	1978	742	-27%	4	1980
1978	742	1981	1024	+38%	1982	777	-24%	4	1982
1982	777	1987	2722	+250%	1987	1738	-36%	5	—
1987	1738	1990	3000	+73%	1990	2365	-21%	3	1991
1990	2365	1994	3978	+68%	1994	3593	-10%	4	—
1994	3593	1999**	10006	+178%					

*Department of Commerce

** March 29

Source: David Poole

Goodyear blimps Spirit of Akron (left), Stars and Stripes and Eagle (in hangar) in Akron, Ohio

PLAYING THE DOW

The Dow Jones Industrial Average isn't just a stock-market gauge. For some people, it's a tool in an investment strategy.

Probably the most popular strategy — and one of the more successful over time — is to invest each year in the ten Dow Jones industrial stocks with the highest dividend yields (the yield is a stock's dividend divided by the share price). From 1973 to 1994, this strategy produced an annual total return of 17.5%, compared with 11.5% derived from investing in all thirty of the Dow industrial stocks, according to the book *The Dividend Investor* by Harvey C. Knowles III and Damon H. Petty.

The strategy hasn't worked quite so well recently, but that hasn't stopped investors from pouring huge amounts of cash into unit trusts and other programs based on it. By some estimates it's as much as $20 billion. In 1998, the ten stocks with the highest dividends returned about 11.5% (including dividends), compared with 18.1% for the industrial average, according to *Barron's* magazine, a sister publication of *The Wall Street Journal*. In 1997, the strategy produced a gain of 21.9% (including dividends), compared with about 24.9% for the 30-stock average.

Barron's calculates that the "Dogs of the Dow," as the ten stocks have come to be known, were narrowly behind the average for the decade ended December 31, 1998, with an 18.1% average annual gain compared with 18.6% for all 30 Dow stocks. But in 1993, the ten "dogs" walloped the 30 Dow industrials with a return of 27.3% compared with 16.8%.

Michael O'Higgins, a money manager

Some investors don't just follow the industrial average. They base their strategies on it.

---

whose Miami, Fla., firm bears his name, says he has used a variation on the strategy from time to time for a couple of decades. In his own twist, Mr. O'Higgins likes to select the five stocks with the lowest prices from among the ten with the highest dividend yields.

"Lower-priced stocks tend to be more volatile," Mr. O'Higgins says. "And since the volatility tends to be on the upside, that's what

you want." Using this refinement, Mr. O'Higgins says, the strategy produced an annual average return of about 18.8% a year for the thirty years through 1998, compared with 12.6% for the 30 Dow industrials. However, he says that in recent years he has come to prefer a strategy that switches between stocks and bonds, which has produced an average annual return of nearly 24% over the same thirty-year period.

At the end of 1998, the ten stocks with the highest yields in the industrial average were J.P. Morgan & Co., Philip Morris Cos., Minnesota Mining & Manufacturing Co., Chevron Corp., General Motors Corp., DuPont Co., Caterpillar Inc., Eastman Kodak Co., Goodyear Tire & Rubber Co. and Exxon Corp.

In the century-plus history of the Dow Jones Industrial Average, dividends have directly accounted for about 40% of investors' returns. Throw in the gains from reinvesting the dividends, and you are talking about roughly half of investors' total returns.

In the broader market, simply buying the highest-yielding stocks is usually considered unwise. A high yield often indicates a depressed stock price, hence, a company that has stumbled. The dividend may soon be cut, or the company may be headed for serious trouble. But partisans of the strategy say the approach works with the Dow industrial stocks. Because the average consists of solid, blue-chip companies with the resources to recover from missteps, they say, a high yield often reflects a temporary slump in the stock price.

Another investment strategy is to buy stocks when Dow Jones & Co. announces that they will be added to the industrial average, and then sell when the addition actually takes effect.

"It works if you're very quick," says Robert Stovall, president of Stovall/Twenty-First Advisers Inc. in New York. "You can scruff a couple of points out of it." But Mr. Stovall notes that such a strategy can hardly provide a steady living for a trader, as changes in the industrial average's roster of companies are usually made less often than once a year.

Mr. Stovall has used a couple of other strategies based on the Dow. One, which ordinary investors can use, is to look at the percentage change in each of the industrial average's 30 stocks and single out those that have done worst over the previous twelve to eighteen months. He recommends that investors "cherry-pick" among these, based on their view of the companies' prospects.

Mr. Stovall says this approach would have led to a big gain in Sears, Roebuck & Co. stocks in the early 1990s, for example. But he wouldn't buy just any stock that has been weak. International Harvester Co. (now Navistar International Corp.) was a weak sister in the industrial average for years, and continued to perform poorly after it was deleted from the average in 1991. He views two companies deleted from the average in March 1997, Woolworth Corp. and Bethlehem Steel Corp., in the same light.

And he adds that this strategy is less appealing now that dividend yields are near all-time lows. When stocks in the Dow 30 were yielding 5% or 6% in the 1970s, it was like being "paid to wait" for the stock price to rise, he says; the average Dow stock was yielding 1.6% at the end of 1998.

For professional money managers who don't manage huge portfolios, Mr. Stovall recommends using the 30 Dow industrial stocks as an index fund — in other words, buying all 30. The results, he says, won't be too far from those of buying all the stocks in the Standard & Poor's 500-stock index, but it's a lot easier to buy thirty stocks than five hundred.

It's an advantage, in his view, that the industrial average is full of big companies that do business worldwide, such as Merck & Co., Boeing Co. and two giant oil companies. That, he says, gives the portfolio "an international flavor."

The Dow's Dividends

Dividend Yield on the Dow Jones Industrial Average Since 1905

Record high (May 1932)	16.6%
Average	4.4
Low (April 1998)	1.5

Source: Ned Davis Research

THE BOTTOM LINE

Do they pay off?

That, of course, is the key question for investors in the stock market.

And the answer has been clear: For anybody who has held on long enough, stocks have always beaten alternative investments such as government bonds and bank accounts.

But before investors turn that fact into strategy, it is important to understand this: History doesn't necessarily repeat itself. What the market did do doesn't guarantee what it will do.

"We really don't know what the future holds, just because the past looked like this," says Peter Bernstein, a New York investment consultant and founding editor of the *Journal of Portfolio Management.*

Perhaps not, but many people believe that, at the very least, the past is a guide. And the past, they say, indicates that equities are the way to go. Consider these numbers compiled by the Chicago consulting company Ibbotson Associates:

- Stocks provided double the compound annual return of U.S. government bonds over the 73 years through 1998 — a juicy 11.2% a year, compared with 5.3% for bonds. Short-term Treasury bills,

with rates comparable to those of bank accounts, delivered a measly 3.8%.
- Despite some stomach-wrenching plunges and bear markets, stocks have made money for investors in every single twenty-calendar-year period since 1925.
- In 98% of those twenty-year periods, stocks did better — often far better — than bonds.

The fact that stocks have performed so well over long periods leads some people to argue they're not that risky at all. "The safest long-term investment has clearly been stocks, not bonds," writes Jeremy J. Siegel, professor of finance at the University of Pennsylvania's Wharton School of Business, in his book *Stocks for the Long Run.* When people save for retirement or other dis-

Stocks vs. Other Investments: % Rate of Return

1926–1998

Source: Ibbotson Associates

tant goals, the real danger is having the purchasing power of their savings eaten up by inflation, he says. Stocks come to the rescue. Their short-term price drops pose no threat, says Mr. Siegel, who has researched investment returns all the way back to 1802. He found that

---

In the long run, nothing has beaten the return on stocks. But is history a guarantee of future success?

---

stocks have had a "remarkable" tendency to keep holders well ahead of inflation. In each of the three major periods he identifies — 1802 to 1870, 1871 to 1925, and 1926 to 1998 — the real, or inflation-adjusted, return on stocks averaged 6.5% to 7.5% a year.

His conclusion: If people are investing for a long time — thirty years, say — even those willing to take only moderate risks should put all their investment dollars into stocks.

Other market watchers, though, get queasy at the suggestion that stocks are certain winners over time. The backward-looking euphoria has gone too far, they say, and people have grown too complacent in believing stocks will always end up rewarding investors.

The arguments made by history lovers are flawed, says Nobel Prize winner Paul A. Samuelson, professor emeritus of economics at the Massachusetts Institute of Technology.

Although monthly performance records go back nearly two hundred years, those figures aren't distinct bits of data like rolls of the dice. "We actually have only one history," which is like a single roll, according to Mr. Samuelson. And one history is too small a sample to conclude that the healthy performance of stocks is "a sure thing," he says.

Mr. Bernstein believes that good times have made investors cocky. They are ignoring the possibility that they may be buying at a cyclical peak, and that an extended bull market has boosted stock prices to a level that makes future disappointments likely.

In the wake of the 1973–1974 bear market, "When the stock market was a screaming buy," Mr. Bernstein says, "nobody was talking about" the market as a sure winner over time.

But today, with so many people convinced stocks can only go up, the market may be due for a painful correction. Even with a

very long horizon, Mr. Bernstein says, "I wouldn't bet the ranch and put 100% of my assets in the stock market."

One of the biggest question marks is the baby-boom factor. Many boomers — heeding warnings that a comfortable retirement is threatened by changes in Social Security and corporate pension plans — have become determined investors in stock mutual funds. Some market watchers believe these purchases will keep the market climbing, perhaps for two or three decades. But the market might slump

after that, they say, as retired boomers start cashing out — and scrambling to beat everyone else who is cashing out.

Why have stocks trounced bonds and other investments over the long term? One explanation is that their value is tied to the nation's economic output. As output grows, so do stock prices and dividends. Bonds, by contrast, have no such link. Their interest payments may be comforting in their regularity, but they're fixed in dollar terms.

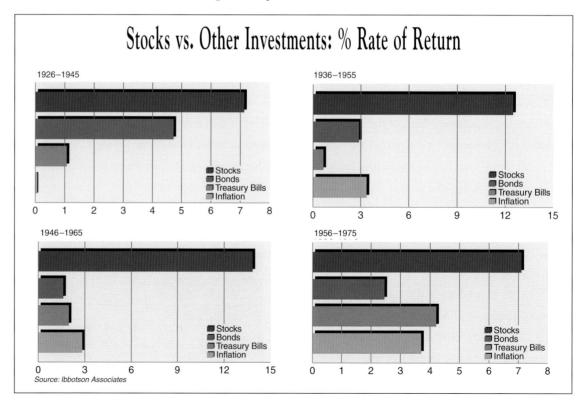

Stocks vs. Other Investments: % Rate of Return

1926–1945

Stocks
Bonds
Treasury Bills
Inflation

0 1 2 3 4 5 6 7 8

1936–1955

Stocks
Bonds
Treasury Bills
Inflation

0 3 6 9 12 15

1946–1965

Stocks
Bonds
Treasury Bills
Inflation

0 3 6 9 12 15

1956–1975

Stocks
Bonds
Treasury Bills
Inflation

0 1 2 3 4 5 6 7 8

Source: Ibbotson Associates

Another explanation: Stocks beat bonds because they must. Without higher stock returns over time, investors wouldn't tolerate big bounces in stock prices. In other words, higher risks deliver higher rewards; if they did not, there would be no reason to buy stocks.

Higher historical returns are "compensation for periods like October 1987, 1973–1974, the Depression years," says Mark Riepe, head of Charles Schwab Corp.'s Center for Investment Research.

Regardless of why stocks have proved to be good investments, investors studying the lessons of the past must look at the right pages in their history books — and at the footnotes. Messrs. Riepe and Siegel caution that the standard Ibbotson data, which track prices from 1926 on, exaggerate the performance of stocks compared with bonds. The margin by

which stocks outperform bonds varies according to time frame; it narrows in Mr. Siegel's much longer time frame of 1802 to 1995 as well as in the more recent twenty-five years on which Mr. Riepe focuses.

For a good part of the more recent time frame — until the early 1980s — interest rates were generally climbing, largely because of rising inflation. So, bond prices, which move in the opposite direction from interest rates, were chronically depressed. Since then, interest rates have generally declined, sending bond prices higher. Market watchers don't expect another decades-long span of rising inflation and interest rates; if they're right, bond prices will stay up.

Investors should also beware of the simplistic suggestion that holding stocks for a long period such as twenty years, ensures an

overall return close to the historical average. It certainly doesn't.

Stock returns over one-year periods since 1925 have varied all over the lot, from a 54% gain to a 43% drop. Compound annual returns over twenty-year periods have been limited to a far narrower band, from a best-case return of nearly 18% to a worst-case return of 3%. But look at the range of dollars: An initial $1,000, compounded for twenty years at that best-case return rate of nearly 18%, grows to $25,163. At 3%, the resulting nest egg is a paltry $1,844.

Time may narrow the range of percentage returns, but it magnifies dollar differences, notes William Sharpe, a Nobel Prize winner and Stanford University finance professor. With a long holding period, he says, "In one sense risk is less, but in another sense it is more."

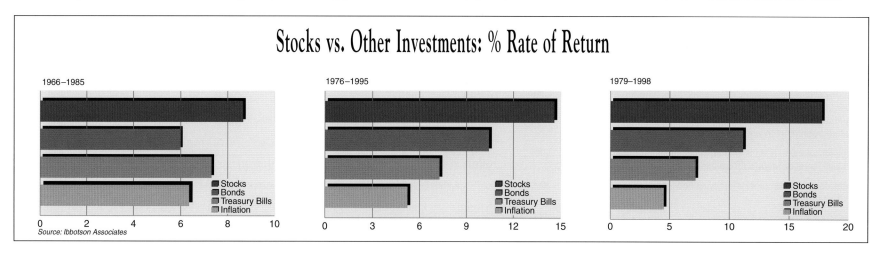

Stocks vs. Other Investments: % Rate of Return

1966–1985

Stocks
Bonds
Treasury Bills
Inflation

0 2 4 6 8 10

Source: Ibbotson Associates

1976–1995

Stocks
Bonds
Treasury Bills
Inflation

0 3 6 9 12 15

1979–1998

Stocks
Bonds
Treasury Bills
Inflation

0 5 10 15 20

HOW TO MAKE $9 MILLION SLOWLY

Why is the Dow Jones Industrial Average the most widely watched financial measure in the world? One reason is that U.S. stocks have been a solid investment.

As the bar chart on page 147 showed, the returns provided over the years by stocks surpass those of other investment assets and the rate of inflation as well. Of course, stock-market returns fluctuate sharply from year to year and even from decade to decade. But measured over long spans, the return from stocks has hovered near 10%.

The Dow Jones Industrial Average has provided an average total return of 9.67% a year, including reinvested dividends, since March 31, 1900, according to Ned Davis

Research Inc. (Good dividend information is unavailable for the pre-1900 period.)

If $1,000 had been invested in the Dow industrials in 1900, the amount would have grown to more than $9 million at the end of 1998. That is testimony not only to the industrial average's good performance, but also to the tremendous power of compounding over long periods.

The Ten Most Widely Held Companies*

1998	1988
Intel	Wal-Mart Stores
PepsiCo	American Family
Merck	PepsiCo
Lucent Technologies	McDonald's
Home Depot	American Telephone & Telegraph
Cisco Systems	Pfizer
AFLAC	Abbott Laboratories
Diebold	General Electric
Motorola	Baxter International
Clayton Homes	Bruno's

*As of December 31, based on number of investment clubs holding stock

Source: National Association of Investors Corp.

Shareownership

Total Number of Shareowners (millions), 1989–1995			
Definition of shareowners	1989	1992	1995
Individuals owning stock directly or through mutual funds, retirement saving accounts or defined-contribution pension plans	52.3	61.4	69.3
Individuals owning stock directly or through mutual funds or retirement saving accounts	42.1	61.5	59.6
Individuals owning stock directly or through mutual funds	31.5	35.3	38.6
Individuals owning stock directly only	27.0	29.2	27.4

According to Ned Davis Research, average compound annual investment returns have been 12.4% on small stocks from January 1926 through December 1998. Over the same time, the average return has been only 5.3% on long-term bonds and 3.9% on Treasury bills. Inflation averaged 3.1% a year.

For the twenty years through December 1998, Ibbotson Associates in Chicago

figures that small stocks have returned an average of 16.0% a year and large stocks 17.8%. That compares with 11.1% for bonds, 7.2% for Treasury bills, 7.0% for commodities, and 1.2% for gold. Inflation during the twenty-year period averaged 4.5%.

Ibbotson uses Standard & Poor's 500-stock index to measure large-stock returns, but the results aren't much different for the Dow industrials. According to Ned Davis Research, since the S&P 500 was invented in 1926, it has returned an average 11.14% a year and the Dow industrials, 10.46%.

DIFFERENT DRUMMERS

There's a saying in the investment community that when the Dow sneezes, the rest of the world catches cold.

The evidence for this bit of wisdom? Largely, the world's reaction to big drops. When Wall Street crashed on October 19, 1987, with the Dow falling 22.6%, traders watched aghast as markets around the world

The Dow moves and the rest of the world reacts. Or does it?

plunged as well. From August 31 to November 30, a period in which the Dow lost 31% of its value, the British market fell 26% and the German market 33%. The 554-point, or 7.2%, drop in the Dow on October 27, 1997, which followed economic turmoil and big declines in Asian markets, also triggered further drops worldwide.

The Dow "cold," however, is largely just a twenty-four-hour bug. True, stock index-

es around the world have a remarkably consistent reaction when Wall Street starts to panic. But over the long term, national stock markets follow national economic and political ups and downs, not the Dow industrials.

The industrial average roughly quadrupled in the decade after November 1987, for example, but the Japanese Nikkei Index fell by more than a third, reflecting domestic economic problems. Meanwhile, emerging economies often have their own agendas: Both the Manila and Makati composite indexes in the Philippines were headed up in October 1987, having just recovered from a coup attempt against the Aquino government in August. Both bourses fell about 12% after the Wall Street crash but recovered within days.

So even though looser capital restrictions, floating foreign-exchange rates and increased international trade have speeded capital movements around the world, no single index — not even the venerable Dow — can influence the pack for long.

The Dow's power to influence foreign markets at all is a relatively recent development. Even at the time of the Wall Street crash of 1929, the

Dow's effect overseas was quite limited. The 12.8% fall on October 28, 1929, immediately ruined many investors in the United States, but European markets took months to react. And even then, the downturn was less severe.

The Depression rendered the Dow even less influential in overseas markets. It left a legacy of high tariffs and other controls, making international trade much less important to national economies and virtually ending international stock investing. So, foreign investors had little reason to keep an eye on the industrial average.

Even during the economic boom of the early 1950s, markets were insular and behaved quite differently. As the Dow soared 262% from early 1950 to the end of 1961, as Germany rebuilt, its market powered ahead 1,253%.

Then in the early 1970s, the rules of the game were dramatically altered. The Bretton Woods agreement, a series of formal accords that defined the post-World War II economic environment, collapsed under the weight of deficit spending by the United States.

In the wake of this, exchange rates were allowed to float, albeit under the watchful eye of central bankers. Controls on the movement of capital across borders were abandoned in the United Kingdom and Japan in 1979 and in France and Italy in the late 1980s.

Under the auspices of the General Agreement on Tariffs and Trade, international trade began to flourish. U.S. trade was particularly robust; the nation's imports and exports jumped to a total of nearly $2 trillion in 1997 from $125 billion in 1970.

At the same time, international investing was undergoing a revolution. Multinational companies, which had been the source of most international investment since the 1950s, were supplanted by fund managers. And after the mid-1980s, managers were aided by a technological revolution that allowed everyone to know what everyone else was doing, and let traders zap orders around the world in an instant.

$\mathbf{A}$s a highly visible proxy for the U.S. market, the Dow's stature in the world arena increased markedly with these developments. According to the Organization for Economic Cooperation and Development, the correlation between

Containerized freight on the dock at the port of Seattle, Wash.

monthly stock-market returns in London and New York rose to 0.59 in the second half of the 1980s from 0.45 before 1973. That means, simply, that 59% of the movements in London stocks can be explained, via complex mathematics, by movements in New York. In the same period, the correlation rose to 0.44 from 0.19 for Japan, to 0.45 from 0.39 for Germany, and to 0.44 from 0.28 for France.

But a closer look shows that the real correlation is among nations' economies, says Campbell Harvey, a professor at the Fuqua School of Business at Duke University in

Durham, N.C. According to Prof. Harvey's research, the correlation among market indexes has been strongest when economic cycles in different parts of the world move together, such as during the oil shocks of 1973 and 1979. During the early 1980s, when the United States went from recession to recovery and Europe just stagnated, the link weakened.

Moreover, the data are skewed by a huge anomaly: the 1987 crash. Leaving it out, the correlation between the Dow and Morgan Stanley Capital International's benchmark of stocks in Europe, Asia and the Far East has been stuck between 0.4 and 0.5 since 1984.

"Just because a market is more integrated with the world capital market, it does not mean that it is more correlated with other equity markets," says Prof. Harvey. "That is more fundamentally determined by the country's industrial portfolio."

William Goetzman, associate professor of finance at Yale University's School of Management, concurs. Reactions to moves in the Dow "can fool the market for a few weeks," he says, "but not for much longer than that."

GOING GLOBAL

There seems to be a lot of money in Genoa, so you shouldn't send our funds there. You can get a better price in Venice or Florence, or here [in Bruges] or in Paris or Montpellier.

That note was sent to Italian financier Francesco Datini by his partner in Bruges, Belgium. It wasn't faxed. It wasn't even cabled. It was written on April 26, 1399, nearly a century before Columbus discovered America.

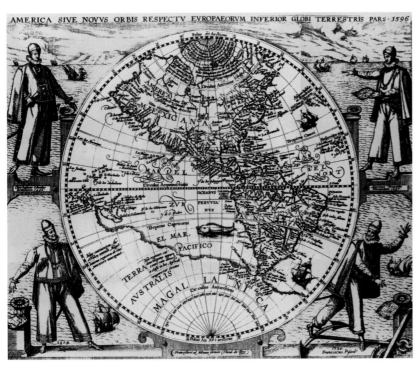

Map of the Americas (engraving, 1590)

As the letter to Mr. Datini shows, international investing isn't new. But over the past few years, a combination of factors has set in motion the biggest cross-border investment boom since before World War I.

The fall of Communism and the adoption of liberal economic policies released two to three billion people into the world's free-market economy. Developing countries and multinational corporations are scouring the globe for capital more intensively than ever before. Barriers to foreign investment are speedily crumbling as country after country sells state-owned industries. At the same time, advances in telecommunications and computerization mean that information is widely disseminated and trades are quickly executed.

Across-the-border stock transactions —

International investing is hotter right now than it has been for a long time.

purchases by investors in one country of stocks that trade in another — soared to $7 trillion in 1998, a sixfold jump from a decade earlier, according to London-based CrossBorder Capital, a financial consulting firm.

Something else is new, too. U.S. investors have joined the party. It used to be the wealth of Britain, Japan and the Netherlands that circumnavigated the globe, seeking out opportunities. Today, the leading investors outside their home turf are the once-parochial Americans. U.S. investors now own more than $1 trillion worth of foreign stocks, up from $44 billion in 1985.

The outflow isn't just from small investors who are putting dollars into their overseas mutual funds. By the end of 1998, U.S. pension funds had committed 10% of their assets to cross-border investments, up from 3.9% in 1990, says InterSec Research Corp., an investment advisory firm in Stamford, Conn.

InterSec predicts that by the year 2003, U.S. pension funds will have some 14% of their assets, or about $1.2 trillion, invested internationally. By 2003, CrossBorder Capital projects, equity trading across national boundaries will have nearly doubled to $12 trillion.

As international investing grows, so does the highly competitive field of developing indexes to reflect the performance of markets around the world. A century after the Dow Jones Industrial Average made its debut to gauge what was then the emerging U.S. stock market, nearly every stock market in the world — from Tokyo to Trinidad and Tobago — has its own index. Moreover, companies such as Morgan Stanley Group Inc., Salomon Inc., Goldman, Sachs & Co. and Dow Jones & Co. have created their own global stock indexes that cover from a few to more than two dozen markets. The Dow Jones Global Index, as of December 31, 1998, included the stock markets of 34 countries.

These measures have given rise to a small but growing trend in international investing: "indexing," which basically means buying every stock in a given index. It is a low-cost, and usually less risky, approach than hiring a money manager to pick individual stocks and countries.

In many ways, today's mutual-fund investors and pension-fund managers are still playing catch-up with their globe-trotting British predecessors. "People now are crazy about international investing," says Prof. William Goetzmann. "But U.S. investment in overseas equities is nothing compared to what British investors were doing."

Back in 1900, Baring Brothers & Co.'s nongovernment bond investment portfolio — a mixture of corporate stocks and bonds — was only 37% invested in the United Kingdom. The United States accounted for 27%, Chile 12% and Argentina 6%. The rest was spread among Austro-Hungary, France, Mexico, Australia, Russia, India, China, Romania and South Africa.

The first major modern stock market was established in Amsterdam in the 17th century. Next came London. In 1688, Joseph de la Vega published a book about how stock markets function that was based on the Amsterdam

Above: A man chisels a piece of the Berlin Wall for a souvenir just after the fall of Communism in East Germany, December 1989
Opposite page: An early print of Dutch tulips

exchange. Its title was *Confusion of Confusions*.

One observer described the London Exchange as "the rendezvous of those who, having money already, wished to own more" with "the more numerous class of men who, having nothing, hoped to attract the money of those who possessed it."

Each of the three great speculative orgies of the 17th and early 18th centuries had an international flavor. During the Dutch tulip mania of the 1630s, single bulbs sold for the equivalent of as much as $50,000 in today's dollars. In the frenzy to buy stocks in John Law's Mississippi Co., before it collapsed on the Paris exchange in 1720, women offered themselves just for the right to buy shares. In London that same year, shares in the South Sea Co. soared 680% in seven months before crashing.

A century later, an enterprising Scotsman was marketing the bonds of a nonexistent Latin American country. For a while, they traded on a par with those of the Kingdom of France.

Inside information? It took on a grand — and overseas — flair. During the War of Spanish Succession in the early 18th century,

Solomon de Medina, a London merchant, purchased the contract to supply the Duke of Marlborough's English army, "and so had a whole network of people" to send him battlefield information, says Larry Neal, professor of economics at the University of Illinois in Urbana-Champaign. As the first person to learn of the English victories at Blenheim, Ramillies and Oudenarde, Mr. Medina profited handsomely.

In 1815, financier Nathan Rothschild repeated the feat when carrier pigeons enabled him to learn of Napoleon's defeat at Waterloo before anyone else in London.

To be sure, there were backlashes against international investing. In 1737, London officials worried about the large number of British government bonds held by Dutch investors. French investors, jealous of the fat profits being earned by their British counterparts a century later, lobbied to prohibit foreign investment in their railroad companies. Both episodes are reminiscent of American alarm over Middle Eastern investment in the United States in the 1970s and Japanese investment in the 1980s.

"International investing goes in cycles," says Michael Howell, head global strategist at CrossBorder Capital. Once a pool of capital has "attacked its own local market with a voracious appetite, it will — like a spreading virus — migrate elsewhere seeking better returns."

Americans were late to join the game. One reason was that their own country was growing so fast, it absorbed nearly every buck they could serve up. In fact, America was built on foreign investment. "In the 19th century, the United States was a big place for direct investment and portfolio investment from Europeans," says Prof. Neal. "It had to compete with other places such as Australia, Canada and Argentina, but it was the big one" of the world's emerging markets.

U.S. investors did venture abroad from time to time. But they often lost their shirts, especially in the Latin American and Weimar Republic bond defaults of the 1930s. World War II didn't help. "Borders were slammed shut, and you couldn't get your money out," says Arthur McCain, a retired vice president at InterSec. "In many cases, assets were literally destroyed."

It wasn't much easier after the war, when United States laws restricted Americans' investment activities abroad. Moreover, "the

155

National flags fly in front of the United Nations building in New York City

U.S. is so huge that people felt they could diversify sufficiently within the U.S. economy," says Prof. Goetzmann of Yale.

Today, the United States no longer represents as big a slice of the world's investment pie as it once did. In 1975, American markets accounted for roughly two thirds of the world's stock-market capitalization. Twenty years later, the share had dropped to about one third. "You can argue it isn't prudent to ignore two thirds of the world's opportunities," says Arnab Banerji, chief investment officer at Foreign & Colonial Emerging Markets Ltd. in London.

Mr. Howell of CrossBorder Capital predicts that by 2010, emerging markets such as Brazil, China and India — but excluding Hong Kong and Singapore — will account for about 16% of the world's stock-market capitalization, up from about 6% at the end of 1998. "Every government wants a presidential palace, an airline and a stock market," he says. "Part of it reflects nationalist ego, but it also represents a way to access global capital."

The explosive growth in cross-border investment and the application of technology to fund management is lending greater importance to indexes designed to gauge foreign stock markets.

Indexes of British stocks were developed as early as the 1880s, those of other countries' markets later. But until computers began being used in the late 1970s to construct portfolios and design futures and options contracts, indexes were little-used curiosity pieces, says Christopher Green, professor of economics and finance at Loughborough University in Loughborough, England. Their wider acceptance, he says, stems from "an increasing emphasis on performance measurement in which money managers are required to meet whatever benchmarks are set for them."

Investors use the indexes as more than benchmarks. InterSec figures that roughly 23% of U.S. institutional international equity portfolios now are deliberately managed so as to match an index. "We see institutions who get frustrated with their active managers' underperformance coming to us," says Jeffrey Davis, a vice president at State Street Global Advisors in Boston, which specializes in index funds. "We're seeing faster growth in our index products...than active managers are getting."

But the percentage of the total amount of U.S. funds invested abroad that is indexed remains tiny, experts say. Patricia C. Dunn, chairman of Barclays Global Investors Inc. in San Francisco, estimates that worldwide, less than 5% of total equity investments are in international index funds, "a real drop in the bucket."

Some investment professionals argue that indexing isn't the way to go. In developing countries, they say, active managers have a better chance of spotting a stock whose prospects aren't well known. "Most of the indices at the moment aren't properly mapping the opportunities," says Mr. Banerji of Foreign & Colonial.

Others say it's too soon to predict how much market share indexing, also called passive investing, will capture. "It might grow some, but the pension sponsors have a difficult time accepting a passive role," says Mr. McCain, the retired InterSec vice president. Indeed, the active international money manager who chooses individual stocks and markets posted a median 10.4% annual return over the ten years through 1998, according to InterSec, compared with the 5.8% return of Morgan Stanley's twenty-country Europe Australasia Far East Index over the same period.

By embracing indexing, a pension sponsor is essentially deciding that he can't hire a manager who will beat the index and that an index's results represent an acceptable return, says Mr. McCain.

"But if you have kids, the fact that the average grade is a C doesn't mean you accept your kid getting a C," he adds. "Also, when you accept indexing, you are accepting the idea that your investment results will be mediocre by definition."

PART VII

THE DOW IN 2100

THE DOW IN 2100

By Peter Francese

Demographic, business and economic trends already in place will exert tremendous influence on the course of the Dow Jones Industrial Average during the next century.

Predicting the future by extrapolating from the past, or even from the present, assumes that a lot of things in the future will be about the same as they are and have been. Indeed, basic human needs and emotions

---

Glimpses of the Future
from the pages of The Wall Street Journal

Scientists leading the $2 billion international Human Genome Project, biology's equivalent of putting man on the moon, expect to unravel the entire structure of human DNA within a few years....

Pharmaceutical researchers are persuaded that detailed knowledge about gene structure will make it easier to design drugs to block the activity of disease-causing genes — or craft copies of missing genes.

— January 21, 1997
Page A13

---

don't change much over many thousands of years. We still live in dwellings and need sleep, food and clothing. We still form families and bear children in much the same, if a much safer, way. We still write and read books, walk on the beach, seek recreation, create art, poetry and music and

obtain an education in ways remarkably similar to the ways of a hundred years ago. A century from now these activities will still be familiar.

What changes over the years and decades are products, tools and materials. No one from a century ago would recognize today's food production methods, manufacturing processes, transportation systems, communications networks or measurement tools. During the next hundred years, those things will no doubt again be changed unpredictably by human curiosity and innovation, creating new industries and destroying old ones.

So we speculate about what the Dow Jones Industrial Average will be in 2100 with absolute certainty that the decades ahead will surprise us time and again.

Still, we are confident that over the next century, as over past centuries, business enterprises will rise and fall, economic conditions will fluctuate and political power will shift. During the 20th century the Dow Jones Industrial Average has changed not only in terms of the number of stocks listed, but also in terms of the industries those stocks represent. In 1900 there were no restaurant chains and it is unlikely that anyone thought of serving food as a potential mass-market enterprise. Instead, in the first industrial average, a commodity-food producer was included (American Sugar) as well as an ancestor of Bestfoods, then called American Cotton Oil. By 2100 new industries and new companies

---

Peter Francese is the founder and former president of American Demographics *magazine. He is currently director of market analysis for Dow Jones & Co.*

will be included in the DJIA; some of them are just emerging now and others we can't even imagine.

Moreover, we can predict that there will be more people on the planet. A population growth curve from 1000 A.D. to today may be seen in Chart I.

In the early stages, growth was very slow, limited by short life spans and lack of food or other resources. But after 1900, growth exploded as improved sanitation, medicine and food production increased both infant and adult survival rates. Because of the law of compound growth, population then started to grow exponentially. In nonhuman life forms — bacteria, for example — the next development is usually that the population dies off quickly because food supplies run out. That is what Thomas Malthus forecast for humans about two hundred years ago.

The difference between us and other life forms, however, is that we attempt to predict the future and, if we don't like the forecasts, to change that future. The most stunning example of this is the one-child policy in China. With a fast-growing country of over one billion people,

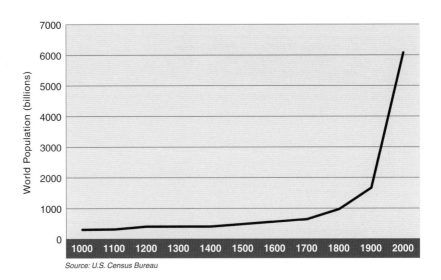

Chart I
World Population, 1000 to 2000

Source: U.S. Census Bureau

A billboard near Xiamen, China, advertising the Chinese government's "One Child Only" policy

but very limited land available for food production, the Chinese government forecast widespread starvation and inevitable civil conflict. As an alternative, they instituted a rigidly enforced policy that permitted each family to have only one child instead of the preferred two or three.

China is still growing, but at a much slower rate than in the past, and famine has been averted. Many other countries with burgeoning populations also have cut their birth rates, using less drastic measures. The net result is that in the next century the curve of human population growth will move from exponential to merely arithmetic growth (Chart II). For every three people on the planet in 1900, there are eight more now, an increase of 267%. But for every three people on Earth today, there will probably be only two more in one hundred years, a 67% increase. That's still a lot of people — perhaps 1 billion being added every twenty

Chart II

World Population 1900 to 2100 — Whither the Dow Jones Industrial Average?

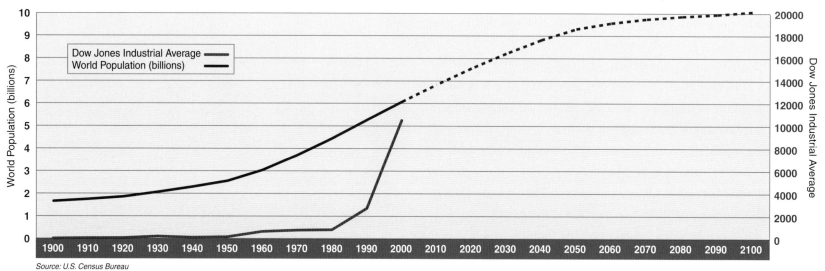

Source: U.S. Census Bureau

to twenty-five years — but slower growth rates means that the increasing efficiency of food production can easily keep up with the demand.

The most likely scenario, given what is knowable today, is that there will be around 10 billion people on the planet by 2100, up from 6 billion today. Some countries (mostly in Europe) will actually decline in population, but overall, the number of people will increase at a slower rate of growth than it did in the past century.

The United States will grow in absolute terms, but perhaps not proportionally. At the beginning of the 20th century, the United States had about 75 million residents, or about

Researchers in Scotland have successfully cloned a grown sheep....perhaps within a few years, the new technique could revolutionize the manufacture of protein-based drugs and other protein products, turning genetically engineered animals into living factories. "It will change the nature of farming and agriculture," said Dr. Caplan, director of the Center for Bioethics at Penn.

— *February 24, 1997*
  Page B1

4.5% of the world's 1.6 billion people. By 2000, the United States is expected to have 275 million people, still about 4.5% of the world's total of 6 billion. By 2100 the United States may have between 400 million and 500 million people, depending primarily on immigration policy. But that much larger number will still account for 4% to 5% of Earth's humans.

The implication is that future growth in the Dow Jones Industrial Average will be driven increasingly by world growth rather than by domestic growth, and that any company hoping to be a component must have a global outlook and worldwide operations.

However, it is economics, not

Several companies are genetically engineering goats and sheep to make them produce milk containing human proteins that may be used to treat cancer, cystic fibrosis and other diseases. A few of these proteins, including an anticoagulant for trauma victims, have reached the stage of human testing....

Other companies say human testing is still a few years off in their efforts to genetically engineer pigs to grow hearts, livers and other organs that could be transplanted into humans without being rejected.

— *February 25, 1997*
Page B1

An irrigation project in Ethiopia, 1974

population, that moves stock markets. If over the next one hundred years the U.S. economy were to grow at the same rate as the U.S. population, we might expect a Dow Jones Industrial Average merely in the 18000 to 20000 range by 2100. That's less than double the level in 1999.

However, recent history has shown that whenever a country's population growth rate slows during peacetime (as it has in China), economic growth accelerates. As world population growth rates, which averaged close to 2% per year during the 20th century, fall below 1% per year in the 21st, long-term economic growth rates may be three to four times that of population. If the increase in the industrial average over the next one hundred years matches the increase over the past twenty-five years, when the Dow went from about 1000 to 10000, then by 2100 the Dow should reach 100000.

As lofty as that number seems from our present vantage point, it is small potatoes by historical standards; it would mean a significant slowing in the price appreciation of the underlying stocks. A $1,000 investment in the 30 Dow stocks in the mid-1970s would be worth about ten times more now. A $1,000 investment today, following the above scenario, would take a century to appreciate by a factor of ten.

In its first one hundred years, the Dow Jones Industrial Average did far better than that. It started at 40.94 on May 26, 1896, and rose to 5762.86 precisely one hundred years later. Suppose that the 21st century

...there isn't enough Nile water to complete the irrigation plans of Ethiopia and Egypt, let alone the other nations that share it.... The Mideast's three main river systems, the Nile, Jordan and Euphrates-Tigris, are all in dispute — and potential flashpoints.

— *August 22, 1997*
Page A1

The members of Generation Y... will hit their teen years just as the next century dawns....

As they try to claim their share of the economic pie, Generation Y's adolescence and young adulthood will be overshadowed by the baby boomers, who will outnumber and outvote them. The ensuing generational battle for the government dollar — pitting Medicare, say, against school construction — will be high on the national agenda for years to come....

Generation Y's skills "must radically improve to prevent a precipitous slide in American wages," warns Marc S. Tucker, president of the National Center on Education and the Economy, a Washington think tank. Not even a bachelor's degree will be an automatic passport to the middle class. "If you don't have a degree you're really cooked, and if you do, you may or may not be cooked," says [a] demographer....

Generation Y will be more tolerant of racial and ethnic differences. Indeed, the term "minority" will lose its literal meaning, when the number of nonwhite teenagers reaches parity with white teenagers by 2040, according to Census Bureau projections.

— *February 5, 1997*
  Page B1

Students in front of the library at American University, Washington, D.C., 1989

proves no worse for the economy, the stock market, and the DJIA than the 20th century was, with its wars, depressions, inflations, and widespread turmoil. Suppose that the DJIA manages to achieve the same percentage gains in its second century. It would enjoy a 140-fold increase from 1996 levels. That means that by the year 2096, it would be trading somewhere around 811000!

How might it get there?

In the century just past, the DJIA was powered by industrial development and burgeoning trade, both within the United States and throughout the world. As the millennium drew to a close, computer technology and increasing economic stability pushed the DJIA higher. The Dow will be likely to need all that and more to repeat its first-century gains in its second. Fortunately, there are ingredients at hand that might provide fuel for an equally spectacular additional increase. The Dow's reaching 100000, let alone 811000, by 2100 would depend on a continuation of the most important demographic trend of the past quarter century — lower worldwide birth rates. Reduced birth rates allow large countries like India and China to shift their focus from maintaining life to bettering the quality of life for their citizens. A release from the intense pressure of rapidly growing populations also sharply decreases the likelihood of warfare, with its devastating human and economic losses.

As the world's population shifts from mostly children to mostly adults, a larger proportion of people are economically active. Personal incomes increase at a faster rate. During the next century, all of the largest countries in the world will have an opportunity to move through a development cycle similar to that of the United States in the past century. In each case, if economic progress is not held back by warfare or repressive governments, and if much of the world embraces free trade and free market development, vast wealth will be created, as markets for consumer and industrial goods flourish.

…grudging but growing acceptance by China's powers-that-be of free elections at the most basic level of governance in China, the village and the urban neighborhood.

…the results of this 10-year-old democratic experiment remain….But a positive trend is unmistakable….It grows out of a spreading recognition within the ruling party of the practicalities of local self-rule. Exercise of the vote helps assuage discontents in a period of rapid change. The economy is becoming too complex and its needs for sometimes painful adaptation too urgent — carrying potential for serious social upheavals — for China to continue to be ruled safely with mandarin-style diktats handed down from Beijing.

Henry S. Rowen, a senior fellow at the Hoover Institution at Stanford…in a brilliant article in *The National Interest*…predicted that China will be a democracy by about the year 2015. He sees budding forms of democracy, largely unnoticed by the outside world….

— *July 21, 1997*
  Page A23

Chinese policemen line up to vote in Beijing's first local legislative elections, December 15, 1998

The world will also need new industries. At the beginning of the 20th century, the industries that showed the most promise for the future were energy, transportation and manufacturing. Great fortunes were made in these industries as they powered the Dow Jones Industrial Average for most of the past century. But today the petroleum and auto industries are consolidating and most domestic manufacturing operations continue to shrink. There will still be a huge demand for manufactured goods, but for the most part, manufacturing capacity exists to serve that need, which implies that growth in that sector may be incremental at best.

In the culture that leaders of global businesses inhabit, where shared values of open markets, hard money and standardized technology increasingly take precedence over old-fashioned nationalism, such transnational combinations (as Daimler-Benz and Chrysler) are logical, and they are becoming more commonplace every day….

More and more, national boundaries, cultural variations and accidents of geography such as the Atlantic Ocean aren't stopping business leaders who see a chance to expand their reach as trade barriers fall, communication becomes cheap and consumer tastes for everything from cola to cellular phones converge.

…The blurring of international business culture into a global unified field — a process celebrated at a schmoozefest for the economic elite each year in Davos, Switzerland — has opened corporate executives to possibilities they and their investment bankers could barely imagine five years ago.

— *May 7, 1998*
  Page A1

Chart III

Population Pyramids for the United States

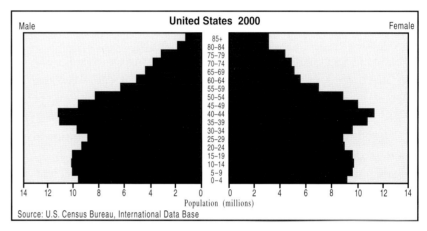

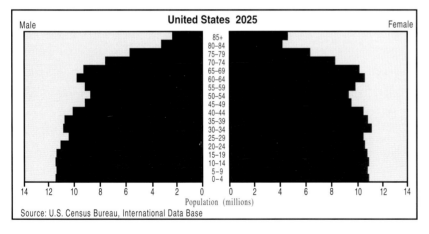

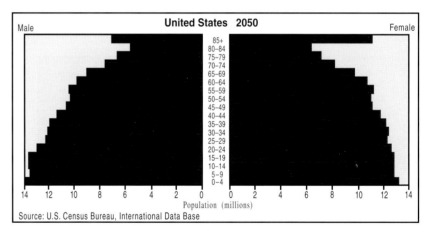

The graph of age by gender in the United States in 2000 clearly shows the baby boomers in their highly productive 30s and 40s as well as showing the result of the baby bust that followed. But in fifty years, according to Census Bureau forecasts, there will be huge increases in the 85-or-older population from about 5 million today to over 18 million in 2050.
Above left: A child with his great-grandfather

Along with computer technology, the industries that now show great promise for the future and seem most likely to power the Dow Jones Industrial Average over the next century are all services or service-related industries:

1. Health care and biotechnology
2. Education
3. Communications and information services
4. Financial services
5. Environmental services
6. Tourism and recreational services

These new growth industries will be driven by demographic changes as well as by new technologies not yet invented.

Health Care and Biotechnology

Two major world issues for the 21st century are the increasingly aged population in the developed world and the need to feed more people with

Senior citizens in a "slimnastics" class, Miami Beach, Fla.

To a startling degree, international executives are adopting business practices made in the U.S. In Japan, dozens of companies are embracing the U.S. emphasis on raising profits, streamlining production and punishing executives when share prices fall or stagnate. Toyota Motor Corp. has bought back its own shares to buoy its stock price, and Sony Corp. has offered stock options to managers; both practices, standard in the U.S., were illegal in Japan until recently. German chemical company SGL Carbon has raised profits with concepts that violate a host of German taboos....

Americanization is fueled by the U.S. economy's remarkable run. Foreigners have concluded that U.S. companies are ascendant in part because of the American focus on the bottom line, efficiency and stock performance — traits for which U.S. managers once were criticized.

— *June 8, 1998*
  Page A1

less land in cultivation and fewer fish in the oceans.

Health care in the United States is already a trillion dollar industry, and U.S. oldsters, the major recipients of that care, account for only about 8% of the world's elderly population. By the middle of the next century the population of elders in the United States is projected to more than double from 38 million in 2000 to 79 million.

But the world's population of people sixty-five years old or older is forecast by the U.S. Census Bureau to increase 250% to about 1.5 billion people by 2050. The worldwide market for pharmaceuticals, diagnostic equipment and other medical devices as well as health care facilities will create the need for huge multinational corporations to efficiently deliver health-related products and services throughout the world.

Another component of the rising demand for health services is that because women live longer than men, a majority of the world's population in the next century will be women. And women traditionally use more health services than men. Women also traditionally have been care givers, so we will probably see much larger numbers of women employed as health care professionals.

Biotechnology is an industry in its infancy. Stories about cloning are big news today, as the Wright Brothers' first flight was nearly a century ago. Genetic engineering holds the promise of a new "green revolution" in which crop yields can be increased and growing times reduced to compensate for the loss of farm land because of residential or other development.

A salmon farm hatchery in New Zealand, 1992

It began with a single 3½-inch floppy disk... it turned into an information wildfire that sent the Starr report almost instantaneously onto millions of computer and TV screens. "Everybody was seeing it at once — Congress, the news media, citizens," said Barry M. Schuler, president of the interactive-services unit at America Online Inc. "When this period of history is written, we may well look on this as defining the medium the way the JFK-Nixon debates defined television."

...But as the Starr report was creating a new model for the dissemination of information, it was also offering an unsettling lesson in the brutal new rules of democracy in the age of the Web. The prosecutor had the extraordinary power to present his combative case against President Clinton directly to the nation, unfiltered by any intermediary....

"I believe we're going to a political system in which there will be a series of pulses, where everyone in the nation will become interested in something, and they will all develop an opinion of it fairly quickly. That model is one that is becoming more and more a part of our society," said Eric Schmidt, an early pioneer of the Internet and now chief executive of software maker Novell Inc.

— *September 14, 1998*
Page B1

It is in aquatic agriculture, however, that the biggest "green" revolution probably will take place. One of the companies in the future Dow industrials index may be a major agribusiness with huge fish farms around the world, which will be needed to offset the dwindling supplies available from ocean fishing. The bottom line in agriculture and in health care in the next century, however, is less reliance on meat from animals, cloned or not, and more reliance on genetically engineered crops and farm-raised fish.

Never mind PCs and mainframes. Think photocopiers, refineries, heart monitors, cameras, and just about anything else that can hold a computer chip. Plug a constellation of devices into the Internet and the myriad gadgets of everyday life will get smarter and more useful. When people hook up their PCs to the World Wide Web, they transform glorified typewriters into windows on a world of information. The Internet can do the same for countless other gadgets....

Developers see air conditioners that can turn themselves on in response to an e-mail message zapped before you leave your office. Everything from a car to a dishwasher could monitor itself, sending out electronic pleas for help when something malfunctions and preventing the repairman from showing up with the wrong parts.

— *August 27, 1998*
   Page A1

Education

The fish hook, and the practice of putting some bait on the end of that hook, have hardly changed for centuries. But the operation of an efficient fish farm requires detailed knowledge of fish diet and life cycles, fish diseases, water quality and temperature requirements, waste disposal, harvesting and shipping methods. It's the same in every industry: The level of knowledge required to be successful has risen far faster than the rate at which it is possible for people to learn on the job.

A major component of the future Dow Jones Industrial Average may be an educational company. Even today, a privately held company known as Phoenix University teaches more than 100,000 students nationwide a variety of skills they need to have successful careers. In a few decades such firms could have a worldwide student body in the millions, many of them accessing course offerings over the Internet. The infrastructure necessary to accomplish that expansion may have to be financed with capital from a public offering of securities.

Communications and Information Services

World economic growth will depend increasingly on a global communications network that provides inexpensive phone service from anywhere. The benefit will be not just in the ability to call home cheaply but in the ability of even modest-sized firms to transmit large data files, fax documents, or conduct video conferences between cities perhaps ten time zones apart.

AT&T is already included in the Dow, and it is a company that probably will be a major factor in this business in the future. Other communications firms will play a role, too, particularly those in wireless communication. Most members of the world's population do not have

Microwave antennas in Magdalena, N.M.

"Europe has to decide what it wants to be," says Norman Davies, the eminent European historian. "In the long run, Europe will certainly move toward unification. But it will be a process of push and pull, and there will be resistance."

Simply defining the word is a chore. For geographers, Europe is a region of 36 countries bordered by Iceland in the west, Turkey in the south, Russia's Ural Mountains in the east and the Arctic Ocean in the North. Politicians says it's a "community," dreamed up to serve various ends. In a world of giant trade blocs where size matters, Europe is a huge merger trying to happen — a group that would give small and medium-sized countries a big voice in return for part of their national sovereignty. In a continent scarred by wars, a unified Europe also is a way to keep the peace and keep Germany in its place.

Indeed, the region is closer to Winston Churchill's vision of a "United States of Europe" than ever before.

— *October 19, 1998*
  Page A1

immediate access to a phone. India, for example, today has fewer than 20 million phones for 1 billion people as opposed to the United States, where there are nearly 200 million phones for 275 million people.

It makes no economic sense to attempt to string telephone wires across India as was done in the United States during the past century. It's quicker and a lot cheaper to go wireless from the start. The multinational firms that make the switching equipment and telephones and operate the fiber-optic and satellite networks are in a much better position to grow and prosper in the next century than are the folks who make copper wire.

The Internet is a major reason communications is such a growth industry. But to continue their rapid expansion into electronic commerce, Internet companies need a broader bandwidth for faster transmission of data than can be accommodated by conventional wired phone lines. Two possibilities now exist: cable and wireless. AT&T, at the close of the millennium, is betting heavily on cable, which may be the best short-term solution. But the United States over the next century, will see broadband wireless or cellular telephone companies emerge to satisfy the worldwide demand for audio and video transmission and high volumes of electronic commerce.

Financial Services

The trend toward privatization of formerly government functions — combined with the desire of people everywhere for a better quality of life — will require enormous capital investments for housing and transportation as well as for food production and distribution systems. Capital

Above: A banner reading "The Euro is Here" is hung outside the Frankfurt, Germany, stock exchange on January 3, 1999, in preparation for the launch of the common European currency the following day
Opposite page: Everyone's favorite, Mickey Mouse

markets exist to finance start-ups and expansion plans, but much of the capital must come from personal savings or investments.

The worldwide decline in the number of children in each family means that both parents can work more hours. Also, more families will be able to invest some money (that previously might have been spent on a fourth or fifth child) in a small family enterprise, an institution that historically has helped to build wealth and create a middle class.

Entrepreneurship in America has created more than one million millionaires just in the past twenty-five years. Financial intermediaries such as banks, insurance companies, mutual funds and security dealers will expand worldwide to invest the trillions of newly created wealth accumulating in developing nations where free markets exist.

Environmental Services

Increased worldwide demand for cleaner air, drinkable water and food free of disease-bearing insects or pathogens means opportunity for firms that can improve the quality of the environment. This includes companies that can help dispose of the world's garbage in a safer manner.

Global environmental firms of the next century will prosper by being able to use the latest biotech innovations to turn toxic waste into benign landfill. Successful firms in this industry will also be able to use wireless remote sensing devices to measure water and air quality and transmit data over the Internet.

Tourism, Travel and Recreational Services

Only one recreation-oriented firm (Disney) is currently part of the DJIA. But will more be added over the next hundred years as emerging middle-class families worldwide spend some of their newfound disposable income on packaged travel and recreation services? The United States is off to a good start in this field: Hollywood sets many of the world's standards in

popular entertainment, and MTV is already available worldwide. It is certainly conceivable that Disney will be joined by other leisure-time giants-to-be.

The bottom line is that slowing population growth is a prelude to dramatic economic growth as women are better able to work outside their homes and as families are better able to invest and save. When families have incomes beyond subsistence levels, they desire a better quality of life. This basic characteristic of human nature is not likely to change over the next hundred years. It will create the opportunity for the new companies in the DJIA to grow and prosper simply by serving that age-old desire for better health, a better home, a better meal and a better education for a better job.

Many of the important pieces are in place for a long period of enormous economic growth. U.S. companies should be able to continue contributing to and profiting from this burgeoning development. Though they will have more and more competition, there is every reason to believe that the Dow Jones Industrial Average's second century can end up being as good a bull run as its first.

INS AND OUTS

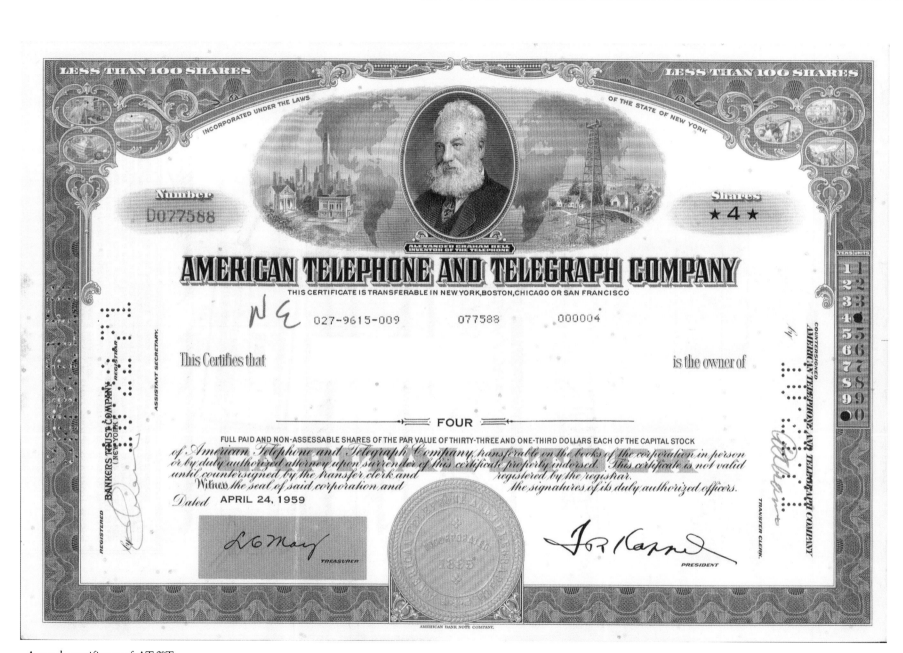

A stock certificate of AT&T

INS AND OUTS

A Guide to Every Company That Has Ever Been in The Dow Jones Industrial Average

It's easy to see the Dow Jones Industrial Average as a monolith. Each day, the average rises, falls, stays flat. Always meaningful, perhaps, but always obscuring the faces behind the wall.

What follows is an attempt to peer, if only for a while, into those faces. Many are instantly familiar. Others might be recognized only by dedicated business wonks: quaint-sounding companies such as American Cotton Oil and Distilling & Cattle Feeding Co.

But, given the serpentine paths these companies have taken over the years, even that distinction is misleading. The two apparent obscurities mentioned above, for example, eventually became Bestfoods Inc. and Millennium Chemicals Inc.

Here, then, is the genealogy of the Dow, along with a comparison of each company's stock performance (excluding dividends) while in the industrial average with the DJIA's performance for the same period.

American Cotton Oil
IN: 5/26/1896   OUT: 4/1/01
Performance: 112%   DJIA Performance: 73%
Founded in 1889 as a successor to the American Cotton Oil Trust, the company sold the cotton-seed-oil business in 1923 and formed Gold Dust Corp., a soap maker. In 1936, Gold Dust was renamed Hecker Products Corp. In 1942, Hecker acquired and took the name of Best Foods Inc., which merged with Corn Products Refining Co. in 1958 to become Corn Products Co. In 1969 the name was changed to CPC International Inc. CPC, based in Englewood Cliffs, N.J., spun off its corn-refining business and changed its name to Bestfoods Inc. on January 1, 1998.

American Sugar Refining Co.
IN: 5/26/1896   OUT: 7/18/30
Performance: -56%   DJIA Performance: 488%
Incorporated in 1891, the company changed its name to American Sugar Co. in 1963 and Amstar Corp. in 1970, distributing its products under the Domino brand name. In 1984, Amstar was taken private, and in 1988 it sold its sugar business to Tate & Lyle PLC, a British sugar refiner and distributor. After the sale, Amstar became essentially a holding company for Milwaukee Electric Tool Co. In 1993, Amstar merged with Essex Industries, a lock and door company, to form Esstar Corp. In 1995, Esstar sold Milwaukee Electric Tool to Sweden's Atlas Copco, then changed its name to Essex Industries. That December, Essex agreed to be acquired by Assa Abloy, a Swedish lock maker.

American Tobacco
IN: 5/26/1896   OUT: 4/21/1899
Performance: 238%   DJIA Performance: 87%
IN: 1/22/24   OUT: 10/1/28
Performance: 11%   DJIA Performance: 160%
Class B:
IN: 10/1/28   OUT: 7/18/30
Performance: -13%   DJIA Performance: 0.2%
IN: 5/26/32   OUT: 10/30/85
Performance: 764%   DJIA Performance: 2,652%
Formed in 1890 by James B. Duke as a consolidation of the principal cigarette factories in the United States, American Tobacco grew to be a monopoly, buying up competitors and exercising tight control over pricing. In 1904, it merged with its holding company, Continental Tobacco Co. The federal government broke up the massive operation in 1911, freeing up such holdings as Liggett & Myers Co., P. Lorillard Co. and R.J. Reynolds. A company called American Tobacco survived the breakup; in 1966, it began diversifying into consumer goods and soon changed its name to American Brands Inc. The company sold its tobacco operations to B.A.T. Industries PLC in 1994, and changed its name to Fortune Brands in 1997.

Chicago Gas
IN: 5/26/1896   OUT: 3/24/1898
Performance: 29%   DJIA Performance: 4.4%
Incorporated in 1855, Chicago Gas was one of a host of utilities absorbed by Peoples Gas Light & Coke Co. in 1897 as part of a massive industry consolidation. Peoples Gas, renamed Peoples Energy Corp. in 1980, is based in Chicago and is the holding company for two local utilities.

Distilling & Cattle Feeding Co.
IN: 5/26/1896   OUT: 4/21/1899
Performance: -18%   DJIA Performance: 87%
IN: 8/13/34   OUT: 6/1/59
Performance: 412%   DJIA Performance: 612%
Formed in 1890 as a successor to the Distillers & Cattle Feeders Trust, the company ran into antitrust trouble in the late 1890s and was broken up, with a handful of operations continuing under the umbrella of American Spirits Manufacturing Co. To cope with Prohibition, American Spirits became U.S. Food Products Corp., which restructured in 1924, becoming National Distillers & Chemical Corp. In 1988, National Distillers sold its liquor business to American Brands and changed its name to Quantum Chemical Corp. Quantum was acquired by Britain's Hanson PLC in 1993. In 1996, Hanson split itself into four businesses, including an independently traded chemical company based in Iselin, N.J., called Millennium Chemicals Inc.

General Electric Co.
IN: 5/26/1896   OUT: 9/14/1898
Performance: -20%   DJIA Performance: 40%
IN: 4/21/1899   OUT: 4/1/01
Performance: 82%   DJIA Performance: -7.6%
IN : 11/7/07
Performance to 12/31/98: 52,970%   DJIA Performance: 18,182%
This industrial giant was formed in 1892 by the merger of Thomson-Houston Electric Co., Thomson-Houston International Electric Co. and Edison General Electric Co., which had been founded by the polymath inventor. In 1919, GE joined with other technology businesses to form Radio Corp. of America, which took over the assets of Marconi Wireless Telegraph Co. of America. Although RCA became an independent company in 1933, GE, now based in Fairfield, Conn., eventually brought it back into the fold, acquiring it in 1986.

Laclede Gas Light Co.
IN: 5/26/1896   OUT: 4/21/1899
Performance: 350%   DJIA Performance: 63%
Formed in 1857, Laclede dominated the natural-gas business in St. Louis as late as 1942. It began by providing gas-powered street lamps to the city, evolving into a full-scale utility in the 1950s. Laclede Gas Co., which dropped the "Light" from its name in 1950, is still active in the distribution and transportation of gas power, and is still based in St. Louis.

National Lead
IN: 5/26/1896   OUT: 10/4/16
Performance: 183%   DJIA Performance: 153%
National Lead, a producer of lead and other chemicals, was incorporated in 1891. In 1971, the company changed its name to NL Industries Inc. Based in Houston, NL is now a worldwide producer and marketer of pigments, dyes and specialty chemicals.

North American Co.
IN: 5/26/1896   OUT: 8/26/1896
Performance: -18%   DJIA Performance: -26%
IN: 10/1/28   OUT: 1/29/30
Performance: 33%   DJIA Performance: 9.2%
North American financed and controlled street railways and natural-gas and electricity businesses from 1890 to 1955. But then the company was dissolved, and one of its units, St. Louis-based Union Electric Co., took control of its assets. At year-end 1997, Union Electric completed a merger with Cipsco Inc., a utility based in Springfield, Ill., to form Ameren Corp., based in St. Louis.

Tennessee Coal, Iron & Railroad Co.
IN: 5/26/1896   OUT: 11/7/07
Performance: 292%   DJIA Performance: 38%
Formed as Sewanee Mining Co. in 1852, the company was reorganized and incorporated in 1860 as Tennessee Coal & Railroad Co. The "Iron" was added in 1881. U.S. Steel Corp. bought the company in the Panic of 1907 — J.P. Morgan, who ran U.S. Steel, agreed to rescue the economy, and trustbuster Theodore Roosevelt agreed not to object to the buyout. Tennessee Coal was a unit and then a division of U.S. Steel until 1964, when it and other operating divisions were merged into the parent company.

U.S. Leather (preferred)
IN: 5/26/1896   OUT: 4/1/05
Performance: 69%   DJIA Performance: 73%
U.S. Leather was one of the nation's largest shoemakers in the first decades of this century. It was succeeded in 1905 by Central Leather Co., and in a 1927 reorganization the company changed its name back to U.S. Leather. The company was dissolved in 1952.

U.S. Rubber Co.
IN: 5/26/1896   OUT: 11/10/1896
Performance: 16%   DJIA Performance: 8.8%
IN: 9/14/1898   OUT: 10/1/28
Performance: -7.5%   DJIA Performance: 318%
Preferred:
IN: 4/1/05   OUT: 3/16/15
Performance: -11%   DJIA Performance: -20%
U.S. Rubber, formed in 1892 as a consolidation of nine domestic makers of rubber products, changed its name to Uniroyal Inc. in 1966. By then, it had tire, plastic and chemical businesses. In 1986, after fighting off a takeover bid, Uniroyal chose to liquidate. The tire division merged with B.F. Goodrich Co.'s tire division to become Uniroyal Goodrich Tire Co., which was acquired by France's Groupe Michelin in 1990. The chemical division became Uniroyal Chemical Inc., purchased by Avery Inc. and taken private in 1989. Renamed Uniroyal Chemical Corp., it went public in 1995, and in 1996, agreed to be acquired by Crompton & Knowles Corp., a specialty chemical maker.

U.S. Cordage (preferred)
IN: 8/26/1896   OUT: 12/23/1896
Performance: 56%   DJIA Performance: 31%
U.S. Cordage was created as a reorganization of the National Cordage Co. trust, which went under during the stock-market panic of 1893. The successor company failed in 1895 and another reorganization followed. A new company, Standard Rope & Twine, eventually ended up as a successor to U.S. Cordage's operations.

Pacific Mail Steamship Co.
IN: 11/10/1896   OUT: 4/1/01
Performance: 43%   DJIA Performance: 59%
This shipping and transportation company, incorporated in 1848, carried people, goods and mail from San Francisco to Asia and South America, adding San Francisco-to-New York routes in the 1920s. In 1938, the company changed its name to American President Lines. American President Cos. became APL Ltd. in 1996, and in 1997 it was acquired by Neptune Orient Lines of Singapore.

Standard Rope & Twine Co.
IN: 12/23/1896   OUT: 4/21/1899
Performance: 14%   DJIA Performance: 93%
Formed in 1895 as part of the U.S. Cordage collapse, Standard Rope & Twine had taken over its predecessor's business by the end of 1896. Standard Rope lasted longer than U.S. Cordage, but collapsed in 1905. The successor to Standard Rope, Standard Cordage Co., was liquidated in 1912.

Peoples Gas
IN: 3/24/1898   OUT: 10/4/16
Performance: 26%   DJIA Performance: 142%
See Chicago Gas.

Continental Tobacco Co.
IN: 4/21/1899   OUT: 7/1/01
Performance: 7.1%   DJIA Performance: 0.5%
Formed in 1898 as a holding company for James B. Duke's American Tobacco Co., Continental was merged into its parent in 1904.

Federal Steel
IN: 4/21/1899   OUT: 4/1/01
Performance: -19%   DJIA Performance: -7.6%
The steelmaker was organized in 1898 in a merger of Illinois Steel Co. and other companies, a transaction bankrolled by J.P. Morgan. In 1901, Mr. Morgan bought out Andrew Carnegie's steel business and combined it with Federal Steel, American Steel & Wire Co. and several other companies to form U.S. Steel Corp.

American Steel & Wire Co.
IN: 4/21/1899   OUT: 4/1/01
Performance: -26%   DJIA Performance: -7.6%
Created in 1897 and incorporated the next year, American Steel & Wire was one of the companies that merged to form U.S. Steel in 1901. In 1986, it was sold to Chicago West Pullman Corp. The company had a public offering in 1988, and was acquired by Birmingham Steel Corp. in 1993.

Amalgamated Copper
IN: 4/1/01   OUT: 7/29/15
Performance: -27%   DJIA Performance: 6.9%
Amalgamated Copper, incorporated in 1899, was a holding company for several mining companies. In 1915, Anaconda Copper Mining Co. took over its operations. In 1971, after the big Chuquicamata mine in Chile was confiscated by the Chilean government and Anaconda lost two-thirds of its copper production, a unit of Atlantic Richfield Co. purchased Anaconda Copper Co. Arco split Anaconda into two divisions in 1973, and sold off pieces of the businesses over the next decade. The only remaining element of Anaconda is Arco Aluminum Co. in Logan, Ky.

American Smelting & Refining
IN: 4/1/01   OUT: 6/1/59
Performance: 531%   DJIA Performance: 808%
Incorporated in 1899, American Smelting & Refining had mining operations in Colorado and Mexico in addition to its plants in Nebraska, Montana and Texas.

In 1975, the company changed its name to Asarco Inc., which remains a leading producer of nonferrous metals, mining about 12% of the Western world's copper, 10% of its silver and 21% of its lead.

International Paper Co.
Preferred:
IN: 4/1/01   OUT: 7/1/01
Performance: -3.6%   DJIA Performance: 8.7%
Common:
IN: 7/3/56
Performance to 12/31/98: 293%   DJIA Performance: 1,752%
Formed in 1898 as a consolidation of 18 paper mills across the Northeast, International Paper moved its newsprint operations to Canada in the 1920s and founded Canadian International Paper Co. The company bought General Crude Oil Co. in 1975, but sold the oil and gas operations to Mobil Oil Corp. four years later. International Paper, now based in Purchase, N.Y., is one of the world's leading producers of printing and writing paper, as well as other wood products.

U.S. Steel Corp.
Common:
IN: 4/1/01   OUT: 5/6/91
Performance: 509%   DJIA Performance: 4,048%
Preferred:
IN: 4/1/01   OUT: 10/4/16
Performance: 25%   DJIA Performance: 46%
J.P. Morgan's U.S. Steel was incorporated in 1901 as a consolidation of several steelmakers. The largest company in the nation at that time, it also owned an extensive system of railroads, as well as interests in ocean shipping, machinery, cement, heavy construction and home building. The company acquired Marathon Oil in 1982 and Texas Oil & Gas in 1986, after which it changed its name to USX Corp. In 1991 and 1992, units became publicly traded; there are separate common stocks for USX-U.S. Steel Group, USX-Marathon Group and USX-Delhi Group, a natural-gas provider. USX itself isn't traded. U.S. Steel remains the nation's biggest steelmaker, but Marathon makes up about two-thirds of USX's sales.

American Car Foundry
IN: 7/1/01   OUT: 10/1/28
Performance: 251%   DJIA Performance: 211%
In 1899, 13 independent railroad-car builders merged to form American Car Foundry. By 1928, the company had moved into trucks and auto parts; at the time of its name change to ACF Industries Inc. in 1968, it also made oil-industry equipment and specialized plastics. The company was bought by Carl Icahn's I.C. Holding Co. in 1984.

Colorado Fuel & Iron

IN: 7/1/01   OUT: 5/12/12
Performance: -74%   DJIA Performance: 16%
A consolidation of Colorado Coal & Iron Co. and Colorado Fuel Co., this maker of steel products was incorporated in 1892. In 1966, the company changed its name to CF&I Steel Corp. It was acquired by Crane Co. in 1969 and spun off to shareholders in 1985. CF&I filed for bankruptcy protection in 1990, and was purchased by Oregon Steel Mills Inc. in 1993.

Central Leather Co.

IN: 5/12/12   OUT: 1/22/24
Performance: -35%   DJIA Performance: 8.6%
See U.S. Leather.

General Motors Corp.

IN: 3/16/15   OUT: 10/4/16
Performance: 46%   DJIA Performance: 83%
IN: 8/31/25
Performance through 12/31/98: 15,726%   DJIA Performance: 6,403%
Established in 1908, GM had become the nation's leading car maker by the early 1930s. Over the decades, the Detroit-based company has amassed a long list of technological advances, including the V-8 engine, introduced in 1914, and the automatic transmission, in 1948. But management missteps and growing competition in the 1970s and 1980s left GM in financial jeopardy by the early 1990s. A board-led management shakeup and a sweeping reorganization returned GM to financial health.

Anaconda Copper Mining Co.

IN: 7/29/15   OUT: 8/31/25
Performance: -39%   DJIA Performance: 86%
IN: 6/1/59   OUT: 8/9/76
Performance: -12%   DJIA Performance: 53%
See Amalgamated Copper.

American Can Co.

IN: 10/4/16   OUT: 5/6/91
Performance: 1,227%   DJIA Performance: 2,745%
American Can, formed in 1901 after a consolidation of several leading container factories, expanded into a wide range of paper goods and then into a variety of other businesses, including mining and recorded-music retailing. In 1986, it changed its name to Primerica and the following year acquired Smith Barney. In 1988, Commercial Credit Co. acquired Primerica, adopting its name. The new Primerica, by then almost exclusively involved in financial services, acquired Travelers Corp. in 1992 and 1993 and renamed itself Travelers Inc.

Also in 1993, the company bought the U.S. retail brokerage and asset-management businesses of Shearson Lehman Brothers Inc. In 1995, the company renamed itself Travelers Group Inc. and in 1998 it merged with Citicorp to form Citigroup.

American Beet Sugar Co.

IN: 10/4/16   OUT: 3/1/20
Performance: -19%   DJIA Performance: -11%
American Beet Sugar, founded in California in the late 1890s, became American Crystal Sugar Co. in 1934. It was bought out by a group of growers in the early 1970s. Still under the American Crystal Sugar name, it remains one of the leading sugar cooperatives in the United States. It is based in Moorhead, Minn.

American Locomotive

IN: 10/4/16   OUT: 10/1/28
Performance: 136%   DJIA Performance: 132%
Incorporated in 1901, American Locomotive dominated the U.S. steam-locomotive industry for decades. During World War II, Alco produced materials for the Allied effort, but fell behind competitors after the war. In 1955, as part of a diversification, the company changed its name to Alco Products Inc. After passing through a series of owners, the company, by then called Alco Power Inc., was bought by Bombardier Inc. of Canada in 1984.

American Telephone & Telegraph Co.

IN: 10/4/16   OUT: 10/1/28
Performance: 35%   DJIA Performance: 132%
IN: 3/14/39   OUT: 1/4/84
Performance: -58%   DJIA Performance: 740%
 "New" AT&T:
IN: 1/4/84
Performance through 12/31/98: 63%   DJIA Performance: 623%
Started in 1885 as a successor to Alexander Graham Bell's eponymous phone company and later merged with equipment pioneer Western Electric Co., AT&T came to dominate the U.S. phone business. To settle a federal antitrust suit, AT&T broke itself up at the start of 1984, remaining in the long-distance and equipment businesses and spinning off the seven giant regional Bell phone companies. It expanded in computers and wireless services in the early 1990s. Its name shortened to plain AT&T Corp., the New York-based company moved to break itself up again in 1996, staying in communications and other services and spinning off its telephone-equipment and computer businesses.

Baldwin Locomotive Works
IN: 10/4/16   OUT: 8/31/25
Performance: 28%   DJIA Performance: 37%
Formed in 1831 by jeweler Matthias Baldwin, the maker of locomotives and industrial equipment became one of the biggest and most widely known steam-engine makers of the 19th century. The company changed its name to Baldwin-Lima-Hamilton Corp. in 1950 after acquiring Lima-Hamilton Corp. BLH was bought by meatpacker Armour & Co. in 1965, which was subsequently merged into a subsidiary of Greyhound Corp. in 1970.

B.F. Goodrich Co.
IN: 10/4/16   OUT: 1/22/24
Performance: -68%   DJIA Performance: -6%
IN: 10/1/28   OUT: 7/18/30
Performance: -64%   DJIA Performance: 0.2%
Formed in 1870 as Goodrich, Tew & Co. — a partnership between Benjamin Franklin Goodrich and his brother-in-law, Harvey W. Tew — the company shortened its name 10 years later. In 1986, Goodrich combined its tire business with Uniroyal's to form Uniroyal Goodrich Tire Co. Goodrich sold its 50% interest in the new company to Clayton & Dubilier, a New York investment firm, the following year. Michelin later acquired Uniroyal Goodrich. Goodrich, based in Akron, Oh., now provides aircraft systems and services and manufactures a variety of specialty chemicals.

Republic Iron & Steel Co.
IN: 10/4/16   OUT: 5/12/24
Performance: -47%   DJIA Performance: -13%
Republic was formed in 1899 as a consolidation of 24 companies operating mills and blast furnaces across the East and Midwest. In 1930, the company was part of another consolidation and became Republic Steel Corp., which eventually merged with LTV Corp., a steel, energy and aerospace company, in 1984. Today, LTV, having shed its other businesses, is the nation's third-largest steelmaker.

Studebaker Corp.
IN: 10/4/16   OUT: 5/12/24
Performance: 18%   DJIA Performance: -13%
Nonpar stock:
IN: 5/12/24   OUT: 8/31/25
Performance: 47%   DJIA Performance: 58%
This auto maker was incorporated in 1911 as a consolidation of Studebaker Brothers Manufacturing Co. and Everett-Metzger-Flanders Co. It merged with

Packard Motor Car in 1954 to form Studebaker-Packard Corp., manufacturing such cars as the Packard Clipper and the Studebaker President. The new entity merged with Worthington Corp. in 1967 and became Studebaker-Worthington Corp., which was acquired by McGraw-Edison Co., an electrical- and mechanical-products maker, in 1979. McGraw-Edison was bought by Cooper Industries Inc. in 1985.

Texas Co.
IN: 10/4/16   OUT: 1/22/24
Performance: -12%   DJIA Performance: -6%
IN: 8/31/25   OUT: 3/17/97
Performance: 15,120%   DJIA Performance: 4,812%
Founded in 1902 by "Buckskin" Joe Cullinan and New York investor Arnold Schlaet, Texaco Inc. was originally known as Texas Co. With the acquisition of California Petroleum Corp. in 1928, Texaco became the first oil company to market in all 48 states. In 1984, Texaco, now based in White Plains, N.Y., acquired another huge operation: Getty Oil Co. However, a jury later found that Texaco had improperly snatched Getty away from another suitor, Pennzoil Co. In 1987, Texaco paid Pennzoil $3 billion to settle the case.

Utah Copper Co.
IN: 10/4/16   OUT: 2/6/24
Performance: -32%   DJIA Performance: -2.0%
Utah Copper Co. was incorporated in 1904, as a reorganization of another company of the same name. In 1936, it merged with Kennecott Copper Corp., which in turn merged with Standard Oil Co. (Ohio) in 1981. British Petroleum Co. took control of Standard of Ohio in 1986. BP sold Kennecott to RTZ Corp., a British mining concern, in 1989.

Western Union Telegraph Co.
IN: 10/4/16   OUT: 10/1/28
Performance: 48%   DJIA Performance: 132%
The company was incorporated in 1851 as New York & Mississippi Valley Printing Telegraph Co., acquiring its more familiar name five years later. In 1987, the company became Western Union Corp., and Brooke Group Ltd. bought a majority stake. Western Union's name was changed to New Valley Corp. in 1991; the company filed for bankruptcy protection later that year. New Valley's money-transfer operations — the bulk of its business — were bought by First Financial Management Corp. in 1994; First Financial later merged with First Data Corp.

Westinghouse Electric & Manufacturing Co.
IN: 10/4/16   OUT: 12/7/25
Performance: 15%   DJIA Performance: 49%
IN: 10/1/28   OUT: 3/17/97
Performance: 1,066%   DJIA Performance: 2,790%
Founded in 1886 by inventor George Westinghouse, who made his mark with innovations in air brakes for trains and railway-signal design, the company introduced, in 1896, the alternating-current system of electrical power that later became the standard for the nation. In 1920, Westinghouse established the first commercial radio station. It shortened its name to Westinghouse Electric Corp. in 1945. Over the years, the Pittsburgh-based company began to concentrate more on industrial and defense equipment. But in 1995 it dramatically changed its business portfolio with the $5.4 billion acquisition of CBS Inc. The company subsequently spun off its industrial businesses and changed its name to CBS Corp.

Corn Products Refining Co.
IN: 3/1/20   OUT: 1/22/24
Performance: 109%   DJIA Performance: 5.2%
IN: 8/15/33   OUT: 6/1/59
Performance: 113%   DJIA Performance: 566%
Corn Products Refining was incorporated in 1906 to absorb a number of other corn- and sugar-products companies. In 1958, Corn Products Refining merged with Best Foods Inc. to become Corn Products Co. That name gave way in 1969 to CPC International Inc. The company, now based in Englewood Cliffs, N.J., spun off its corn-refining operations in 1997 and changed its name to Bestfoods.

E.I. Du Pont de Nemours & Co.
IN: 1/22/24   OUT: 8/31/25
Performance: 31%   DJIA Performance: 45%
IN: 11/20/35
Performance to 12/31/98: 6,356%   DJIA Performance: 6,161%
Incorporated in 1915, the progenitor of today's DuPont Co. was formed to take over the operations of E.I. du Pont de Nemours Powder Co., which through various incarnations, had been making explosives since 1802. The company, now based in Wilmington, Del., had moved into a broader chemical business by the 1920s. Among DuPont's many advances were the refrigerant Freon, produced in a joint venture with GM in 1931; Teflon, created in 1938; Dacron and Mylar, in the 1950s; and Lycra, introduced in 1963.

Mack Trucks Inc.
IN: 1/22/24   OUT: 5/26/32
Performance: -71%   DJIA Performance: -49%
Mack was incorporated in 1916 under the name International Motor Truck Corp., and adopted its more familiar sobriquet in 1922. The company merged with Signal Oil & Gas Co. in 1967; it was spun off in 1983, with French car maker Renault SA increasing its stake to 40%. In 1990, Mack became a wholly owned subsidiary of Renault.

Sears, Roebuck & Co.
IN: 1/22/24
Performance to 12/31/98: 371,211%   DJIA Performance: 9,343%
Founded in 1886 as R.W. Sears Watch Co. by Richard W. Sears — Alvah Roebuck was made a partner several years later, but left because of ill health in 1895 — Sears, Roebuck & Co. was strictly a catalog merchant until 1925, when it opened its first retail store. In 1931, Sears formed Allstate Insurance Co.; in 1981, it bought Coldwell, Banker & Co., a real-estate firm, and Dean Witter Reynolds Inc., a brokerage firm. In 1993, Sears closed its catalog operations and began to divest its nonretail operations, offering chunks of Dean Witter — renamed Dean Witter, Discover & Co.— and Allstate Corp. in public offerings. Today, the Hoffman Estates, Ill., company operates department, furniture, hardware and automotive stores.

Standard Oil Co. of California
IN: 2/6/24   OUT: 8/31/25
Performance: -21%   DJIA Performance: -4%
IN: 7/18/30
Performance to 12/31/98: 7,092%   DJIA Performance: 3,717%
This was the Western arm of the Standard Oil "octopus" founded by John D. Rockefeller in 1870. As of 1899, Standard Oil's many operations were controlled under the umbrella of Standard Oil of New Jersey, which the federal government broke up into 33 companies in a 1911 antitrust action. The California operation, now based in San Francisco, changed its name to Chevron Corp. in 1984.

F.W. Woolworth Co.
IN: 5/12/24   OUT: 3/17/97
Performance: 1,154%   DJIA Performance: 7,651%
The biggest nickel-and-dime operation of them all was incorporated in 1911 to consolidate the assets of several retailers. In 1963, the company bought shoemaker and retailer G.R. Kinney Corp. from Brown Shoe Co. Based in New York, it dropped its initials and became simply Woolworth Corp. in 1989. The company closed the last of its variety stores in the United States in 1997 to focus on footwear and sporting goods, and became Venator Group in 1998.

International Harvester Co.
IN: 8/31/25   OUT: 5/6/91
Performance: 101%   DJIA Performance: 1,984%
This maker of farm equipment was incorporated in 1902, in the merger of McCormick Harvesting Machine Co., Deering Harvester Co. and several smaller manufacturers. The new company controlled 85% of the U.S. farm-equipment market. In 1911, the federal government filed an antitrust suit against the company, which agreed, years later, to sell several of its subsidiaries. In 1985, International Harvester sold its agricultural-equipment business to the Case unit of Tenneco Inc., and the following year changed its name to Navistar International Corp. Navistar's principal business is making medium- and heavy-duty trucks and diesel engines. The company is based in Chicago.

Kennecott Copper Corp.
IN: 8/31/25   OUT: 12/31/25
Performance: 0.9%   DJIA Performance: 11%
This mining and copper-products company was incorporated in 1915, acquiring the property of Kennecott Mines Co. and Beatson Copper Co., among others. In 1936, the company merged with Utah Copper Co.; in 1981, it was bought by Standard Oil of Ohio. British Petroleum took control of Standard Oil of Ohio in 1986; in 1989, BP sold its minerals unit — primarily Kennecott — to RTZ Corp., a British mining company.

U.S. Realty & Improvement Co.
IN: 8/31/25   OUT: 12/7/25
Performance: 17%   DJIA Performance: 9.2%
Incorporated in 1904 as a successor to U.S. Realty & Construction Co., the real-estate firm became Realty-Sheraton Corp. through a 1941 merger. In 1947, under the name Sheraton Corp. of America, the company became the first hotel stock listed on the Big Board. In 1968 Sheraton became a subsidiary of International Telephone & Telegraph Co., which later became ITT Corp. ITT, by then a hotel and gaming company, was acquired by Starwood Hotels & Resorts Worldwide Inc. early in 1998.

Allied Chemical & Dye Corp.
IN: 12/7/25
Performance to 12/31/98: 3,046%   DJIA Performance: 6,403%
Formed in 1920 as a consolidation of five companies, the maker of chemicals and other products trimmed its name to Allied Chemical in 1958. It changed its name again in 1981, to Allied Corp., to reflect its diverse businesses. Two years later, the company acquired Bendix Corp., giving it a significant footing in the aerospace industry. In 1985, Allied merged with Signal Cos. and began divesting businesses such as Union Texas Petroleum. AlliedSignal Inc. dropped the hyphen in 1993.

Famous Players-Lasky Corp.
IN: 12/7/25   OUT: 5/26/32
Performance: -95%   DJIA Performance: -65%
Incorporated in 1916 as a successor to Famous Players Film Co. and Jesse L. Lasky Feature Play Co., the company's business was producing movies and operating theaters in which to show them. A succession of name changes began in 1927, first to Paramount Famous Lasky Corp., in 1930 to Paramount Publix Corp. and, in 1935, to Paramount Pictures Inc. In 1948, the Supreme Court ordered motion-picture companies to give up control of their theater chains. The theater operation became United Paramount Theaters, which in 1953 bought the fledgling ABC television network. The Paramount movie studio was bought in 1966 by Gulf & Western Industries Inc., the diverse conglomerate. In the 1980s, G&W whittled down its sprawling collection of companies, and in 1989 changed its name to Paramount Communications Inc. Viacom Inc., the entertainment and publishing company, acquired Paramount in 1994.

Remington Typewriter Co.
IN: 12/31/25   OUT: 3/16/27
Performance: 118%   DJIA Performance: 14%
In 1873, Milwaukee inventor Christopher Shoales persuaded the owners of E. Remington & Sons, a firearms maker that made occasional forays into sewing machines and agricultural equipment, to help him develop his version of the typewriter. The typewriter operation, sold in 1886, became Remington Typewriter Co. (The gunmakers became Remington Arms Co.) After a 1927 merger with Rand Kardex Corp., Remington Typewriter became Remington Rand Inc. and branched into adding machines and other business systems. In 1955, the company merged with Sperry Corp. to become Sperry Rand Corp. Sperry dropped the "Rand" in 1979, and around that time, sold its typewriter business. In 1986, Sperry was bought by Burroughs Corp. The combined entity, renamed Unisys Corp., is based in Blue Bell, Pa.

United Drug Co.
IN: 3/16/27   OUT: 10/1/28
Performance: -33%   DJIA Performance: 47%
Incorporated in 1902, this drug maker and distributor was taken over by Drug Inc., a holding company, in 1928. When the holding company was split up in 1933, United Drug Inc. emerged as one of five surviving companies. The company changed its name to Rexall Drug Inc. in 1946, taking the name of its widely known Rexall brand. Rexall became Dart Industries Inc. in 1969, and in 1980 merged with Kraft Inc. to form Dart & Kraft Inc. Dart & Kraft spun off to shareholders most of the company's nonfood businesses and changed its name to Kraft Inc. in 1986. Two years later, Kraft was bought by Philip Morris Cos.

Atlantic Refining Co.
IN: 10/1/28   OUT: 7/18/30
Performance: -20%   DJIA Performance: 0.2%
Incorporated in 1870, Atlantic Refining became one of the world's largest makers of lubricating oils, gasoline and other petroleum products. The company merged with Richfield Oil in 1966 and changed its name to Atlantic Richfield Co. Today's Arco is a product of yet a third merger — with Sinclair Oil Corp. in 1969. In 1977, the company merged Anaconda Copper Mining Co. into one of its subsidiaries. Los Angeles-based Arco also has interests in chemicals and coal.

Bethlehem Steel Corp.
IN: 10/1/28   OUT: 3/17/97
Performance: 58%   DJIA Performance: 2,790%
Formed in 1857 as Saucona Iron Co., the company changed its name to Bethlehem Steel Co. in 1899, and upon its 1919 incorporation, to Bethlehem Steel Corp. The company, based in Bethlehem, Pa., has made steel for some of the nation's most notable structures, including the Empire State Building and the Golden Gate Bridge. Today, it is the No. 2 steelmaker in the United States.

Chrysler Corp.
IN: 10/1/28   OUT: 6/29/79
Performance: -39%   DJIA Performance: 251%
The company was formed in 1920 when Walter P. Chrysler, an executive late of General Motors, took over Maxwell Motor Corp. He changed the company's name five years later. In 1980, Chrysler was rescued from the brink of bankruptcy when the federal government guaranteed more than $1 billion in loans. In 1987, the company acquired American Motors Corp. and its Jeep line and subsequently became one of the most profitable vehicle makers of the 1990s. In 1998, Chrysler merged with Germany's Daimler-Benz AG to form DaimlerChrysler AG.

General Railway Signal Corp.
IN: 10/1/28   OUT: 7/18/30
Performance: -24%   DJIA Performance: 0.2%
General Railway Signal, incorporated in 1904, started out as a maker of railway safety devices. The Stamford, Conn., company, which dropped "Railway" from its name in 1962, has since become more diverse in its product line: It makes a wide range of equipment, from valves and pumps to telecommunications gear. In 1991, General Signal sold its General Railway Signal operation to Sasib SpA, an Italian maker of railway equipment and industrial machinery.

International Nickel Co.
IN: 10/1/28   OUT: 3/12/87
Performance: -42%   DJIA Performance: 845%
Incorporated in 1902, this nickel and copper company was acquired by an unrelated corporation, International Nickel of Canada, in 1928. International Nickel changed its name to Inco Ltd. in 1976 and today produces more than 25% of the world's nickel, as well as copper, precious metals and cobalt.

Nash Motors Co.
IN: 10/1/28   OUT: 7/18/30
Performance: -58%   DJIA Performance: 0.2%
IN: 5/26/32   OUT: 3/14/39
Performance: -9.5%   DJIA Performance: 202%
Incorporated in 1916, the car maker merged with Kelvinator Corp., a maker of household and refrigeration equipment, in 1937, becoming Nash-Kelvinator Corp. The new entity changed its name to American Motors Corp. in 1954 after a merger with Hudson Motor Car Co. In 1968, AMC sold its Kelvinator division to White Consolidated Industries Inc., a maker of industrial machinery. AMC was acquired by Chrysler in 1987.

Postum Inc.
IN: 10/1/28   OUT: 10/30/85
Performance: 1,267%   DJIA Performance: 473%
Incorporated in 1922 as Postum Cereal Co., this packaged-foods maker changed its name to Postum Inc. in 1927, and to General Foods Corp. in 1929 after buying the Clarence Birdseye firm. Its divisions came to include such widely known brands as Jell-O gelatin, Maxwell House coffee and Oscar Mayer hot dogs. The company became a subsidiary of Philip Morris Cos. in 1985.

Radio Corp. of America
IN: 10/1/28   OUT: 5/26/32
Performance: -93%   DJIA Performance: -79%
RCA was formed in 1919 as a partnership that came to include such industrial giants as GE, Westinghouse, AT&T and United Fruit (which relied on radio to contact its far-flung field operations). The partners took over Guglielmo Marconi's U.S. radio operations and agreed to share important patents for the new wireless technology. Under pressure from the Justice Department, the corporate sponsors withdrew from RCA in 1933, leaving it an independent company. RCA held the controlling interest in the first true radio network, National Broadcasting Co., and was a pioneer in the development of television technology. In 1986, RCA was bought by one of its old parents: GE.

Standard Oil Co. (New Jersey)
IN: 10/1/28

Performance to 12/31/98: 109,090%   DJIA Performance: 3,725%

As of 1899, the New Jersey arm of Standard Oil was an umbrella for John D. Rockefeller's numerous oil operations. The federal government closed the umbrella in 1911, breaking Standard Oil into 33 different companies. The one that kept the name Standard Oil of New Jersey was renamed Exxon Corp. in 1972. Now based in Irving, Texas, Exxon is the nation's largest oil company, and it also has interests in refining and marketing chemicals and in the coal, mineral and power-generating businesses. In December 1998, Exxon agreed to acquire Mobil Corp., another Standard Oil descendant, for $75.3 billion in stock, the largest takeover ever.

Texas Gulf Sulphur
IN: 10/1/28   OUT: 5/26/32

Performance: -79%   DJIA Performance: -79%

Incorporated in 1909, the company — which had pared its name to Texasgulf Inc. — was purchased by Société Nationale Elf Aquitaine of France in 1981. Texasgulf was acquired by Potash Corp. of Saskatchewan in 1995.

Union Carbide & Carbon Corp.
IN: 10/1/28

Performance to 12/31/98: 2,940%   DJIA Performance: 3,725%

The chemical maker, founded in 1917, trimmed its name to Union Carbide Corp. in 1957. Union Carbide grew through the 1970s, with a range of products that included Prestone antifreeze, Glad bags and Eveready batteries. Then in 1984, a gas leak at Union Carbide's plant in Bhopal, India, killed more than 2,000 people in what quickly was branded the worst industrial accident in history. The tragedy left Union Carbide weakened and vulnerable to a takeover. In 1986, the company fended off a hostile bid from GAF Corp. but to repay debt it had taken on in the GAF fight, it sold a number of businesses, leaving it considerably smaller. Today, Union Carbide, based in Danbury, Conn., is a chemical and polymer company.

Victor Talking Machine Co.
IN: 10/1/28   OUT: 1/8/29

Performance: 35%   DJIA Performance: 24%

Victor Talking Machine Co. was incorporated in 1901 to make and sell sound-reproduction machines. The company was bought by RCA in 1929.

Wright Aeronautical Corp.
IN: 10/1/28   OUT: 9/14/29

Performance: 208%   DJIA Performance: 53%

This maker of aircraft motors was incorporated in 1919 to acquire a portion of the assets of Wright-Martin Aircraft Corp. In 1929, it merged with Curtiss Aeroplane & Motor Co. and Wright Aeronautical Corp. to form Curtiss-Wright Corp., now based in Lyndhurst, N.J.

National Cash Register Co.
IN: 1/8/29   OUT: 5/26/32

Performance: -92%   DJIA Performance: -83%

Founded by John H. Patterson in 1884 as a maker of simple machines that helped merchants mechanically record transactions and payments, the company went public in 1925 with an offering of $55 million of shares, at that time the largest public offering in U.S. business history. The company trimmed its name to NCR Corp. in 1974; by that time, it had expanded into such businesses as electronic data processing and, later, banking systems and computer equipment and services. NCR was acquired by AT&T in 1991. Spun off by AT&T in 1996, it is once again an independent company headquartered in Dayton, Oh.

Curtiss-Wright Corp.
IN: 9/14/29   OUT: 7/18/30

Performance: -69%   DJIA Performance: -34%

Incorporated in 1929 as a consolidation of several aviation-related businesses, by 1941 it had $1 billion in orders. By 1945, Curtiss-Wright was second only to General Motors in producing goods for the nation's war effort. But after the war, its enormous plant capacity sat idle. The company's share of total U.S. aviation sales plunged to 10% in 1947 from 50% in 1934. Today, the company, based in Lyndhurst, N.J., makes flight systems and other aerospace components, as well as electronic control valves for a variety of uses.

Johns-Manville Corp.
IN: 1/29/30   OUT: 8/30/82

Performance: -59%   DJIA Performance: 241%

This maker of asbestos, building materials and assorted insulation products was incorporated in 1926 as a reorganization of another company of the same name. In 1981, the company became simply Manville Corp. It struggled through bankruptcy-law proceedings for much of the decade, trying to resolve thousands of claims from victims of asbestos-related illnesses. A trust for handling victims' claims today owns 80% of the company's shares. After emerging from bankruptcy, Manville became a holding company in 1990, with mineral, mining, forest-product and building-product operations. In 1995, it completed the spinoff of its mining unit, and in 1996 sold its forest-product unit. Now simply a building-products maker, Manville has changed its name to Schuller Corp.

Borden Co.

IN: 7/18/30 OUT: 11/20/35
Performance: -66% DJIA Performance: -39%

Gail Borden Jr. & Co. was founded in 1857 by the inventor of the same name, who had patented a method for condensing milk. In 1858, the name was changed to New York Condensed Milk Co.; in 1875 it began selling milk in liquid form. New York Condensed Milk was also the first company to sell milk in bottles, beginning in 1885. The company reorganized in the late 1890s as Borden Condensed Milk Co., and in 1919, the name was shortened to Borden Co. In 1928, the company diversified into a wide range of dairy products, with adhesives following soon after; later it moved into a broad range of consumer products. The Columbus, Oh., company went private in 1995.

Eastman Kodak Co.

IN: 7/18/30
Performance through 12/31/98: 6,225% DJIA Performance: 3,717%

This photography and imaging company was incorporated in 1901, several years after its founder, George Eastman, had popularized the camera. (Reportedly, he chose the name Kodak because it wasn't easily mispronounced and K was the first letter of his mother's maiden name.) Today, Kodak, based in Rochester, N.Y., is moving into the world of digital electronics, which includes products such as "filmless" cameras.

Goodyear Tire & Rubber Co.

IN: 7/18/30
Performance through 12/31/98: 4,261% DJIA Performance: 3,717%

The maker of rubber products was formed in 1898. In 1925, Goodyear made the Pilgrim, its first blimp filled with helium, and in 1961, Goodyear blimps moved into their most recognizable role: providing a bird's-eye view of sporting events for television broadcasts. The largest U.S. tire maker, this Akron, Oh., company also makes and sells vehicle parts as well as industrial rubber products and rubber-related chemicals.

Liggett & Myers Tobacco Co.

IN: 7/18/30 OUT: 5/26/32
Performance: -62% DJIA Performance: -79%

Formed in 1873, the partnership between John Edmond Liggett and George S. Myers was snapped up by American Tobacco Co. in 1899. When the U.S. government broke up American Tobacco in 1911, Liggett & Myers was reborn. Among its brands were Chesterfield and Lark cigarettes. In the late 1960s, the company moved into dog food and importing and selling alcoholic beverages. In 1976, it restructured, and the parent company was renamed Liggett Group Inc. Britain's Grand Metropolitan PLC bought Liggett in 1980, and changed the name to GrandMet USA. The tobacco operations were bought in 1986 by Bennett S. LeBow, who consolidated them under his Brooke Group Ltd. umbrella.

Hudson Motor Car Co.

IN: 7/18/30 OUT: 5/26/32
Performance: -92% DJIA Performance: -79%

Incorporated in 1909, Hudson Motor Car Co. built mechanical equipment in addition to automobiles. In 1954, Hudson merged with Nash-Kelvinator Corp., and the resulting company became American Motors Corp. AMC was acquired by Chrysler in 1987.

United Aircraft & Transport

United Air Transport:

IN: 7/18/30 OUT: 5/26/32
Performance: -87% DJIA Performance: -79%

United Aircraft:

IN: 8/15/33 OUT: 8/13/34
Performance: -53% DJIA Performance: 70%
IN: 3/14/39
Performance through 12/31/98: 8,726% DJIA Performance: 5,976%

Founded in 1929, UAT became a partnership among several aviation companies, including Boeing Airplane & Transport Corp. and Pratt & Whitney. The partnership was an umbrella for two publicly traded companies: United Aircraft Corp., which made planes, and United Air Transport Corp., which flew them. In 1934, Congress decided that builders and airlines should be separate entities. UAT was broken up, with the survivors continuing on as United Air Lines Transport Corp., Boeing Airplane Co. and United Aircraft Corp. United Air Lines, of course, went on to become a major carrier; Boeing let "Airplane" fly away from its name in 1961, and was added to the Dow 26 years later. United Aircraft is in the Dow today under the name it adopted in 1975: United Technologies Corp. Now the company makes everything from helicopters to elevators.

Drug Inc.

IN: 5/26/32 OUT: 8/15/33
Performance: 59% DJIA Performance: 93%

The drug holding company was incorporated in 1928. In 1933, it was split into five companies: Sterling Products Inc., whose North American operations are now part of Bayer AG of Germany; United Drug Inc., which changed its name to Rexall Drug Inc. and is now part of Philip Morris Cos.; Bristol-Myers Inc., which merged with Squibb Corp. in 1989 to become Bristol-Myers Squibb Co.; Vick Chemical Inc., now a unit of Procter & Gamble Co. known as Richardson-Vicks; and Life Savers Corp., whose namesake product line is now owned by RJR Nabisco Holdings Corp.

International Business Machines Corp.
IN: 5/26/32   OUT: 3/14/39
Performance: 204%   DJIA Performance: 202%
IN: 6/29/79
Performance through 12/31/98: 404%   DJIA Performance: 990%
Incorporated in 1911 as Computing-Tabulating-Recording Co., a purveyor of scales, adding machines and other business equipment, CTR became IBM in 1924. IBM grew to dominate the market for mechanical tabulating machines, prompting a government antitrust decree in the 1950s. About the same time, IBM made a belated entry into electronic computers. It went on to dominate that market as well, leading to another antitrust investigation. But the government dropped its long-running attempt to break up IBM in 1982. IBM subsequently saw its position challenged by the rise of personal computers and the near collapse of its mainframe computer franchise. In recent years, the Armonk, N.Y., company has refocused its products and returned to profitability.

Loews Corp.
IN: 5/26/32   OUT: 7/3/56
Performance: 22%   DJIA Performance: 892%
Loews began life in the early '20s as a string of movie houses and in 1924 acquired and consolidated three film studios: Metro Pictures, Goldwyn Pictures Corp. and Louis B. Mayer Productions. In the late 1940s, the federal government's threat of antitrust action led to the separation of MGM. Brothers Preston and Laurence Tisch bought a controlling interest in Loews in 1959, and took the company into such diverse fields as cigarettes, insurance, watchmaking and offshore drilling. The company sold its theater operations in 1985.

International Shoe Co.
IN: 5/26/32   OUT: 8/15/33
Performance: 29%   DJIA Performance: 93%
International Shoe, incorporated in 1921, adopted the name Interco in 1966. In 1991, Interco filed for relief under the federal bankruptcy code; it emerged a year later. By 1995, Interco had spun off several shoe subsidiaries and become a major maker of residential furniture, changing its name to Furniture Brands International Inc. in 1996.

Coca-Cola Co.
IN: 5/26/32   OUT: 11/20/35
Performance: 1,186%   DJIA Performance: 193%
IN: 3/12/87
Performance through 12/31/98: 1,012%   DJIA Performance: 305%
Atlanta pharmacist John Pemberton first brewed Coca-Cola in 1886, hawking it as a tonic for a plethora of illnesses. In 1891, pharmacist Asa Candler bought

the company for $2,000 and promoted the flagship beverage as a soft drink. The company, based in Atlanta, was incorporated in 1891. In 1894, a retailer in Vicksburg, Miss., started selling the beverage in bottles. In 1919, the company was acquired by Atlanta banker Ernest Woodruff, with an investment group, for $25 million. His son, Robert Winship Woodruff, was soon appointed president, beginning more than six decades of successful leadership that built the company into a marketing giant.

Procter & Gamble Co.
IN: 5/26/32
Performance through 12/31/98: 61,172%   DJIA Performance: 18,266%
Procter & Gamble, founded by soap maker James Gamble and candle maker William Procter in 1837, stuck to candles, glycerine, soap and oils in its early years. In 1879, the Cincinnati company had its first hot seller in Ivory soap, which the company assured consumers was "99 $44/100$% pure." Its next big hit was Crisco. Tide detergent, introduced in 1946, is America's top seller in its category.

National Steel Corp.
IN: 11/20/35   OUT: 6/1/59
Performance: 2,123%   DJIA Performance: 339%
National Steel was incorporated in 1929, as a merger of Weirton Steel, Great Lakes Steel and Hanna Iron Ore Co. After a restructuring, National Steel became a subsidiary of National Intergroup Inc. in 1983. Soon after, employees led a buyout of the Weirton Steel division. In 1984, NKK Corp. of Japan bought a controlling stake in National Steel.

Aluminum Co. of America
IN: 6/1/59
Performance through 12/31/98: 392%   DJIA Performance: 1,327%
Incorporated in 1888 as Pittsburgh Reduction Co., Alcoa adopted its present name in 1907. The company's first offering: an aluminum teakettle. Today, Alcoa, based in Pittsburgh, is the world's largest producer of aluminum, with operations in 28 countries. It also makes many nonaluminum products, including plastic bottle caps and electrical distribution systems for cars.

Owens-Illinois Glass Co.
IN: 6/1/59   OUT: 3/12/87
Performance: 451%   DJIA Performance: 252%
This maker of glass containers was incorporated in 1907 as Owens Bottle Machine Corp., later changing its name to Owens-Illinois Glass, then to simply Owens-Illinois Inc. The Toledo, Oh., company was bought out in 1987 by Kohlberg Kravis Roberts & Co. It was taken public again in December 1991, with KKR retaining a 30% interest, and now trades on the New York Stock Exchange.

Swift & Co.
IN: 6/1/59   OUT: 6/29/79
Performance: 59%   DJIA Performance: 31%
The food and chemical maker was incorporated in 1885, and changed its name to Esmark in 1973. Esmark was acquired by Beatrice Co. in 1984; Beatrice, in turn, was bought by Kohlberg Kravis Roberts & Co. in 1986. In 1990, KKR sold Swift's meat line to ConAgra Inc., now the nation's largest independent food concern.

Minnesota Mining & Manufacturing Co.
IN: 8/9/76
Performance through 12/31/98: 521%   DJIA Performance: 834%
This diversified manufacturer was formed in 1902 by five businessmen who wanted to mine raw materials for grinding wheels. In 1925, it produced its first major innovation, masking tape: Two-tone paint jobs were in vogue for automobiles, and auto shops needed an easy way to block off sections of the car that had already been painted when applying the second color. Later, the company would venture into audio and video tape, as well as data storage for computers. Nearly 80 years after its founding, the St. Paul, Minn., firm introduced another product that has become nearly ubiquitous: Post-it notes.

Merck & Co.
IN: 6/29/79
Performance through 12/31/98: 1,868%   DJIA Performance: 990%
The progenitor of this drug maker was E. Merck, a German company with roots stretching back to the 17th century. In the early 1890s, it decided the best way to deal with a nagging problem in its U.S. operations — its labels were being put on other companies' drugs — was to send George Merck to the United States to open a branch of the company. Thus, Merck & Co. was founded in New York in 1891. During World War I, Merck was forced to sever its ties to its German sibling, and in 1953 it merged with Sharp & Dohme, a pharmaceutical maker with extensive overseas distribution networks. Now based in Whitehouse Station, N.J., Merck has such discoveries to its credit as vitamin B_{12}, cortisone and streptomycin.

American Express Co.
IN: 8/30/82
Performance through 12/31/98: 912%   DJIA Performance: 927%
American Express Co. was founded in 1850 as a joint-stock association, when Henry Wells merged Wells & Co. with other express carriers Livingston & Fargo and Butterfield, Wasson & Co. (Wells and Fargo would found the bank that bears their name two years later.) In 1891, the American Express Travelers Cheque was created. The American Express Card was launched in 1958, and American Express Co. was incorporated in 1965.

Philip Morris Cos.
IN: 10/30/85
Performance through 12/31/98: 1,641%   DJIA Performance: 567%
Philip Morris started humbly in 1847 as a London tobacconist's shop owned by an entrepreneur of the same name. The firm made its first cigarettes in 1854; in 1901 it was appointed tobacconist to King Edward VII. A year later, Gustav Eckmeyer, who had been Philip Morris's sole agent in the United States since 1872, formed Philip Morris & Co. in New York. In 1924, the company introduced Marlboro cigarettes. Three decades later, the company acquired Benson & Hedges. Soon afterwards, the company changed its name to Philip Morris Inc. In the 1980s, Philip Morris snapped up Kraft and General Foods, broadening its consumer-product business. As part of a restructuring, Philip Morris Cos. became the holding company for its operations.

McDonald's Corp.
IN: 10/30/85
Performance through 12/31/98: 416%   DJIA Performance: 567%
In 1948, Dick and Mac McDonald started a drive-through hamburger shop in San Bernardino, Calif. Ray Kroc, a milkshake-machine salesman, was impressed enough to buy franchise rights in 1954. Mr. Kroc opened his first McDonald's in 1955, in Des Plaines, Ill. — the site has since become a McDonald's museum — and bought out the brothers in 1961. In 1967, McDonald's invaded Canada; four years later, outlets appeared in Japan, Germany, Australia, Guam and the Netherlands. Today, McDonald's has more than 15,000 restaurants around the world.

Boeing Co.
IN: 3/12/87
Performance through 12/31/98: 180%   DJIA Performance: 305%
See United Aircraft & Transport.

Caterpillar Inc.
IN: 5/6/91
Performance through 12/31/98: 270%   DJIA Performance: 212%
This heavy-equipment maker began as Caterpillar Tractor Co. in 1925, a merger of C.L. Best Tractor Co. and Holt Manufacturing Co. Mr. Holt had introduced the "track" design for heavy-machinery wheels in 1904, and coined the name Caterpillar for his products. The company boomed during the Depression by selling tractors to the state farms of Russia, then embarking on a plan to mechanize agricultural production. Caterpillar also introduced its first diesel engines during that time. The company, based in Peoria, Ill., dropped "Tractor" from its name in 1986, but continues to make agricultural tractors as well as construction and other earth-moving equipment.

Walt Disney Co.

IN: 5/6/91

Performance through 12/31/98: 194%   DJIA Performance: 212%

Founded as Disney Brothers Studio in 1923 by Walter E. and Roy O. Disney, the company was incorporated in 1938 as a consolidation of Walt Disney Productions, Walt Disney Enterprises, Disney Film Recording Co. and Liled Realty & Investment Co. Seventeen years later, after a string of hit films, the company opened Disneyland in Anaheim, Calif.; in 1971, Disney World opened near Orlando, Fla. In 1986, the company dropped "Productions" from its name and in 1996, acquired Capital Cities/ABC Inc.

J.P. Morgan & Co.

IN: 5/6/91

Performance through 12/31/98: 95%   DJIA Performance: 212%

In 1861, J.P. Morgan founded this company in New York to act as an agent in bills of exchange for George Peabody & Co., a London merchant bank that financed trade between Europe and the United States. In 1935, banking laws forced the company to choose between commercial banking and securities underwriting; it opted for the former. Some employees, including three partners, withdrew from the company and formed an investment bank, Morgan Stanley & Co. J.P. Morgan & Co. incorporated in 1940, and in 1959 merged with Guaranty Trust Co. to form Morgan Guaranty Trust Co. A decade later, J.P. Morgan & Co. became the bank holding company for Morgan Guaranty.

Citigroup

IN: 3/17/97

Performance through 12/31/98: 43%   DJIA Performance: 32%

Created by the 1998 merger of financial-services giants Travelers Group and Citicorp. See American Can.

Hewlett-Packard Co.

IN: 3/17/97

Performance through 12/31/98: 23%   DJIA Performance: 32%

Founded in 1939 by electrical engineers Dave Packard and Bill Hewlett, the company began operations in a Palo Alto, Calif., garage. Its first product was an audio oscillator used to test sound equipment. Hewlett-Packard expanded into such fields as medical electronics and analytical instrumentation in the 1960s; its first computer was a controller for some of its test and measurement systems. Hewlett-Packard introduced a desktop scientific calculator in 1968 and a hand-held scientific calculator four years later. By the 1980s, it was offering a full range of computers and had moved into the printer market. It is still based in Palo Alto.

Johnson & Johnson

IN: 3/17/97

Performance through 12/31/98: 45%   DJIA Performance: 32%

Johnson & Johnson began operations in 1886, about a decade after the discovery that airborne germs were a source of infection in the operating room. It was incorporated in 1887; mass-produced antiseptic dressings made of cotton and gauze followed a few years later. Band-Aid adhesive bandages were introduced in 1921, about the same time as Johnson's Baby Cream. McNeil Laboratories Inc., the maker of Tylenol, was acquired in 1959. Still based in New Brunswick, N.J., Johnson & Johnson today makes a variety of surgical and diagnostic products, as well as pharmaceuticals and personal care products.

Wal-Mart Stores Inc.

IN: 3/17/97

Performance through 12/31/98: 182%   DJIA Performance: 32%

The first Wal-Mart store was opened in Rogers, Ark., in 1962, by Sam Walton after his chain of variety stores in Arkansas and Kansas was hit by competition from regional discounters. There were 276 Wal-Mart stores by 1980, and the following year the company branched out into warehouse stores with its first Sam's Club, in Midwest City, Okla. The first Supercenter, with a complete grocery department and 36 departments of general merchandise, opened in 1988. Based in Bentonville, Ark., the company today has some 3,000 stores in eight countries.

The 12 Original Dow Companies

American Cotton Oil
American Sugar Refining Co.
American Tobacco
Chicago Gas
Distilling & Cattle Feeding Co.
General Electric Co.
Laclede Gas Light Co.
National Lead
North American Co.
Tennessee Coal, Iron & Railroad Co.
U.S. Leather
U.S. Rubber Co.

The 30 Dow Companies (as of 10/29/99)

AlliedSignal Inc.	Goodyear Tire & Rubber Co.
Aluminum Co. of America	Hewlett Packard Co.
American Express Co.	International Business Machines Corp.
AT&T Corp.	International Paper Co.
Boeing Co.	Johnson & Johnson
Caterpillar Inc.	McDonald's Corp.
Chevron Corp.	Merck & Co.
Citigroup	Minnesota Mining & Manufacturing Co.
Coca-Cola Co.	J.P. Morgan & Co.
Walt Disney Co.	Philip Morris Cos.
DuPont Co.	Procter & Gamble Co.
Eastman Kodak Co.	Sears, Roebuck & Co.
Exxon Corp.	Union Carbide Corp.
General Electric Co.	United Technologies Corp.
General Motors Corp.	Wal-Mart Stores Inc.

On Nov. 1, 1999, Home Depot Inc., Intel Corp., Microsoft Corp. and SBC Communications Inc. were substituted for Chevron Corp., Goodyear Tire & Rubber Co., Sears, Roebuck & Co. and Union Carbide Corp.

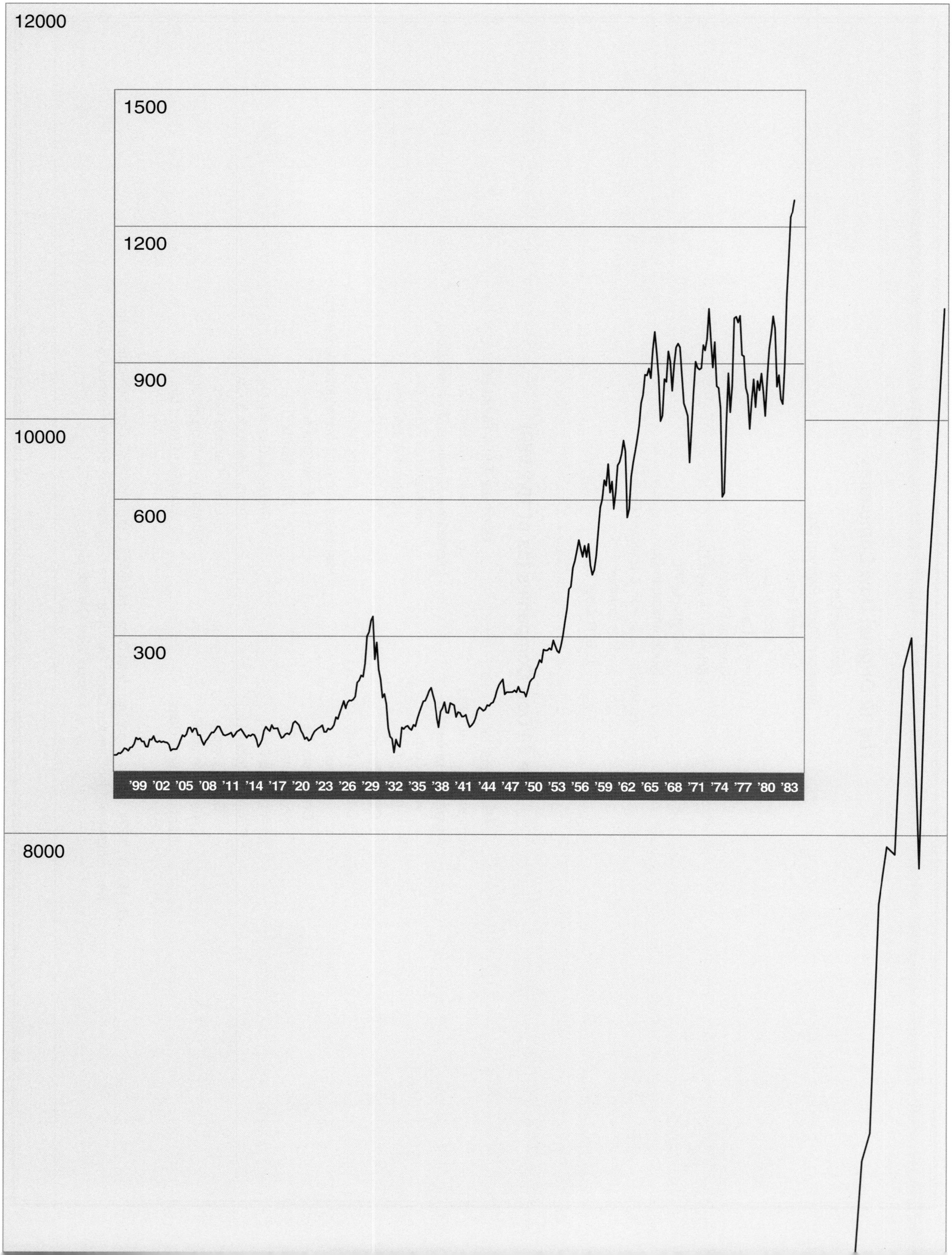

| | '99 '02 '05 '08 '11 '14 '17 '20 '23 '26 '29 '32 '35 '38 '41 '44 '47 '50 '53 '56 '59 '62 '65 '68 '71 '74 '77 '80 '83 |

300

600

900

1200

1500

8000

10000

12000

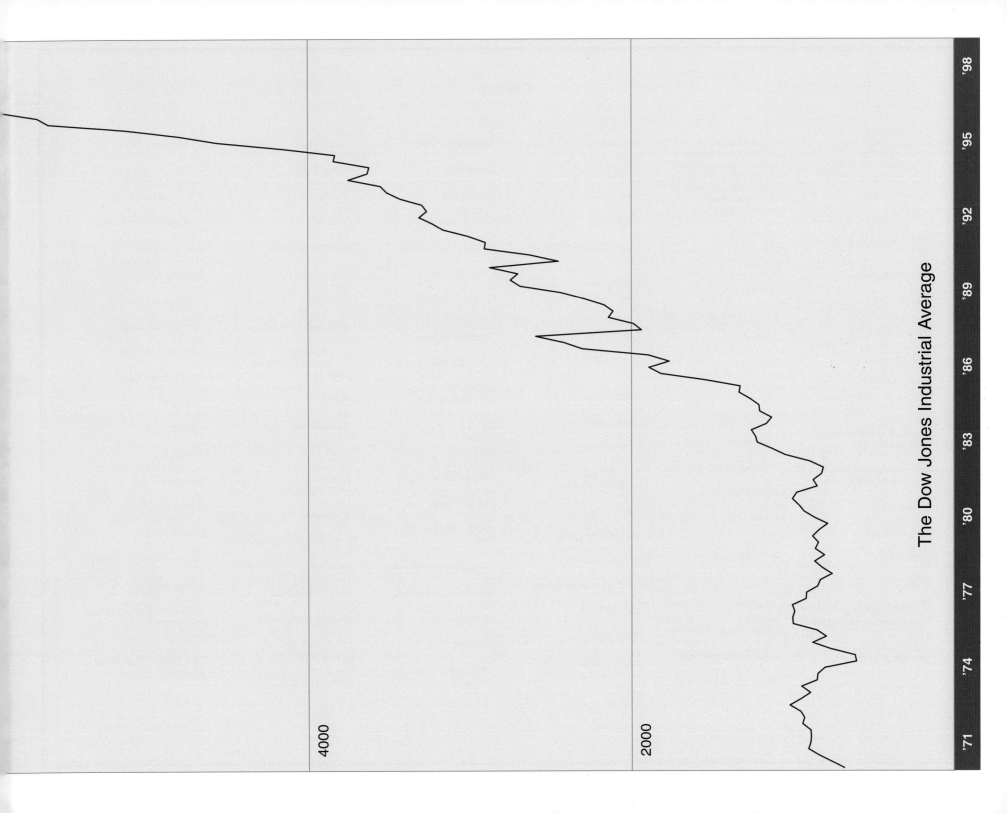

The Dow Jones Industrial Average

Credits

Key to picture position:
(L) = left, (C) = center, (R) = right,
(T) = top, (B) = bottom,
and combinations such as (TL) = top left

Part I

9
[Panic at Wall Street (engraving)]
CORBIS

10
CORBIS/The Mariners' Museum

12,13
CORBIS

14,15,16,17
Dow Jones & Co.

Part II

19
CORBIS/Charles E. Rotkin

20
CORBIS/Museum of Flight

21
Property of AT&T archives. Reprinted
with permission of AT&T

22
CORBIS/Schenectady Museum, Hall of
Electrical History Foundation

23
CORBIS/Bettmann

24
CORBIS/Leif Skoogfors

25,26
CORBIS/Bettmann

27, 29
CORBIS

30
(TL) CORBIS/Patrick Bennett
(C) CORBIS/Richard Hamilton Smith

31
(BL) CORBIS/Charles E. Rotkin
(TR) CORBIS/Charles E. Rotkin

32
CORBIS/Jim Sugar Photography

33
(TL) CORBIS/Bettmann
(TC) CORBIS/Richard Cummins
(TR) CORBIS/Schenectady Museum,
Hall of Electrical History Foundation
(BL) CORBIS/Richard Cummins
(BC) CORBIS/Bettmann
(BR) CORBIS/Robert Holmes

34
CORBIS/Bettmann

35, 36, 37
CORBIS/Bettmann

39, 40, 41, 42
CORBIS/Bettmann

43
Courtesy of the Ellen and Arthur Liman
Collection at the Museum of American
Financial History

44, 45
CORBIS/Bettmann

46
CORBIS/AFP

Part III

49
CORBIS/Bettmann

50
CORBIS/Vince Streano

51, 52, 53
CORBIS/Bettmann

54, 55
Dow Jones & Co.

56
(BL) CORBIS
(TR) CORBIS/Bettmann

57
CORBIS

58
(L) CORBIS
(C) CORBIS
(R) CORBIS/Underwood & Underwood

59, 60
CORBIS/Hulton-Deutsch Collection

61
CORBIS/Underwood & Underwood

62
CORBIS/Bettmann

63
CORBIS/Bettmann-UPI

64
CORBIS/Bettmann

65
CORBIS

66
(TL) (BR) CORBIS/Hulton-Deutsch
Collection

67
CORBIS/Schenectady Museum, Hall of
Electrical History Foundation

68
(L) CORBIS
(R) CORBIS/Minnesota Historical
Society

69
CORBIS

70
CORBIS/Bettmann

71
CORBIS/Bettmann-UPI

72, 74
CORBIS/Bettmann

75
(TL) CORBIS/Bettmann
(BR) CORBIS/Bettmann-UPI

76, 77
CORBIS

78
(TL) CORBIS/Flip Schulke
(TR) CORBIS/Bettmann
(B) CORBIS/Bettmann

79
CORBIS/Hulton-Deutsch Collection

80, 81
CORBIS/Bettmann

82
CORBIS/Owen Franken

85
Courtesy of The Vanguard Group

86, 87
CORBIS

88
CORBIS/Franklin McMahon

89
CORBIS/Bettmann

90
Dow Jones & Co.

91, 92, 93
CORBIS/Bettmann

95
CORBIS/Françoise de Mulder

96
CORBIS/Yves Debay

98
CORBIS/Wally McNamee

99
(TR) CORBIS/Robert Maass
(B) CORBIS/Franz-Marc Frei

100
CORBIS/Wally McNamee

101
(L) CORBIS/Wally McNamee
(R) CORBIS/Robert Maass

Part IV

103
CORBIS/AFP

104
CORBIS/Matthew Mendelsohn

105
CORBIS/Gail Mooney

106
CORBIS/Joseph Sohm;
ChromoSohm Inc.

108, 109
Courtesy of Chicago Board of Trade

110
CORBIS/The Mariners' Museum

111
CORBIS/Kevin R. Morris

112
CORBIS/AFP

113
(TR)CORBIS/Reuters Newmedia Inc.
(BL) CORBIS/Paul A. Souders

115
Dow Jones & Co.

116
Courtesy of CNBC

117
(BL) (TR) CORBIS/AFP

119
CORBIS/AFP

120
CORBIS/Charles O'Rear

Part V

124, 126
CORBIS/Bettmann

127
CORBIS/Raymond Gehman

129
(BL) CORBIS/Bettmann
(TR) Omaha World-Herald/Jeff
Beirmann

Part VI

133
CORBIS/Bettmann

134, 135
CORBIS

136
(L) CORBIS
(R) CORBIS/Bettmann

137
CORBIS/Bettmann-UPI

138
CORBIS/Minnesota Historical Society

139
CORBIS AFP

140
(L) (R) CORBIS/Bettmann

141
CORBIS/Roger Ressmeyer

142
CORBIS/Joseph Sohm;
Chromosohm Inc.

144
Courtesy of Goodyear

152
CORBIS/Michael T. Sedam

153
CORBIS

154
CORBIS/Owen Franken

155
CORBIS/Historical Picture Archive

156
CORBIS/Paul Almasy

Part VII

159
CORBIS/Charles O'Rear

161
CORBIS/Wolfgang Kaehler

163
CORBIS/The Purcell Team

164
CORBIS/Richard T. Nowitz

165
CORBIS/AFP

166
CORBIS/Bob Krist

167
CORBIS/Bettmann

168
CORBIS/Natalie Fobes

169
CORBIS/Charles O'Rear

170
CORBIS/AFP

171
CORBIS/Kelly-Mooney Photography

Ins and Outs

174
Courtesy of the Museum of American
Financial History

Book Design/Photo Editor

Valerie Bowe